STAR WARS
EMPIRE AT WAR

W9-CKJ-383

PRIMA Official Game Guide

Michael Knight

Prima Games
A Division of Random House, Inc.

3000 Lava Ridge Court, Ste. 100
Roseville, CA 95661
1-800-733-3000
www.primagames.com

The Prima Games logo is a registered trademark of Random House, Inc., registered in the United States and other countries. Primagames.com is a registered trademark of Random House, Inc., registered in the United States. Prima Games is a division of Random House, Inc.

Product Manager: Mario De Govia
Editor: Rebecca Chastain
Senior Project Editor: Brooke N. Hall
Design & Layout: Winter Graphics North

ISBN: 0-7615-5165-4
Library of Congress Catalog Card Number: 2005925100
Printed in the United States of America

05 06 07 08 DD 10 9 8 7 6 5 4 3 2 1

CONTENTS

A long time ago, in a galaxy far, far away....

Twenty-nine years ago a cultural phenomenon was born. Starting with a black screen of scrolling golden letters, a new universe was introduced to the world, with heroic Rebels fighting against a tyrannous Empire. Jedi became a familiar word, and everyone realized that Darth Vader was the ultimate villain. Six movies, more than a hundred books, and dozens of computer and video games later, the legend continues with no end in sight.

Now players everywhere can place themselves in the command chair of both the Rebel Alliance and the Galactic Empire in the newest release, **Star Wars®: Empire at War™**. Rather than fighting as a single person, you have the power to control massive fleets, relentless armies, and even the ultimate super weapon—the Death Star—with the power to destroy entire planets.

While all of this power can be intoxicating, it is nothing if not used with strategy and tactics. Don't let a single X-wing fighter bring down your hopes and aspirations to control the galaxy. Be ready to fight, attack, and defend, for this is an Empire at war.

This guide has been written after much consultation with high-level tacticians—both Imperial and Rebel—to help you achieve your goals of victory. The first chapter covers the game's basics and gets you ready to take command of all types of units, from infantry squads to space fleets. You also learn about the economics necessary to fund your war machine. The second section, Tactics for Conquering the Galaxy, focuses on the tactics needed to defeat your enemies on land or in space. It is important to know the people and equipment under your command as well as those of your enemies. Find information on units and structures for the Rebels, the Empire, and the common or non-aligned in the next three sections, respectively. One of the game's highlights is the Rebel and Imperial Campaigns, which lead you through a story of the Galactic Civil War from both opposing points of view. Complete walkthroughs including maps for each Campaign are covered in The Rebellion Campaign and The Empire Campaign sections. Next up are the Galactic Conquest missions, followed by information, tips, tactics, and maps for both the Skirmish and multiplayer games.

Begin with the Galactic Command Training section to get you started. Then, if you want to get into the action, skip ahead and play the Rebel Campaign. You can then read the previous chapters to gain a greater insight into the intricacies of the game and how best to wage war on a galactic scale as well as during tactical battles.

Acknowledgments

I would like to thank Bertrand Estrellado and Christopher Gross at LucasArts for all their support and help during this project; Eric Brummel, my guide through the campaigns; Nick Dengler for his Galactic Conquest insight; and the rest of the testing staff at LucasArts for their tips and hints. I am also grateful for Mario De Govia and Rebecca Chastain at Prima Games for helping make this book a reality.

Last, but certainly not least, I want to express my love and gratitude for my wife Trisa and all the support and care she provides. Hugs and kisses go out to our four children—Beth, Sarah, Connor, and Tanner—all of whom are growing in their interest and knowledge of the **Star Wars** universe.

Welcome recruits! You have been chosen to be a commander rather than just a foot solider or pilot. Instead of carrying a blaster rifle, you will be armed with the latest in communications and surveillance equipment to allow you to monitor the status of your troops across the galaxy, send them into battle against the enemy, and even take charge of the battles, both on the ground and in space. However, before you can get into the war, you must first become familiar with how to interface with your troops.

Getting Started
The Main Menu

When you first begin the game, you find yourself at the Main menu. Here you have six different options. Let's take a look at each in turn.

Menu Option	Description
Tutorial	This launches seven training missions that teach you the basics of the game.
Single Player	This leads to another menu where you can select to begin a New Campaign, play a Galactic Conquest mission, or play a Skirmish battle.
Multiplayer	This allows you to host or join a game over a LAN or the Internet.
Load Game	If you have previously saved a game, select this to rejoin the action where you left off.
Options	Here you can edit both audio and video settings, set up network settings for multiplayer games, configure keyboard "hot keys," and adjust settings for gameplay.
Exit Game	This is the escape pod back to the real world. Use at your own risk.

Types of Games

Star Wars: **Empire at War** offers several different types of games. This is much more than a standard real-time strategy game. It offers both strategic and tactical levels of play. After you play through the tutorials, which are covered in greater detail later in this chapter, you will have learned enough to play each of the various types of games. Following is more information on them.

The Campaigns

You can choose from two different campaigns: the Rebel Alliance or the Galactic Empire. The campaigns feature a story line as you seek to take control of the galaxy. During each campaign, you must complete certain objectives. These essentially break down the campaign into a series of linked missions. You play the campaigns at the strategic level and then fight ground and space battles at the tactical level when you engage the enemy. "The Imperial Campaign" and "The Rebel Campaign" sections of this guide contain more information for the two campaigns, including complete walkthroughs.

Which side you will choose to play as—the Rebellion or the Empire?

Galactic Conquest

These missions allow you to play both strategic and tactical battles as you try to take control of all the planetary systems in the mission and/or complete other objectives along the way. The Galactic Conquest missions can be small or quite large depending on the number of planetary systems involved. Check out the "Single Missions" section for more information on these games.

TIP

For those who want to play only a strategic game without having to personally lead their troops in each tactical ground and space battle, you can have the computer auto resolve each battle (you cannot auto resolve campaign missions). However, for this method, the game just considers the strength of each side's army or fleet to determine the winner. The commander's genius is not factored in.

Skirmish Battles

If you just want to play a land or space tactical battle, without having to worry about the strategic level, then you want a Skirmish battle. Unlike the campaigns and Galactic Conquest games, the Skirmish battles let you build units during the course of the battle. You usually start with only a few units and must create an army or fleet while fending off your enemies' attacks and also take the battle to them. The "Skirmishes" section contains additional information on Skirmish battles as well as details on each of the maps.

Multiplayer Games

You can also compete against other players in both strategic and tactical battles during multiplayer games. The host of the game selects the type of game and all the options. For more information on multiplayer games, go to the "Multiplayer" section.

The Game Screen

No matter what type of game you are playing, the game screen is essentially the same. Both the strategic and tactical levels of the game share almost the same elements—the only differences being the controls available at each level. Therefore, you do not have to learn a completely new interface for each level. By breaking down the game screen into its four main elements, you can better see their function and how to use them in your quest for control of the galaxy.

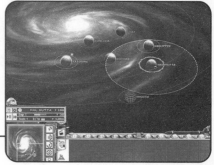

The screen during the strategic level of a game

Game Window

The upper three-quarters of the game screen is the game window. Here you see the game being played out. At the strategic level, you have a view of the galaxy where the individual planetary systems act as spaces for moving fleets, armies, and heroes. During tactical battles, the window shows either the battleground on the surface or the area of space above for ground and space battles. In all cases, you can scroll your view using either the arrow keys or by moving your cursor to the edge of the window in which you wish to scroll. Within the game window, you can select various units and even give them orders.

Data Bar

On the screen's left side, immediately below the game window, is the data bar. The four buttons on the left allow you to access information such as a technology tree, or look at your objectives—both assigned and completed. You can also pause the game or speed it up here. The information area of the data bar varies depending on the level. At the strategic level, the right side of the bar lists the planetary system you have selected, with the amount of credits it provides per day. Below that is shown how many game days have elapsed since the start of this game, and how many credits you earn per day. The lowest level lists the technology level for your side, the number of units you have in the system and the maximum number allowed, and finally your total credits.

Minimap

The minimap is below the data bar. At the strategic level, this shows the galaxy with the planetary systems included in the mission. Select systems by clicking on them in the minimap, then click on the magnifying glass in the map's lower left corner to zoom in to give production orders and assign units to fleets. During tactical battles, you can see the locations of your units and any enemy units you have detected. Friendly units are displayed in green, while enemy units are red. You can even use the minimap to give movement orders to selected units. The buttons along the right side of the minimap vary depending on whether you are at the strategic level or the tactical battle level.

Minimap Buttons

Strategic	Tactical
View planet credit value toggle	Special Attack (bombing run on land, ion cannon or hypervelocity gun in space)
View planet's space station level and ground structure slots	Place beacon
View planet's special ability and weather	Call for reinforcements
Bring heroes to the top of the unit stack	Retreat from battle
Main menu	Main menu

Command Bar

The command bar focuses on the game's units. During the strategic level, you can select from space and ground units and structures to produce. The unit production queue is along the top of the command bar. Because ground units are produced on the planet while space units are produced in orbit, you can have both types of units in production at the same time.

The command bar during a land battle

The command bar lets you give orders to units during tactical battles. The six order buttons along the left side allow you to give advanced movement orders to the currently selected units, which appear in the unit area to the right. While you can give attack and movement orders with the mouse and cursor, sometimes you'll want to use the order buttons to ensure that your troops act as you desire.

Tactical Order Buttons

Order	Description
Attack	Attack targeted object with selected units.
Attack Move	Selected units move to the targeted location, attacking enemies within range along the route.
Guard	Click this button, then right-click on a friendly unit to command your troops to follow and protect the target. Guarding units will chase enemies only a short distance before returning to the guarded unit.
Move	Selected units move to the targeted location, ignoring all enemies along the route.
Set Waypoint	Selected units move to the targeted point on the map. You can continue clicking the map to create a path for the units to follow until waypoint mode is turned off.
Stop	Cancels any previous orders and stops your troops where they are. The Troops will still engage enemy units within range after stopping.

Above the advanced movement order buttons is a button with a clapboard on it, like you would see on a movie set. Click on this button to activate the cinematic camera mode. This zooms in on the action and lets you view the battle up close. You can't give orders in this mode, however. Move the mouse to return to the normal view.

Tutorial 01: Basic Land Combat

The best way to learn the game basics is to play through the provided tutorials. Even if you are a veteran of real-time strategy games, it's a good idea to play these quick missions to learn the nuances of this particular game. So go ahead and load up the first tutorial.

The tutorials help you learn how to play the game at the strategic level, plus how to command your units during both land and space battles.

Starting with the Galactic View

The tutorial begins at the strategic level with the screen showing several planetary systems in the area. During campaigns and Galactic Conquest games, this is the view that you always begin with. You are a Rebel commander charged with the defense of the Wookiee homeworld—Kashyyyk. You do not need to produce any units during this mission. In fact, you don't do anything on the galactic view except watch an Imperial invasion force move from Nal Hutta to Kashyyyk, precipitating a battle on the planet's surface.

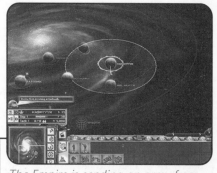

The Empire is sending an army from Nal Hutta to invade Kashyyyk.

Gaining Ground—the Land Battle

BRIEFING

A platoon of Rebel infantry has been dispatched to locate a lost squad that was last seen performing a routine perimeter sweep.

Imperial forces have detected the Rebel presence on Kashyyyk. During the course of this mission, you need to gather your troops and defend the Alliance base. At the beginning of the mission, you command a single squad of Rebel soldiers. The tutorial quickly goes over the minimap and special abilities. Then it's time to get started.

Select the squad of Rebel soldiers by left-clicking on them. Notice that a click selects all five individual soldiers that make up this squad. Rather than giving orders to a single soldier, you give orders to a squad. Information on the selected squad is displayed on the command bar. Here you can view the status of the unit and even activate special unit abilities.

OBJECTIVE

1. *Find the missing patrol squad.*

NOTE

Depending on the type of infantry squad, you may have different numbers of troops in a squad at full strength. However, as they take damage during combat, squads can be whittled down to a single soldier.

The location your squad must move to is indicated on the minimap by a green bull's-eye marker. To order your selected squad to move to this point, either right-click on the marker on the minimap, or right-click on the map. The location is to the southeast. To scroll the map, either use the arrow keys or move the cursor to the screen's right edge. When you scroll to the objective location, you see blue arrows pointing to the location on the game window. Move your squad to this position.

Once you arrive at the location, you find the lost squad. Take control of both squads by holding the left mouse button and dragging a box around them. You can select several units or even your whole army using this method. You can also double-click on a unit to select all visible units of that type.

The lost squad is found.

OBJECTIVES

2. Find the jamming device.
3. Destroy the jamming device.

Your new task is to find a jamming device. Move both of your squads north to the objective marker. Once you have found the jamming device, with both squads still selected, move the cursor over the device and right-click to order your squads to attack. The Rebel soldiers fire their blasters at the jamming device until it is destroyed.

Click on the cinematic action mode button to watch your troops fire on the target.

TIP

Change the camera in tactical mode by pressing CTRL +center mouse button. Reset it to its default position by pressing END .

OBJECTIVE

4. Advance to the Rebel base.

Now just get your two squads to the Rebel base in the northwest. Try right-clicking on the bull's-eye marker on the minimap to send your troops back to their base to complete this objective.

OBJECTIVES

5. Construct a bacta healing station.
6. Construct a turret.

Once your troops arrive at the Rebel base, you receive two new orders. Additional squads of troops at the base are now under your command. Your task is to build a bacta healing station as well as an anti-infantry turret. To accomplish this task, locate the build pads near the walls to the east of the base. Right-click on a build pad to open a construction menu. Build the bacta healing station at the southern pad, and the anti-infantry turret on the northern pad. These two structures come in handy during the upcoming Imperial attack. During actual missions, you can choose from a variety of structures to build at these types of pads.

Once the bacta healing station is completed, left-click on it to select it. A green circle appears around the station. This represents the range of the station. Infantry units within this range are healed. Note how far the range circle extends and try to keep your infantry within this range during the upcoming battle so that they are automatically healed as they take damage from enemy fire.

The green circle indicates the healing range of the bacta healing station.

OBJECTIVE

7. Defend the Rebel base.

Besides the squads of Rebel soldiers at the base, you also have a new type of unit—the Plex missile soldier. These squads consist of three soldiers each armed with a rocket that causes a lot of damage to enemy vehicles and structures. The anti-infantry turret that you constructed also aids in base defense. Select it and right-click on enemy units to order it to fire at them. However, the turret automatically fires on any enemy units that come into range.

TIP

When you hold the cursor over a unit, either friend or enemy, an info box is projected onto the screen by your astromech droid. This provides information about the unit and lists the types of enemies that the unit is strong or weak against. For example, the Plex missile soldiers are strong against AT-ST walkers, but weak against stormtroopers. Learn the strengths and weaknesses of your troops and the enemy units to maximize your firepower against the enemy while minimizing your casualties.

Move your squads of Rebel soldiers so they are positioned in the opening between the two walls east of your base. Click on the special ability button in the command bar for your infantry to order them to take cover. This orders your infantry squads to take evasive maneuvers and spread out. As a result, damage from enemy fire is reduced. However, your unit also moves slower. Because you are just defending right now, movement speed is not an issue. Before long, squads of Imperial stormtroopers advance toward your base from the east. Order all of your Rebel solider squads to fire on them. However, keep your plex mission soldiers back until you have taken out most of the stormtroopers and the AT-ST walkers arrive on the scene. Select all of your plex missile soldiers by double-clicking on one of the squads. Then order them to attack the walkers while your Rebel soldier squads deal with any remaining stormtroopers.

Imperial AT-ST walkers arrive after a wave of stormtroopers. Your Plex missile soldiers work best against these vehicles.

OBJECTIVE

8. Capture reinforcement points.

After the Imperial attack has been repulsed, it's time to move out. Order all of your squads to advance east to the first reinforcement point. Capturing reinforcement points prevents the enemy from landing even more troops. To capture a reinforcement point, you must eliminate all enemy units in the area and remain near the reinforcement point until it turns green. Position your troops near the first reinforcement point. The Imperials may already have more troops on the way, so watch for Imperial shuttles dropping off stormtroopers to retake the point. As before, let your Rebel soldiers deal with the stormtroopers.

Once the first reinforcement point is under your control, move your army to the second one in the northeast corner.

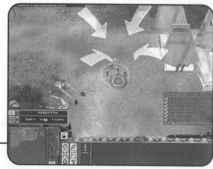

Rebel soldiers prepare to fight against the stormtroopers that will disembark from this Imperial shuttle to try to retain the reinforcement point. Once you take it, the Imperials can no longer bring in reinforcements here.

TIP

While paused, you can queue up structures to build, but you cannot move units or change the composition of your fleets.

OBJECTIVE

9. Retreat from Kashyyyk.

After taking control of both reinforcement points, you receive the order to retreat from Kashyyyk. Your superiors have decided to save your troops rather than lose them to the large force the Imperials are sure to land later. Retreating allows you to save your units from certain destruction whenever you are faced with overwhelming odds. Remember, you can always return to a battle later with additional units.

Select the retreat button on your command bar next to the minimap. Once the retreat order is given, a countdown timer appears, showing how much time remains until the battle ends. You must get all of your units within range of the reinforcement points to get them off the planet surface. Your troops are more vulnerable to enemy fire as they prepare to leave the planet. However, because you have eliminated all of the enemies on the map, you do not have to worry about that during this mission.

Once the timer reaches zero, the first tutorial mission is complete. You have learned the basics of a tactical land battle and are ready to advance to the next tutorial. You can continue to it immediately, or play it at a later time. However, be sure to go through the rest of the tutorials before playing a regular mission.

Tutorial 02: Basic Galactic Controls

During this second tutorial, you learn to use the galactic view to move units around the galaxy. As you continue to command Rebel forces, you also learn about some of the Rebels' special abilities that allow them to fight effectively against the enormous military might of the Empire.

OBJECTIVES

1. *Move troops into orbit over Kashyyyk.*
2. *Move fleet to Bothawui.*
3. *Combine fleets at Bothawui.*
4. *Move fleet into orbit above Ryloth.*
5. *Move fleet to surface of Ryloth.*
6. *Zoom in to Ryloth.*

TIP

More buildings of a certain type will increase production (i.e., five barracks). If using multiple super weapons (i.e., Ion cannons), the recharge is reduced for the amount of buildings for that type. The more you have, the shorter the refresh.

Because you have successfully retreated from Kashyyyk, you can continue to command the surviving forces from that battle within the galactic view. This view allows you to manage the resources on all of your planets, including the economy, bases, and units. You see your troops on the surface of the planet Kashyyyk in the galactic view. Here units are represented by stacks of units known as fleets. The strongest unit within a fleet is always displayed on top. Transports are inherent with land units so you do not have to build these space vessels to move land units from one planet to another. Move your ground forces into orbit by dragging them from the surface of Kashyyyk into one of the available slots located above the planet. This prepares them for space travel.

The Rebel Alliance has taken control of Bothawui. This system now appears green to show that it's under friendly control. To move your fleet of ground units to this system, drag them from Kashyyyk's orbit to one of the two empty slots over Bothawui. The view shows your fleet moving to the new system. Now combine your fleet from Kashyyyk with the fleet already at Bothawui. Combining two fleets creates a single fleet that is larger and more powerful. To combine your fleets, simply drag and drop one fleet icon onto another. If you ever do this accidentally, you can separate them again.

The Rebel fleet moves to Bothawui.

Mon Mothma gives you a short briefing on resources, which are simplified into credits. Each system that you control provides credits at the end of each galactic day. To obtain more resources, you must claim another planet. This increases the total number of credits you collect daily, and also increases the total number of units that you can support. Ryloth is currently unoccupied. This means that is should be an easy planet to capture.

To begin the process of capturing Ryloth, move your forces into orbit above Ryloth by dragging your fleet into one of the orbital spaces. To capture a planet, your forces must occupy the planet's surface. To do this, simply move your fleet into the ground slot located near the planet's center. Don't worry about having space units in your fleet stack. Only ground units will actually land. Because there was no resistance, you automatically take control of Ryloth once your troops touch down on the surface.

Let's take a closer look at Ryloth. To access a more detailed view of a planet, select the planet, and then click on the magnifying glass—the zoom-in icon—in the bottom left corner of the minimap.

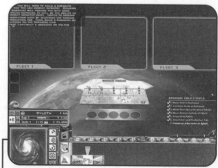

The planet zoom-in view shows the ground forces, structure slots, and fleet slots in orbit.

OBJECTIVES

7. *Select the land production tab.*
8. *Construct a barracks on Ryloth.*
9. *Recruit 2 infantry platoons.*
10. *Select the space production tab.*
11. *Construct a space station on Ryloth.*
12. *Construct 2 X-wing squadrons.*

The zoomed-in view of Ryloth shows several different things. Along the top are the spaces for three different fleets. These are the same as the slots in orbit above the planet on the galactic view. On the planet's surface are ground force squares that represent the number of ground units you can have on this planet. Below that are circles that represent the capacity of the planet for structures. Ryloth can have five structures. This capacity varies from planet to planet. Therefore, it is impossible to build every single structure on one planet. During missions, you must have certain planets specialize in different structures.

To start building, first click on the land production tab at the command bar's bottom left. This brings up a selection of three structures that can be built on Ryloth. You need to build a barracks before you can recruit infantry units. Building a barracks provides you with the basic ground defenses, as well as the ability to recruit infantry units. Click on the barracks icon in the command bar to begin building a barracks. Constructing multiple buildings of the same type on a planet gives you bonuses such as faster build times for specific units, but remember—each planet has a limited capacity for structures. Once the barracks is completed, the land production bar shows additional structures that can now be built, plus two types of infantry. Click on the infantry platoon button twice to recruit two infantry platoons.

You need to build a space station before you can build space units. Building a space station provides the basic space defenses as well as the ability to build space units. Switch to the space production mode by selecting the space production tab, just above the land production tab. Then build a space station by clicking on the space station icon. To protect the space around the planet, you also need to create a space fleet. Now that you have created a fully operational space station, you can build ships. Click twice on the

X-wing fighter icon to build two squadrons of these fighters. Now that you have learned how to build units, click on the zoom-out icon on the minimap.

OBJECTIVES

14. *Recruit a smuggler on Bothawui.*
15. *Siphon credits from Nal Hutta.*
16. *Steal technology from Nal Hutta.*
17. *Construct a base shield generator.*
18. *Zoom in to Bothawui.*
19. *Create a raid fleet.*
20. *Zoom out from Bothawui.*
21. *Deploy a raid fleet to Tatooine.*

Whenever you capture a planet, you are rewarded with credits. Use credits to purchase new units, structures, and upgrades. You receive money from all of the planets under your control at the end of the galactic day. The more planets that you control, the more credits you receive. Smugglers can provide useful additional income. Click on Bothawui to select this planet. Then select the land production tab and click on the smuggler icon to recruit a smuggler. A smuggler appears in orbit over Bothawui. Smugglers can siphon away credits from enemy-controlled systems. To do this, click on the smuggler to select this unit. In addition to the orbital slots that appear over planets, a steal credits slot appears near enemy-controlled planets. Move the smuggler to the slot by Nal Hutta to begin siphoning credits from the Empire.

Send the smuggler to Nal Hutta to steal credits from the Empire.

The Rebel Alliance gains new technology by stealing it directly from Imperial planets. Use the heroes C-3PO and R2-D2 to accomplish this task. They appear in orbit over Bothawui. Click on their icon to select them. Notice that a steal slot appears near Nal Hutta. Drag the droids to this slot to begin stealing technology. A steal technology window appears. To get more detailed information, hover the mouse cursor over any item and a tool-tip is displayed. Choose a technology to steal from the Empire by selecting it from the available list. Whenever the Rebel faction exhausts all possible technology options, they advance to the next technology level. Click on any of the options to complete this objective.

C-3PO and R2-D2 can steal Imperial technology for the Rebels.

Your next task is to construct a base shield generator. You do not have to zoom in on a planet to construct structures or get new units. Click on the ground production tab and then on the base shield generator to begin constructing it. Structures that require power to function, such as the base shield generator, cause a power generator to be built automatically.

NOTE

Having a power generator built automatically does not count against the number of structures you can build on a planet.

The Galactic Empire's large and powerful navy allows it to maintain control of the galaxy. Because the Rebel Alliance can rarely go toe to toe with Imperial fleets, the Rebels have a way around this threat. They can use raid fleets to bypass space battles within enemy territory by moving directly to a planet's surface. This allows the Rebel Alliance to reinforce friendly planets blockaded by enemy space units, or even capture undefended enemy planets. Zoom in on Bothawui. Create a raid fleet by dragging the ground unit to one of the fleet positions in orbit. Now zoom out from Bothawui.

Drag the squad of Rebel soldiers to a fleet slot to create a raid fleet to send to Tatooine.

Your final objective is to deploy a raid fleet to Tatooine. You need to bypass the Imperial space units positioned above Tatooine. To do this, simply drag the Rebel raid fleet from Bothawui to the raid slot located on Tatooine. This places the infantry units directly on Tatooine's surface. As a result, the Rebels gain control of Tatooine—right from under the noses an Imperial fleet in orbit above the desert planet. Once this is accomplished, you have completed the second tutorial.

Tutorial 03: Basic Space Combat

For this tutorial, you now command Imperial forces. Here you learn about space combat. Selecting and giving orders to units is very similar to ground combat, so you should have no trouble. However, combat in space offers some unique challenges.

OBJECTIVE

1. Move attack fleet to Kashyyyk.

You begin with a fleet in orbit over Nal Hutta. Your first task is to engage the enemy. To attack the Rebel space forces located above Kashyyyk, drag the Imperial fleet from Nal Hutta to Kashyyyk. Moving a fleet into orbit above an enemy planet initiates a space battle.

You must send your fleet to Kashyyyk to attack the Rebels there.

Empire at War—Space Battle

BRIEFING

After being defeated on the surface of Kashyyyk, an Imperial Officer now attempts to uncover the source of the new resistance movement.

OBJECTIVE

1. Follow the Imperial Officer.

As soon as your fleet arrives in orbit over Kashyyyk, you automatically begin a battle against the Rebel forces on the space tactical map. You begin with a force of three TIE scout squadrons and three *Tartan*-class patrol cruisers. Your task is to follow the Imperial Officer who is aboard the shuttle. Start off by double-clicking one of the TIE scout squadron icons to select all three squadrons. You can also select fighter squadrons by clicking on one of the individual units. Once the scouts are selected, press (CTRL)+(1). This creates a group that you can quickly select in the future by just pressing (1). Use the same method to select all three cruisers and assign them as group 2 ((CTRL)+(2)).

The Imperial fleet arrives over Kashyyyk.

The TIE scouts have the sensor ping ability. When these units are selected, click on the special ability button in the command bar. This changes the mouse cursor to a reticle with a green circle around it. You can move this around the map and then left-click to reveal any enemy units that might be in range of the sensor ability. The cruisers, on the other hand, have the ability to boost weapon power. Activating this ability increases the damage they inflict on the enemy.

OBJECTIVE

2. Eliminate enemy fighter units.

The minimap shows certain areas as light blue. These are nebulae. While in these areas, your units can't use their special abilities, so try to avoid them. Lead with your cruisers as you follow the shuttle to the north where you run into four squadrons of Rebel fighters—Z-95 Headhunters. Select your cruisers, activate their special ability, and then order them to fire on the Rebel squadrons by right-clicking on the targets.

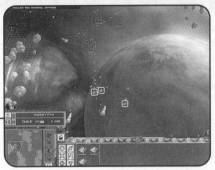

Use the cruisers to attack the Rebel fighters.

Each of your units has a health bar, which appears as a green line when the unit is selected. As units take damage, this bar becomes shorter and turns yellow to indicate some damage, and then turns red when the unit approaches maximum damage and destruction. Some units, such as your cruisers, also have a blue bar. This represents the shields. As a cruiser takes laser fire, its shield absorbs the damage and the bar shortens. Once the shield has been completely reduced, further attacks damage the cruiser's health. Shields slowly recharge. Therefore, after this first engagement, let your cruisers restore their shields to maximum strength before continuing.

OBJECTIVES

3. Follow the Imperial Officer.
4. Eliminate the frigate ship.

The Imperial Officer's shuttle continues to the east after the first fight. The next engagement pits you against more fighters and a Nebulon-B frigate. This is a tougher unit to destroy because it has several weapons and shields. You can destroy the hard-points on larger ships such as the frigate or space stations to disable critical parts such as weapons, shields, and engines. Therefore, during this fight, order your TIE scouts to go after the Y-wings while cruisers use their special ability and target the frigate's shields. Once they are down, take out the weapons' hard-points until the frigate is destroyed. Concentrate on the frigate because it is the biggest threat to your cruisers.

Concentrate your cruisers' fire on the frigate's shields and then weapons.

OBJECTIVES

5. Deploy all reinforcement units.
6. Follow the Imperial Officer.
7. Eliminate the Rebel space station.

After you've destroyed all Rebel units in this second engagement, you receive some reinforcements. To bring reinforcements into a battle, select the reinforcements button, then drag and release the ships into space from the reinforcements window. Remember, reinforcements can be released only in open space away from enemy structures and other hazards. For this tutorial, you have received two *Acclamator*-class cruisers. Once you deploy these vessels, the *Acclamators* launch a squadron of TIE fighters and a squadron of TIE bombers. Assign the *Acclamators* to group 3 and the squadrons to 4 and 5 respectively so you can quickly call them up during the fighting.

Use the various units of your fleet to their strengths. Don't forget those special abilities.

Now head north to locate the Rebel space station. Order your *Acclamators* to target the station's shields and be sure to use the boost weapon power ability. Order your TIE bombers to go after the shields while your cruisers and TIE fighters take on the squadrons of Rebel fighters. Keep up the attacks, just like you did against the frigate, until the space station is destroyed and the tutorial is complete.

Tutorial 04: Advanced Galactic

During this tutorial, you learn more about the galactic mode and discover some of the Empire's ways of dealing with the Rebellion.

Kashyyyk is yours for the taking.

OBJECTIVE

1. Capture the Kashyyyk System.

Because there are no Rebel forces on Kashyyyk, the Empire can capture the planet without a land battle. Whenever you capture a planet, you are rewarded with credits, as well as the ability to support more units. The more planets that you capture, the larger your forces can become.

For this invasion, you only need the ground unit on Nal Hutta. Drag the unit to a space slot above Nal Hutta. Then drag this fleet to a space slot above Kashyyyk. Once the fleet is in orbit over Kashyyyk, you can then drag it to the surface of the planet to capture it. Notice that control of Kashyyyk changes from neutral to Empire and you receive quite a few credits for your effort. This is important to remember. Not only do you increase the amount of credits you receive at the end of each galactic day, but you also get an immediate bonus for the capture itself. The capture has also increased the total number of units that you can build from 22 to 25. Furthermore, a trade route now connects Kashyyyk and Nal Hutta, increasing the total number of credits generated by the connected planets. Trade routes also increase the movement speed of any friendly fleets traveling along their path.

OBJECTIVES

2. Upgrade space station on Nal Hutta.
3. Construct research facility on Nal Hutta.
4. Upgrade to technology level 2.

Upgrading your space station makes it a stronger defensive structure. This also allows you to support more units and produce more types of units. Switch to space production mode by selecting the space production tab. Then upgrade your space station by clicking on the space station icon. In addition, your space station receives a garrison force of TIE fighters, TIE bombers, and a Tartan cruiser. The space station can now produce several other types of space units besides probe droids.

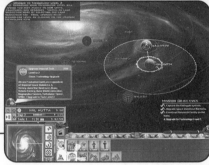

By upgrading your technology level, you gain access to more advanced and powerful units and heroes.

Your next task is to construct a research facility. Click on the land production tab to see the units and structures you can construct on Nal Hutta. Now click on the research facility icon. The research facility allows the Empire to advance their technology level. Unlike the Rebels, who have to steal technology, the Empire conducts its own research.

Once the research facility is completed, a new option appears on the control bar. Click on the upgrade Imperial technology icon. Once this research is complete, you can produce new space units, ground units, and structures, and even upgrade to technology level 3.

OBJECTIVES

5. Recruit a bounty hunter on Nal Hutta.

6. Neutralize a smuggler on Nal Hutta.

Whenever a planet's total credit value is modified, this is visible at the planet itself. Notice the red "minus" sign next to the credit symbol by Nal Hutta. This means that the credits generated at Nal Hutta have been reduced by the presence of an enemy smuggler. Bounty hunters are minor heroes who can travel the galaxy undetected by hostile fleets to find and neutralize other heroes. They are great for getting rid of smugglers.

From the land production mode of the control bar, click on the bounty hunter icon to recruit one to your force. When you click on the bounty hunter in the space slot above Nal Hutta, a neutralize hero slot appears near the planet. Drag the bounty hunter fleet to the slot. This opens a neutralize hero window. If there were more than one hero here, you could select the bounty hunter's target. However, there is only a single smuggler in the window at this time. The number below the smuggler icon is the fee you must pay the bounty hunter to get rid of the smuggler. Minor heroes are eliminated from the game permanently while major heroes, such as Han Solo and Chewbacca, are removed temporarily until they respawn.

Bounty hunters are useful for eliminating enemy hero units such as smugglers.

OBJECTIVES

7. Deploy probe droid to Corellia.

8. Deploy probe droid to Ryloth.

It seems that the smuggler came from Corellia. You now must find out what is located at this planet. To receive information on nearby enemy systems, the Empire must use probe droids. Whenever a probe droid is deployed to the surface of a planet, information about that planet is revealed to the Empire. Click on the space production tab to access space units. Click on the probe droid icon twice. You need a second probe droid for the next task. Once the first probe droid is complete, click on it and drag it to the spy slot near Corellia. When it arrives, it shows you that units are in orbit and on the planet's surface.

The probe droid has discovered pirates at Corellia.

The units at Corellia have a yellow border around their icons. This identifies them as pirates. While they are hostile to the Empire, these aren't the Rebels you're looking for. Gather more information about nearby enemy planets by deploying your second probe droid to the ground slot of Ryloth. When it arrives, you see that Ryloth contains a Rebel garrison on the surface of the planet.

OBJECTIVES

9. Construct 2 Acclamator ships.
10. Recruit a field commander.

Before you can attack the Rebels at Ryloth, you must build up a fleet. To begin with, click on the Acclamator-class cruiser icon twice to order two of these space vessels for your fleet. Most Imperial ships, such as the Acclamators, contain TIE bomber units. Whenever these units, or Y-wing fighters for the Rebels, are in orbit above an enemy planet, you can use bombing run attacks while you are involved in a land battle at that planet. Always bring bomber units when invading an enemy planet.

Imperial capital ships all carry a complement of TIE fighters and TIE bombers. You do not construct these units separately. They are a part of the capital ship and launch automatically whenever the capital ship goes into battle. As you build the Acclamators, notice that each takes up three unit capacity points. Larger ships significantly impact the maximum unit capacity provided by the planets and space stations. Once that limit is reached, you cannot create new units until more planets are acquired.

Your final task is to recruit a field commander. These units provide combat bonuses to all friendly units within a battle. You must have an officer academy to recruit a field commander. Switch to the land production mode by selecting the land production tab. Because Nal Hutta already has an officer academy, click on the field commander icon to recruit one of these units. Once the field commander is successfully added to your forces, the fourth tutorial ends.

Imperial capital ships are very powerful due to their weapons and the squadrons of TIE fighters and TIE bombers they carry.

Tutorial 05: Advanced Land Combat

This tutorial continues where the last left off. You located the Rebels on Ryloth and are now going to invade and take control of the system.

OBJECTIVES

1. Combine all fleets located on Nal Hutta.
2. Deploy land units to the surface of Ryloth.

First, combine the land units on the surface of Nal Hutta with the space units orbiting over the planet. To do this, simply click on the ground forces and drag them up to the same orbital slot as the space units. Now send your combined fleet to Ryloth by dragging your fleet to one of the orbital slots above Ryloth. Finally, to begin your invasion, click on your fleet and drag it to the slot on the planet's surface to send your ground troops into action and begin a tactical land battle.

Send your fleet to Ryloth to begin the invasion.

Imperial Policy—Tactical Land Battle

BRIEFING

Imperial forces have located a Rebel base on Ryloth and are poised to launch a full assault on the Rebel position.

OBJECTIVE

1. Capture the reinforcement point.

Your troops land in the map's southwestern corner. The initial force consists of two speeder bikes and three squads of stormtroopers. Because you do not control a reinforcement point, you have to capture one before you can land the rest of your ground troops. The first reinforcement point is to the northeast. Before moving out, organize your units into groups. Double-click on one of the speeder bikes to select both of these units. Then press (CTRL)+ 1 to assign them to group 1. Use the same procedure to assign the three stormtrooper squads to group 2. This allows you to quickly call up each group as needed.

Speeder bikes make a hit-and-run attack using their thermal detonators.

Send your speeder bikes toward the reinforcement point to see if any enemies are around it. You find some Rebel soldiers, so drop thermal detonators near them and then rush back to your landing spot for safety. Now bring up your group of stormtroopers to fight any survivors. Before a reinforcement point can be captured, the area surrounding it must be clear of enemy units. Then you must have an infantry-type unit, or hero, nearby to turn it to your side. As your stormtroopers come in contact with Rebel soldiers, order them to use their take cover ability. Slowly advance past the reinforcement point so that your units are the only ones near it until you take control.

TIP

Speeder bikes can use the thermal detonator ability for hit-and-run attacks. To use this ability, select a speeder bike unit, and then click on the thermal detonator ability icon on the command bar. This causes the speeder bike to drop a thermal detonator at its location. After a few seconds, the detonator explodes and damages nearby enemy units.

OBJECTIVE

2. Deploy all reinforcements.

Land reinforcements can be deployed only in controlled areas known as reinforcement points. Conquering reinforcement points is of particular strategic importance. The number of units you can bring into any reinforcement point is determined by the total of all of your reinforcement points' capacities. These are denoted by the number shown at the reinforcement points and their total is listed in the data bar. Once you reach the total capacity for your reinforcement points, you can no longer bring down any more units until you capture more reinforcement points. Click on the call-for-reinforcements button near the minimap and a reinforcements window opens. Drag the field commander and the company of stormtroopers to the area around the reinforcement points to call them in. A short time later, a couple shuttles land and drop off your troops.

TIP

Foul weather can reduce the effectiveness of your units. You must account for weather changes whenever you are engaged in battle on a planet's surface. An icon in the screen's upper right corner informs you of any modifications to the battle such as weather. Here on Ryloth, you find yourself in the middle of a sandstorm. This weather reduces rocket accuracy by 50 percent. Luckily for you, your troops are not using rockets.

OBJECTIVE

3. Destroy the Jawa sandcrawler.

When you invade a planet's surface, it is vital to maintain control of as many reinforcement points as possible because you can deploy reinforcements only near areas that you control. If the defender gains control of a reinforcement point, you cannot deploy reinforcements there. While you do not have any more reinforcements for this mission, it is always good practice to defend your reinforcement points.

Some Jawas to the northeast are the nearest threat. Send your group of three stormtrooper squads, group 2, to attack the Jawas and destroy their sandcrawler. As long as the sandcrawler is on the map, it will continue to spawn groups of Jawas who will attack your troops and try to take your reinforcement point. Order your group to attack the Jawas first. Meanwhile, group your new company of stormtroopers, two squads, into group 3 while you assign your field commander unit to group 4. The field commander increases the health of your units, so keep him back from the fighting while your stormtroopers take out the Jawas.

Stormtroopers attack the Jawas and destroy their sandcrawler.

NOTE

Beware of indigenous units, such as Jawas. These forces continue to attack until their habitat has been destroyed. On some other planets, the indigenous units may be friendly and you can even take control of them to help you win a battle.

Near the reinforcement point, you find a build pad. Move a unit near it to take control of it. Click on it and you can then build a small structure. Because some of your troops may need healing, build a bacta healing station there. If you later need something else, you can click on the structure and choose to sell it. Then you can build another structure on the now-empty build pad.

OBJECTIVES

4. Advance on the Rebel base.
5. Destroy the power generator.

With the Jawas eliminated, it's now time to take the battle to the Rebels. Get your troops together and order them to move to the northwest. Be sure to deactivate their take cover ability so they walk faster. However, before you attack the main Rebel base, you need to deal with some of its defenses. Base shield generators provide the defender with a significant advantage by blocking blaster fire and reducing the movement speed of enemy units. Base shield generators require power generators to function. This means that if you destroy the power generator, the base shield will be disabled.

TIE bombers make a run against the Rebel power generator.

As your troops follow the path to the northwest, you see the Rebel power generator. It is protected by a couple of squads of Rebel soldiers. Rather than assaulting this position, try bringing in some heavier firepower. Because bombing units are in orbit above this system (the TIE bombers stationed on the Acclamator-class cruiser), bombing runs are available in this battle. Select the bombing run icon on the command bar and then target a visible area to bomb by left-clicking on the battlefield. Choose a point between the Rebel soldiers and the power generator. After a few seconds, several TIE bombers fly by and drop bombs on the position, often killing all of the infantry and destroying the power generator. This knocks out the Rebel shields over their base. After ordering a bombing run, you have to wait before you can call in another run. You can now advance toward the power generator's location to take control of two build pads and build structures on them if you so desire.

OBJECTIVE

6. Eliminate the Rebel base.

It's time to attack the Rebel base. Lead with your stormtroopers and order them to take cover as soon as they come into contact with the Rebel soldiers. Don't forget to use your speeder bikes to rush in and drop thermal detonators near enemy units. They will not harm your troops. You can also call in bombing runs to destroy the structures or for killing enemy troops. As with thermal detonators, the bombs won't hurt your troops—so call them in as close as you want. Continue until you have destroyed all of the enemy infantry units and their structures to complete this tutorial.

Imperial troops move in to destroy the Rebel base and eliminate all enemy units.

Skirmish Tutorials

The remaining two tutorials, numbers 6 and 7, cover the game's Skirmish mode. Skirmishes are a different type of game than the Campaigns and Galactic Conquest missions. They function more like a traditional real-time strategy (RTS) game and therefore have their own unique features and differences. For more information on the Skirmishes, check out the Skirmishes section. It covers the last two tutorials and provides all you need to know to skirmish your way to victory.

May the Force Be with You!

After reading through this chapter and completing the first five tutorials, you are ready to get into the real game. It is suggested that you play the Rebellion Campaign first, followed by the Imperial Campaign. These games not only provide a lot of story line, but the mission structure of these games helps prepare you for the Galactic Conquest missions, which are much more open. Be sure to check out the Tactics section for a detailed look at tactics you can use in both the galactic mode and in ground and space tactical battles. The next three sections contain information on the units and structures in the game along with tips on how to use them to your advantage. Finally, for intel on all the planetary systems in the galaxy, check out the section titled Planetary Systems of the Galaxy.

Now what are you waiting for? The galaxy is yours to conquer.

Star Wars Empire at War features several different types of games all in one package. There is the strategic-level galactic game where you produce units and fleets and move them from system to system as you take control of the galaxy. As your fleets come in contact with other fleets, then you must fight a tactical space battle. However, to take control of a system, you must land troops on the surface and fight a tactical land battle. Therefore, in order to master this game, you must become proficient in all three different parts of the game.

This chapter focuses on ground combat and space battles. For galactic strategy, turn to the Rebel Campaign and Empire Campaign sections, which describe each side's strategies in the Campaign mode, and the Galactic Conquest section, which offers general strategies for that mode.

Ground Combat

You engage in ground combat whenever opposing ground forces meet on the surface of the planet. You can fight ground battles in the Campaigns, during Galactic Conquest games, and also during Skirmish games. Therefore, it is important to know how best to use your troops to achieve a victory over your enemy.

Ground combat begins when enemy units land on a planet's surface.

Reinforcement Points

During ground battles, reinforcement points are extremely important. You must control these to land reinforcements during the battle. On some maps, the reinforcement points have a capacity value that allows you to land that value of units on the map. The total unit capacity for your army on the map is equal to the sum of the capacity values of the reinforcement points that you control. This only applies to the attacker. The defender can have all of their units on the map at the beginning of the battle.

Due to the capacity values, it is important for both the attacker and defender to take control of the reinforcement points. The attacker needs them to increase the number of units that can be fielded, while the defender wants to deny them to the attacker and thus limit the units to fight against. In fact, if the defender can take over all of the reinforcement points, the attacker can't bring down any more reinforcements until regaining control of one of those points.

Many reinforcement points have build pads near them. These are great places to build turrets to help defend the reinforcement point. However, attackers can use these build pads to construct bacta healing stations and repair stations—creating an impromptu base where units can regain their health before going back into battle. When you are the attacker, always leave at least one combat unit behind to defend your reinforcement point with the highest capacity value. If you lose all of your reinforcement points, you are in trouble. Artillery units are a good candidate for this type of job. Just be sure to have a turret or other unit out in front to act as a spotter so the artillery can fire on enemies as they approach, before they get close enough to attack your artillery units.

Reinforcement points allow the attacker to bring down additional units.

TIP

When on a planet where the indigenous population is your ally, use these infantry units to protect your reinforcement points while you use your combat units for going on the offensive. The indigenous units automatically respawn at their dwellings when they are destroyed.

Terrain

The planet surfaces on which you fight are never flat and open. Vegetation, water, lava, escarpments, and even buildings break up the terrain, forcing units to move along paths to get across the map. These paths limit movement and even create choke points or narrow areas that are more easily defended by a few units. Some units, such as airspeeders, can fly right over terrain to move to their objectives. Repulsor vehicles such as the T2-B and 2-M tanks can move across deep water that prohibits the movement of other ground units. Therefore, when you are preparing to invade or defend a planet, it is important to take into account the terrain.

Some of the above barriers, such as escarpments and vegetation, can block direct fire between units on opposite sides. However, artillery units can fire right up and over these, allowing them to attack enemies without exposing themselves to return fire.

Good Ground

Good ground is a feature found on most maps. It consists of a small, open fortification that can be used by infantry. This feature provides additional protection for infantry located within its walls, decreasing the amount of damage they receive from enemy direct fire—however, this does not apply to artillery fire or bombing run attacks. Infantry units in good ground can hold out much longer than if they were out in the open. Because good ground is often located near reinforcement points, position infantry squads there to protect the location.

Good ground gives infantry units within it a defensive bonus.

Ground Units

Units used to fight battles on the surfaces of planets can be categorized into four groups—heroes, infantry, vehicles, and artillery. Due to the rock, paper, scissors aspect of the game, it is important to use the right unit for the task at hand.

TIP

A good ground force includes a variety of units. You will have a very difficult time invading or defending a planet with only a single type of unit.

Heroes

Heroes are some of the most powerful units in the game due to their special abilities and their increased amount of health, which lets them survive on the battlefield much longer than a typical infantry unit. Therefore, it is often a good idea to bring along a hero for a ground assault mission to give your faction an advantage.

Heroes such as the Emperor have special abilities that can really add to your forces.

Heroes have different abilities. Darth Vader and the Emperor are very destructive, able to take on groups of enemies single-handedly. Others, such as Obi-Wan Kenobi, are less powerful at fighting, but can support the other units in your force. Han Solo can briefly disable vehicles with his EMP burst while Chewbacca can hijack an enemy vehicle and use it against them. R2-D2 and C-3PO, which together make up a single unit, have no combat capability.

However, they can take control of enemy turrets—including turbo-laser towers—and can also repair your vehicles. Heroes can also fight conventionally with either their blasters or lightsabers as their special abilities recharge after use. However, keep a close eye on them. They are not immortal. If they get caught in an artillery barrage, they will take damage and can even be killed.

NOTE

Colonel Veers, an Imperial hero, appears on the battlefield in his own modified AT-AT walker, the *Blizzard 1*. This functions like a normal AT-AT walker with the addition of the maximum firepower ability.

Infantry

Infantry is one of the weakest units in the game. However, it is also very important during ground battles. Infantry units, including heroes, are the only units that can take control of locations such as reinforcement points and build pads. Therefore, it is important to take along infantry and use them in battle even if it takes up a capacity slot that could be filled with a higher-firepower vehicle. Most infantry has the same special ability—take cover. This orders the units to spread out and decreases the damage they take from enemy fire. However, it also slows their movement.

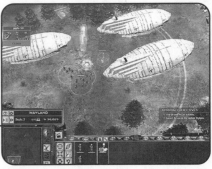

Infantry are necessary for taking control of locations and great for defending your reinforcement points to keep those new units coming.

Infantry comes in groups of soldiers called squads. Each soldier has its own health meter and takes damage individually. As soldiers are lost, the squad loses firepower. Healing a squad at a bacta healing station or through hero abilities returns the health of the remaining soldiers to maximum level. It does not replace lost soldiers. Infantry is very vulnerable on the battlefield. Artillery and bombing runs can quickly wipe out an entire squad. In addition, tanks and other ground vehicles that do not use repulsor technology can drive right over enemy infantry, smashing them into the ground. Therefore, keep your infantry behind your vehicles or protected inside good ground. In most cases, leave infantry back at your base or reinforcement points for defense—then bring them forward when you need to capture a location.

The Empire has only one type of infantry—the stormtroopers. They are best used against enemy infantry. The Rebels, on the other hand, have three different types of infantry, and it is important to use the right kind of infantry for the correct task. The Rebel soldiers are similar to the stormtroopers and best used for fighting enemy infantry. Plex soldiers are specialized for attacking enemy vehicles. Finally, the infiltrators are experts at not only attacking enemy infantry, but also destroying structures.

Vehicles

Most of the combat on a planet's surface takes place between vehicles. Most vehicles come in groups that form platoons or companies. It is a good idea to keep vehicles in these groups rather than sending them off on their own. This allows the vehicles within a group to combine their firepower and cause more damage to the enemy.

Group vehicles of the same type together and order them to concentrate their fire on a single target to destroy it quicker. Then select another target for the group. This minimizes the damage your vehicles take over the course of an engagement because each enemy you destroy means less firepower aimed at your units.

Not all vehicles are the same. While they may be capable of attacking all types of units, many are specialized and more effective against certain types. TIE maulers, with their laser cannons and fast speed, are best used against infantry. However, put them up against tanks and they will be wiped out. Repulsor tanks, including the Rebel T2-B and the Imperial 2-M, are equipped with shields that absorb laser damage as long as they remain online. Each hit they take reduces the shield level. However, shields recharge over time.

Because each type of vehicle has both strengths and weaknesses, vary your forces. For example, the Imperials should use TIE maulers and AT-STs together, with the maulers concentrating on infantry while the walkers take care of vehicles and turrets. The Imperial AT-AT is powerful and can take lots of damage, but it's very vulnerable to the tow cable attack by Rebel airspeeders. An AT-AA makes a great escort because it can shoot down the airspeeders and keep your AT-ATs moving forward rather than toppling to the ground.

Artillery

Artillery deserves a separate category. This destructive unit can wipe out an enemy force almost single-handedly. Yet the downside to artillery is its slow speed and vulnerability to enemy fire. Artillery is a support unit. In order to fire, you must first deploy it. When you want to move it, the artillery units first undeploy, and then move. Therefore, artillery units can't move and fire at the same time and require a couple seconds to transition from one mode to the other.

Keep your artillery behind your other units for protection, and use their long-range firepower to clear the way.

Artillery units are great for defending a base or reinforcement point. Position them away from the entrances, but within firing range so that they can hit enemy units as they approach. Also use artillery during advances against enemy positions. Lead with other vehicles and have the artillery follow. When you come across the enemy, quickly order the artillery to deploy—it automatically fires at enemy units while you concentrate on controlling your other units. Artillery makes short work of turrets and infantry and is also effective against vehicles and structures.

A unique aspect of artillery is that its weapon range is farther than its sight range. Therefore, it can attack targets that it can't see on its own. Use other units that are cheaper or can take more damage as spotters. Artillery can attack whatever you can see through the fog of war. When defending a base with artillery, turrets can act as your spotters at the entrance, allowing you to keep the artillery safely back where the enemy can't see it.

TIP

Rebel artillery units come with spotter droids. You do not have to send these droids out to personally view enemy units for your artillery to attack. Instead they have a sensor ping ability that allows you to briefly remove the fog of war from a part of the map. Use this for targeting not only your artillery, but also bombing runs. Because the spotter droids can do this from anywhere on the map, keep them in a safe spot where the enemy won't destroy them.

While not really artillery, bombing runs are similar. If you have bomber units in orbit over the planet—Y-wings for the Rebels or capital ships carrying TIE bombers for the Empire—you can call in bombing runs. This orders three bombers to fly in from off the map and lay down a large area of destruction that destroys infantry and light vehicles and causes a lot of damage to turrets and structures. Because of the firepower provided, always bring bombers along with your invasion force. Once you have ordered a bombing run, you can't call in another until the bombers reload. Therefore, it's best to use them against concentrations of enemies or to clear a path for your units through enemy defenses.

The defender during a ground battle not only has the units already positioned on the planets, but also has garrison units provided by structures. For example, barracks provide additional infantry. When the garrison unit is destroyed, another spawns at the structure. Therefore, it's a good idea to build barracks and vehicle factories on those planets bordering the enemy. This only applies to Campaign and Galactic Conquest games—not Skirmishes.

Invading a Planet

When landing a force on the surface of a planet to take control of system, you are often at an initial disadvantage. You can only bring down as many units as the reinforcement point allows. Therefore, you must land as many units as possible and then send them to capture other reinforcement points to increase your unit capacity and bring even more units into battle.

Take out power generators before rushing in to attack an enemy base.

However, before leaving your landing zone, take control of any nearby build pads and construct turrets to defend this location while you advance on other reinforcement points. As you move out, look for build pads along your way. You can see the pads even through the fog of war. However, you can't tell if there is a turret or other structure on them until you come into sight range. Engage turrets with the right type of unit. Use vehicles to take out anti-infantry turrets and infantry for anti-vehicle turrets. Bombing runs (if you have them in orbit) or artillery units (if you've purchased them) work even better. However, don't try to rush past a turret or you will take unnecessary damage. Instead, destroy it and then take control of the build pad and construct your own turret or other structure.

You do not have to take control of all reinforcement points. Some may be too difficult or dangerous to get to initially. Therefore, get the easiest ones first and make do with the units you can get. Next, go after the power generator if the enemy has turbolaser towers or a shield generator. Locate this with fast units that can quickly move about the battlefield. Then either call in a bombing run or bring forward some units to attack the power generator. This makes the attack on the enemy base much easier.

As you advance, take time to build turrets on build pads.

TIP

The sooner you can attack the enemy base and destroy the structures, the fewer enemy garrison units you will have to deal with.

Before rushing to the enemy base, make sure you have a bombing run ready to go. You can use it to take out turrets and structures or clusters of units if the enemy has been stockpiling them at the base. Concentrate on the structures that have powerful garrison units, such as the advanced vehicle factory and heavy vehicle factory, because you don't want any more units coming from these.

Once the enemy base is in ruins, just mop up any remaining units to win the battle.

Defending a Planet

As the defender, you have the advantage of having all your units ready to go, as well as the garrison units you receive from your production structures. Because you have more units initially, it's important to use your advantage while you have it. Send infantry to take control of any reinforcement points the enemy does not yet have and to build turrets at build pads. Meanwhile your main force heads to the enemy landing zone to attack enemy units and to try to take control of the reinforcement point to prevent the enemies from landing any more troops. If you can get some artillery down near the enemy landing zone, you can quickly turn it into a kill zone.

Call in bombing runs on enemy reinforcement points as they are landing troops.

You may not always have enough units to rush the enemy landing zone successfully. Therefore, you have to play a bit more conservatively. If you have a power generator, defend it and build turrets near it. This keeps your powered structures—shield generator and turbolaser towers—operating and helps you defend the planet. Use your units for hit-and-run attacks, trying to take over reinforcement points the enemy fails to defend. This usually causes them to send units from their attack force back to reclaim the reinforcement point and weaken their attack force. As the defender, you do not have access to bombing runs. Therefore, you have to rely on artillery for your heavy firepower. If you have a heavy vehicle factory, artillery units spawn there as the structure's garrison force.

Combine different types of units into a force so that you can take on whatever the enemy sends your way.

Space Battles

Space battles are different from ground battles. However, some of the tactics remain the same. A space battle occurs when two opposing fleets occupy orbital slots over the same planet. These battles are won by eliminating the enemy from the map.

Asteroids and Nebulae

Space maps have their own unique types of terrain. On some maps, asteroids act as a semi-permeable barrier. Small ships such as corvettes, as well as fighters and bombers, can move through asteroid fields without any problems. However, larger capital ships can't move through them. If they try, they take damage and can be destroyed. As a result, asteroids can form choke points in space, forcing a fleet to move through narrow openings and limiting maneuverability. These choke points serve as great spots for targeting missile barrages and positioning defending units.

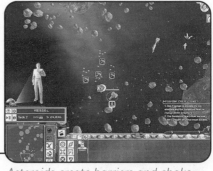

Asteroids create barriers and choke points in space.

Nebulae, on the other hand, are areas of space containing highly energetic ionized particles. All space units can move through nebulae without taking damage. However, while within a nebula, a unit cannot use its special abilities. Therefore, it is best to try to avoid nebulae. On the other hand, as the defender, position your units so that the enemy has to move through a nebula to get to you. This allows you to use your special abilities, but denies your enemy the same capability.

Space Stations

Space stations can be constructed during the galactic mode of a game by the system's owner. Each space station is armed with defensive weapons as well as a garrison of units. The higher the space station's level, the more defenses and the greater the number and types of garrison units. The attacker must destroy the enemy's space station to win the battle. Therefore, it is important to understand how a space station operates. Like a capital ship, a space station has hard-points. Most of these are weapon batteries or launchers. Destroying these hard-points limits the space station's ability to fire at enemies.

Space stations are an important part in a system's defenses and can fight off small to medium enemy fleets on their own.

The shield generator should be the main target when attacking a space station. Once it is destroyed, the space station loses its shields and becomes vulnerable to laser fire. The second target, once the shields are down, is the hangar. As long as this hard-point exists, the space station can continue to spawn garrison units. Take out the hangar, and you prevent additional garrison units from spawning. Next, go after the proton torpedo and concussion missile launchers because these weapons can penetrate the shields of your capital ships. Finally, take out the rest of the hard-points to destroy the space station.

Space Units

Space units come in all sizes from the smallest fighter to the largest Star Destroyer. Like ground units, each space unit has its own strengths and weaknesses. Therefore, use each type to maximize its effectiveness against the enemy.

TIP

When building a fleet, be sure to include all types of units. If you just go for all capital ships, you leave yourself open to attacks by smaller units that capital ships are not equipped to defend against.

Fighters

Fighters are the smallest space units and are best used against enemy fighters. Rebels must build their fighters separately while Imperial fighters are included with their capital ships. Even though fighters may not have a lot of firepower, it's still important to include them in your fleets. Fighter squadrons are great for swarming over enemy ships and space stations, diverting fire away from your large ships and allowing them to move in for the attack.

Mass your fighters and bombers together to attack capital ships and space stations.

Bombers

Bombers, like fighters, are either ordered separately by the Rebels or included with Imperial capital ships. Their role is to attack enemy space stations and capital ships to take out vital hard-points such as shields. Because bombers are armed with proton torpedoes, they can attack right through the shields and cause structural damage. By themselves, bombers are very vulnerable. Therefore, group them with fighters and order the entire group to attack. The fighters don't cause much damage, but they help divert the enemy fire from the bombers and overwhelm the defenses.

Use bombers to take down the shields and other hard-points on space stations.

Corvettes

Corvette-type ships, including both the Corellian corvette and the Tartan patrol cruiser, are built for attacking fighters and bombers. Place them between your capital ships and the enemy to engage enemy bombers and then fighters. They can also attack enemy corvettes. Their laser batteries do not offer enough firepower for them to be effective against capital ships. However, if necessary, order them in to attack to divert fire away from your own capital ships.

Corvettes can screen your capital ships against enemy fighters.

Missile Cruisers

Missile cruisers are the artillery of space battles. They have long-range firepower but are very vulnerable to attack. Because they fire concussion missiles, they cause structural damage to enemy units, passing right through shields. In addition, their area barrage ability lets them plaster an area of space. Group several missile cruisers for these area barrages. Even the most powerful capital ship cannot move through such a barrage without being severely damaged or destroyed. Keep your missile cruisers behind your capital ships for protection. They are also great for attacking space stations because their barrages can damage multiple hard-points at once.

The missile cruisers' area barrages can be devastating to capital ships.

Imperial Capital Ships

Imperial capital ships carry squadrons of TIE fighters and TIE bombers along with their other weaponry. The smaller capital ships, such as the Acclamator, are best used against enemy corvettes, while the Star Destroyers are meant for taking on Rebel capital ships. Most of these ships can boost their firepower. What this does is hold the fire of all the ships' batteries and then lets them loose in one powerful volley. This is best used when targeting a single enemy. An Imperial fleet is always built around capital ships and you should have lots in your main space fleet. Also spread them around the galaxy to help defend your border planets. In fact, Imperial capital ships with some Tartan cruisers can take on most Rebel fleets that try to invade your space.

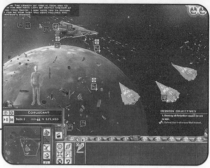

Imperial capital ships can put out a lot of firepower with their special ability activated.

TIP

After destroying the weapons hard-points on an enemy capital ship, do not finish it off. Instead, let it float around and take up a capacity slot so the enemy can't bring in a reinforcement for it.

Rebel Capital Ships

Rebel capital ships include the frigates as well as the Mon Calamari cruisers. Their special ability is to boost shield strength, allowing them to take more damage during a battle. Unless you have the cruisers, don't take on the large Imperial capital ships with just your frigates alone. If you do have to fight, send your fighters and bombers in first to take out their shields and hangar. This keeps the enemy busy while your frigates attack at long range. The Mon Calamari cruisers, on the other hand, have the firepower to duke it out with the Imperial capital ships. However, still use fighters and bombers to divert fire away from your cruisers.

Most Rebel capital ships are smaller and less powerful than their Imperial counterparts.

TIP

Because the Rebels lack the same firepower in their space fleets as the Imperials have, always keep in mind that you can retreat—especially if the enemy is stronger than you anticipated or things are not going your way. Don't stay and lose your entire fleet. Instead, move your fleet away from the enemy, activating speed or shield boosts, and then give the retreat order.

Satellite Defenses

Some space maps have satellite pads that function like surface build pads. Move one of your units next to it to take control. Then build lasers to use against fighters or missiles for larger enemy ships. While it costs some credits to build these, they give your fleet some additional firepower and are especially useful for the defender.

Planetary Weapons

Each faction has its own planetary weapon that can be used to attack enemy units in space. The Rebel ion cannon can disable an enemy capital ship, impairing its shields, movement, and firing rate for a limited time. First, target the largest Imperial ships that offer the biggest threat. Then ignore these disabled ships while you deal with the active enemies. They also make important targets for missile barrages, because the ion cannon must recharge after each shot. However, if you fire it as soon as it is ready, you can have up to three enemy ships disabled at one time. These disabled ships still count toward the enemy's capacity on the map, so this makes your job as a defender a lot easier.

The Imperials, with their emphasis on firepower and destruction, have the hypervelocity cannon as their planetary weapon. The projectiles pass right through enemy shields and cause structural damage, making it easier for your fleet to finish off the enemy ship. This weapon also requires recharge time after each shot. Build these weapons on your planets that border enemy territory to make it a lot easier to prevent the enemy from taking control of your systems.

The Rebel Alliance is a much smaller force than the military of the Galactic Empire. They often have to make do with lighter units that use tactics and cunning to make up for firepower. The key to victory is knowing how to use each type of unit to its maximum potential.

Heroes
Mon Mothma

Mon Mothma is the Rebel Alliance's quiet conscience and central leader. Born on Chandrila, Mon Mothma received her political training early in life. Her father was an arbiter-general for the Old Republic, while her mother served as a planetary governor. She was the youngest person elected to the Old Republic Senate and became a senior senator. Due to her great wisdom, Mon Mothma quickly realized that the Old Republic was crumbling. When Supreme Chancellor Palpatine was granted emergency powers at the dawn of the Clone Wars, she worked with Senators Padmé Amidala and Bail Organa to quietly petition senators who opposed his rule. They banded together to challenge Palpatine, but the villain became too powerful when he eradicated the Jedi Order and proclaimed himself Emperor. Mon Mothma remained committed to the principles of democracy, using the political influence she had left to help create the Rebel Alliance.

Stats

Unit Type: Galactic and Space Hero
Special: Defensive Morale Boost (when in combat), 25% production discount on the Galactic Map
Good Against: None
Vulnerable To: All

Notes

Though Mon Mothma provides a morale boost while in combat, she should stay as far away from combat as possible. In many games, if she is killed, you lose. She helped form the Rebel Alliance and is vital to its continued existence. She is also very useful to you in terms of economy. You receive a 25 percent discount on all costs at the planet where she is located. This goes for recruiting troops, constructing vehicles or space vessels, and even building structures. Early in a game, when credits are few, move her to your planets before making a purchase. This helps your credits go much farther and gives you an advantage over the Empire.

Captain Raymus Antilles

Captain Raymus Antilles belongs to the same bloodline as that of Queen Breha of Alderaan, though he himself holds no royal title. Antilles is level-headed, schooled in diplomacy, and a capable pilot. He is also a brave Rebel sympathizer and skilled at running Imperial blockades, but he lacks experience leading ground troops. He is being groomed to be the sole captain of the *Tantive IV*, a Corellian corvette. Currently he shares this position with his mentor, Captain Colton, who plans to retire from active piloting duty to teach full time at Aldera University. For some of his more dangerous missions, Captain Antilles often pilots another vessel—the *Sundered Heart*, a modified starship of the same class as the *Tantive IV*. Antilles received the starship as a gift for running aid and medical supplies past several Imperial blockades. The *Sundered Heart* was later modified with additional weapon capabilities needed in the event of Imperial entanglements.

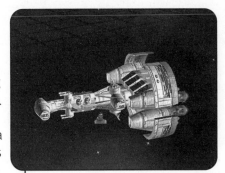

Stats

Unit Type: Space Hero
Special: Weaken Enemy, Boost Engine Power
Good Against: TIE Fighters, TIE Bombers, Pirate Fighters
Vulnerable To: Acclamator Cruisers, Victory-Class Star Destroyers, Imperial Star Destroyers

Notes

Captain Antilles is often required to lead raids during Campaign missions. He is available only during space battles and never goes to the surface for land combat. His ability to boost engine power allows him to attack an enemy and then quickly get away before taking too much damage. In addition, his weaken enemy ability allows you to target an area. All enemies within that area have the damage they inflict against you reduced for a limited time. Using this ability on a large capital ship or several smaller ships and fighters can turn a battle in your favor.

Artoo-Detoo/See-Threepio (R2-D2/C-3PO)

R2-D2 and C-3PO are a dynamic droid duo with a knack for being in the wrong place at the right time. Artoo is a brave droid that was assigned to Queen Amidala's royal starship during the Trade Federation blockade of Naboo. Artoo repaired the damaged deflector shield generator, allowing the vessel to escape. Like all astromech droids, Artoo has built-in tools that he uses to interpret networks and repair vehicles. Artoo converses in a dense electronic language consisting primarily of beeps, chirps, and whistles. He can understand most forms of human speech but must have his own communications interpreted by a starship's computers or his counterpart C-3PO. C-3PO is a protocol droid built from scrap parts by a young Anakin Skywalker. He remained on Tatooine when Anakin left to join the Jedi Order and he was reunited with Anakin years later. After the Clone Wars, the two droids were commissioned to the care of Raymus Antilles.

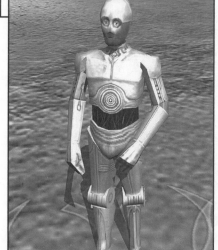

Stats

Unit Type: Ground Hero
Special: Control Turret, Repair Vehicle
Good Against: Turrets
Vulnerable To: All

Notes

These two droids comprise a single unit. When you select them, you give orders to both at the same time. On the ground, they are a hero unit with some important abilities. R2-D2 can slice into the controls of an enemy turret and take control of it, turning it to your side so that it begins firing at your enemies. Furthermore, as an astromech, this little droid can repair your vehicles in the field. This can be handy when you lack a repair station.

R2-D2 and C-3PO also act as a unit on the galactic map. While they do not engage in battles, they can move about the galaxy in their own ship, which can't be detected by enemy units. Therefore, you can send them to systems as spies to see what the enemy has in orbit. You can also use them to steal technology from enemy systems that the Rebels can then use to begin producing new types of units and structures. You should always be using these droids for either stealing or scouting. They can be worthwhile during land battles as long as you protect them.

Han and Chewie (Han Solo and Chewbacca)

Born on Corellia, Han Solo was a hot-headed teenage swoop racer who enrolled in the Imperial Academy, but his stubborn nature and belief in fairness derailed his military career. Han Solo and Chewbacca met when Han's group of TIE fighters attacked Chewie's slave ship. Han boarded the ship and found an injured Chewbacca in the pilot's seat. Han's superior ordered him to bring him the Wookiee's hide, but Han refused the order. After his discharge, Solo took up a life of questionable repute, taking on mercenary jobs and running a regular glitterstim-spice smuggling route for the likes of crime lord Jabba the Hutt. Saving Chewbacca's life resulted in a "life debt" from the Wookiee. Chewbacca became first the protector and then the best friend of the Corellian. He serves as first mate to Han as they embark on a smuggling career, aided by the swift *Millennium Falcon*, which Han won in a game of sabacc from Lando Calrissian.

Stats

Unit Type: Space and Ground Hero
Special: Invulnerability (Space), EMP Burst (Han only),
Steal Vehicle (Chewie only), Sprint (Ground)
Good Against: Vehicles
Vulnerable To: Unknown

Notes

During space battles, both Han and Chewie work together aboard the *Millennium Falcon*. This ship is good for moving quickly around the battlefield. It can briefly become invulnerable to enemy fire. This makes the ship great for moving in close to cause some damage, and then getting away when the ability wears off. The *Millennium Falcon* is good against TIE fighters and TIE bombers, and it is vulnerable to Tartan cruisers.

   Han and Chewie are separate units during ground battles. Both enjoy the sprint ability that allows them to run quickly for a limited time. Use it to get away from the enemy or to rush in and use their other abilities. Han can let loose an EMP burst that disables all nearby enemy vehicles. Use him to sprint out into a group of vehicles and then EMP them. Chewbacca, on the other hand, is great at hijacking enemy vehicles. Use this ability to take over any enemy ground vehicle and use it as your own. When he decides to get out, he sets the vehicle to self-destruct so that it can't be used against you.

Commander Ackbar

In his youth, Ackbar served as Coral City's representative to the Calamarian Council and became a major political figure on the watery world of Mon Calamari. When Imperial forces enslaved his people, he was forced into servitude as Grand Moff Tarkin's interpreter. During his time in servitude, Ackbar secretly learned about many of Tarkin's projects, strategies, and battle tactics. When he was eventually rescued by the Rebellion, the knowledge he had acquired proved most useful to the Alliance. Ackbar's greatest contribution to the Alliance may have been convincing his own people, the Mon Calamari, to join the Rebel cause. Once they committed to the Rebellion, the Mon Cal donated several powerful star cruisers and hordes of skilled technicians and pilots. Ackbar captains a Mon Cal cruiser named *Home One* that serves as his personal flagship.

Stats

Unit Type: Space Hero
Special: Boost Shield Power, Redirect All Fire Power
Good Against: Acclamator Cruisers, Tartan Patrol Cruisers,
Broadside Cruisers
Vulnerable To: TIE Bombers

Notes

Commander Ackbar appears in space battles aboard his flagship cruiser. He brings a lot of firepower into the battle. During battles, he can boost his shield power, allowing him to take more laser damage. This can even be used once shields have gone down to quickly restore them to full power. Ackbar can also order friendly nearby ships to redirect all of their firepower against his selected target. This creates a massive amount of firepower on one target, often quickly destroying it. Ackbar's flagship is the most powerful Rebel space unit in the game, so don't use it carelessly during a battle.

Red Squadron

Red Squadron is an X-wing fighter team that was created early in the Galactic Civil War. The pilots in Red Squadron were drawn from several other groups including the Ecliptic Evaders, the Tierfon Yellow Aces, and the Dantooine Squadron. These pilots were known for their daring piloting and tactics, making Red Squadron the most highly skilled and sought-after flying unit in the Rebel Alliance fleet. Red Squadron was often chosen for dangerous missions requiring their unique set of piloting skills. Throughout the war, Red Squadron saw many pilots come and go, but at its initial formation, the fighter group was commanded by Garven Dreis whose designation was Red Leader. Other notable pilots in Red Squadron early on in the Galactic Civil War were Wedge Antilles (Red 2), Biggs Darklighter (Red 3), John D. Branon (Red 4), Luke Skywalker (Red 5) and Jek Porkins (Red 6).

Stats

Unit Type: Space Hero
Special: Lock Wings, Lucky Shot
Good Against: TIE Fighters, TIE Bombers, Death Star
Vulnerable To: Tartan Patrol Cruisers

Notes

Red Squadron is a group of X-wing fighters of which Luke Skywalker is a part. They can lock their s-foil wings flat rather in the X formation in order to fly faster during a battle. This comes at a cost in the damage they can inflict while their wings are locked. In addition, Luke Skywalker's use of the Force allows the squadron the lucky shot ability, which increases their accuracy and damage against a target. However, what makes this unit invaluable is that it is the only unit in the game that can destroy the Death Star. When you see the Death Star headed to one of your systems, send Red Squadron as a part of the fleet to intercept the Death Star. After you have destroyed the Death Star's escort fleet, if Red Squadron is still in the battle, they automatically destroy the Death Star. If not, then the Death Star will destroy your planet.

Obi-Wan (Obi-Wan Kenobi)

As a Padawan learner, the young Obi-Wan Kenobi was apprenticed to Qui-Gon Jinn. Although Obi-Wan was heavily influenced by the teachings of many leading Jedi, he was uniquely guided by the teachings of his Master. When Obi-Wan was on the verge of becoming a Jedi Knight, he and Qui-Gon were sent to resolve a trade dispute on Naboo. Obi-Wan and Qui-Gon found themselves battling the Trade Federation and later a mysterious Sith warrior named Darth Maul who killed Qui-Gon. They also discovered a young boy on Tatooine named Anakin Skywalker with tremendous affinity for the Force. Obi-Wan promised to take young Anakin as his Padawan, regardless of the Jedi Council's reservations about the boy's future. This promise later led Obi-Wan to confront Anakin in an attempt to steer him back to the light side of the Force. When that failed and Emperor Palpatine assumed control, Obi-Wan went into hiding on Tatooine to secretly watch over and protect Anakin's son, Luke.

Stats

Unit Type: Ground Hero
Special: Force Protect, Force Heal
Good Against: None
Vulnerable To: Darth Vader

Notes

Obi-Wan is a great hero to include in your land battles. While he is not all that great in combat, he can help other units in your force. With his Force protect ability, he can decrease the amount of damage nearby units receive from enemy fire. He can also use the Force to heal Rebel infantry. Obi-Wan is not available during the Campaign game.

Kyle Katarn

Kyle Katarn is a man who has seen all sides of the Force. Born on Sulon, the moon of Sullust, Kyle came from farmer stock and had a close-knit family. While training at the Imperial Academy, he was dealt a crushing blow: An Imperial notification tricked him into believing his parents were killed in a Rebel ambush. Vowing revenge against the Alliance, Katarn joined the special ops division of the Imperial Army. However, he soon discovered the true face of the Empire after learning that they were responsible for the death of his family. His hatred grew for the Empire's underhanded ways. Katarn ended his Imperial service when he elected to help Jan Ors escape from their clutches. Having gone rogue and now freed from his Imperial post, Katarn took work as a mercenary-for-hire, pirate, and reluctant Rebel operative flying a ship named the *Moldy Crow*. Along with Ors, he helps the Alliance fight against the Empire and undermine the Imperial war machine.

Stats

Unit Type: Ground Hero
Special: Thermal Detonator, Sprint
Good Against: Vehicles
Vulnerable To: Unknown

Notes

Kyle Katarn is available only during ground battles. However, his abilities can come in handy. Like Han Solo and Chewbacca, Katarn can briefly sprint. He can also throw a thermal detonator a short distance, which can destroy a vehicle or other units within the blast proximity. Use Katarn to support other units rather than on his own.

Ground Units

Rebel Soldiers (SpecForces Infantry Platoon)

The SpecForces are the ground troops of the Rebel Alliance. They are assigned to fleets to be sent on detached duties to sectors that need them. Infantry platoons or Rebel soldiers are organized into formal units, much like the Imperial Army. However they rarely operate in the field in such units. Instead, they are divided into task forces, consisting of as many soldiers and as much equipment needed to carry out a specific military objective.

Rebel soldiers are trained to use a variety of tactics, easily adapting to different environments and finding ways to take cover and hold a position in any situation. Hand blasters are standard for every Rebel soldier, but some divisions have been known to specialize in particular equipment for some of the more dangerous missions.

Stats

Primary Manufacturer: Various Recruiting Locations and Training Facilities
Unit Type: Infantry
Special: Take Cover
Good Against: Stormtrooper Companies
Vulnerable To: TIE Maulers, Scout Troopers, Anti-Infantry Turrets

Notes

Rebel soldiers are the common infantrymen of the Rebellion. Their main purpose is to fight stormtroopers, and they can take control of locations such as reinforcement points and build pads. Like all infantry units, Rebel soldiers can take cover. This orders a squad to spread out, reducing the damage they take from enemy fire, but also reducing their movement speed and their ability to avoid being run over by enemy vehicles. A company contains three squads of five soldiers each.

Plex Missile Soldiers (SpecForces PLX Missile Soldier Platoon)

Several divisions of the Rebel Alliance SpecForces carry specialized equipment for more dangerous missions. SpecForces Plex missile soldiers carry PLX-2M missile tubes as standard equipment for those tough jobs. Rebel field commanders often use Plex soldier companies to get the door open for them when troops get pinned down by menacing Imperial ground vehicles and turrets.

Plex soldiers are trained to use a variety of tactics, easily adapting to different environments and finding ways to take cover and hold a position in any situation. Plex soldiers carry PLX-2M missile tubes as standard equipment over the hand blaster for missions where an added punch is needed to crack through a tough position.

Stats

Primary Manufacturer: Various Recruiting Locations and Training Facilities
Unit Type: Infantry
Special: Take Cover
Good Against: AT-STs, 2-M Repulsor Tanks, TIE Maulers
Vulnerable To: TIE Maulers, Stormtrooper Companies, Anti-Infantry Turrets

Notes

Until the Rebels get the T4-B tank, the Plex soldiers are an important unit to use against enemy vehicles. However, when facing large groups of vehicles, they are vulnerable. There are two squads of three soldiers each in a company.

Infiltrators (SpecForces Infiltrators)

Infiltrators are among the most feared of the SpecForces and are specially chosen for their distinct hatred of the Empire. These elite forces are known for their ability to slip through tight Imperial security and sabotage important installations and ships. They're equally comfortable on abduction and rescue missions.

Much like the rest of the SpecForces, infiltrators were trained to use a variety of tactics and weapons. Most stick to a basic weapon layout to stay light on their feet, but many infiltrators carry sniper rifles and thermal detonators as well. Infiltrators have rarely been seen leaving the scene of the deadly explosion they caused.

Stats

Primary Manufacturer: Various Recruiting Locations and Training Facilities
Unit Type: Infantry
Special: Thermal Detonator
Good Against: Stormtrooper Companies
Vulnerable To: TIE Maulers, Anti-Infantry Turrets

Notes

These elite infantry are great for taking out stormtroopers from a distance. Also use them to sneak into enemy bases and blow up structures with their thermal detonators.

T2-B Repulsor Tank

To protect its standing with the Empire, Yutrane-Trackata agreed to produce mining vehicles and other equipment solely for Imperial use on Aridus. Seeing an opportunity to undermine Imperial authority, Rebel leaders paid Yutrane-Trackata to supply Chubbit resistance fighters on Aridus and the Rebellion with new tanks through several carefully planned raids on its factories there. The raids allowed the Rebellion to acquire several new pieces of technology, including the T2-B repulsor tank.

The T2-B repulsor tank is the second in the T2 series of tanks housing four fire-linked blaster cannons, shields, and a sophisticated array of sensors. The firepower on these tanks isn't the most impressive, but the sensor array allows the tank driver to easily spot and call out targets to other Rebel forces in the battle.

Stats

Primary Manufacturer: Yutrane-Trackata
Unit Type: Tank
Special: Hunt for Enemies
Good Against: Anti-Infantry Turrets, TIE Maulers, SPMA-T
Vulnerable To: AT-ATs, 2-M Repulsor Tanks, Anti-Vehicle Turrets

Notes

T2-B tanks are the first ground vehicles the Rebels can access. Because they glide above the ground using repulsor technology, these vehicles can move across all types of terrain including deep water, allowing you to hit the enemy where they won't expect it. These tanks are also equipped with shields, allowing them to take more damage than basic Imperial vehicles. When a T2-B has its shields reduced, pull it back from the fight and allow its shields to recharge before sending it back in. This allows it to last much longer during a battle. You can order these units to hunt for enemies. They then move out around the map looking for and engaging enemies on their own. However, this is often a good way to lose your tanks, so try to keep them near the rest of your units where they can provide and receive mutual support. There are five tanks per company.

T4-B Heavy Tank

A tank acquired from a Rebel Alliance raid on Aridus and the heaviest armor unit in the Alliance's arsenal, the T4-B is an updated model of the T3-B heavy tank and a larger tracked cousin of the T2-B repulsor tank. Manufactured by Yutrane-Trackata, T4-B tanks are expensive to produce and few in number. Not many of these tanks were seen in the Galactic Civil War because the Rebel Alliance had little opportunity to use the few they had.

T4-B tanks boast twin fire-linked medium laser cannons and triple-fire concussion missile launchers that can cause substantial area of effect damage. The tracked design prevents the tank from traveling over certain types of terrain but still allows it to easily clear any obstacle placed in its way.

Stats

Primary Manufacturer: Yutrane-Trackata
Unit Type: Heavy Tank
Special: Rocket Weapon
Good Against: AT-STs, 2-M Repulsor Tanks, AT-ATs
Vulnerable To: AT-ATs, Anti-Vehicle Turrets

Notes

The T4-B tank is a powerful weapon in the Rebel arsenal. It fires laser cannons normally. However, you can use its ability to fire rockets instead. Click on the ability icon and the tank fires concussion missiles. It's advisable to keep your tanks in rocket firing mode because these rockets cause a lot of damage not only to where they hit, but also to nearby units. A company of three tanks can wreak havoc when targeting the same enemy unit. The rockets are especially effective against stormtroopers, with a single hit taking out an entire squad. Once you have the technology to produce these tanks, you should land at least one company during every ground battle.

MPTL-2a Artillery

After suffering setbacks in early ground battles, Alliance military personnel sent several requests to Loratus Manufacturing to commission a new artillery unit to replace the MPTL used very early in the Galactic Civil War. The 2a model is lighter and faster than its predecessor, but the range and stability tested poorly during field tests, requiring the addition of stabilizers that are deployed in order to fire its torpedoes.

When deployed, the MPTL-2a can fire torpedoes over long distances with the help of a spotter droid or scout unit that can paint targets. Without the droid or spotting unit, the range and accuracy of the MPTL can be severely hampered. The MPTL-2a is slow moving and vulnerable to attack, and it generally requires an armed escort.

Stats

Primary Manufacturer: Loratus Manufacturing
Unit Type: Artillery
Special: Deploy/Undeploy
Good Against: Anti-Infantry Turrets, Anti-Vehicle Turrets, Stormtrooper Companies
Vulnerable To: AT-ATs, 2-M Repulsor Tanks, Scout Troopers

Notes

The MPTL-2a artillery unit is very powerful. They can attack enemy units at long range and cause a lot of damage to an area rather than a single target with volleys of torpedoes. The only downside is that these units are slow and very vulnerable to enemy fire, and they must deploy after moving before they can fire. They are great for defense. When on offense, bring them up with the rest of your attack units, deploy them, then send in your other units and use the artillery to attack turrets and groups of infantry and vehicles. Each company includes two MPTL-2a artillery units as well as two spotter droids. The spotter droids have the sensor ping ability. Keep them back at your base where it is safe, and use this ability to view an area of the battlefield that you can't see due to the fog of war. This allows you to fire at enemy units in this area with your artillery. You can also use the spotters to call in bombing raids when you do not have other units in the vicinity to locate the target zone. Always park these units next to your turrets or with other units for defense.

Assault Speeder (T-47 Airspeeder)

The Incom T-47 airspeeder was deployed in small numbers by the Rebel Alliance throughout the Galactic Civil War. Like all airspeeders, they rely upon repulsorlift drive units and high-powered afterburners to reach speeds in excess of 1,000 kilometers per hour. Rebel engineers modified the T-47s for combat in different environments, often for use as a cheap and fast attack craft to hold off Imperial assaults.

Each heavily armored airspeeder carries a Rebel pilot and a rear-facing gunner, who controls the craft's twin laser cannons. Assault speeders are also equipped with harpoon guns and tow cables, which gunners have improvised uses for in addition to attaching to cargo bins for transport.

Stats

Primary Manufacturer: Incom
Unit Type: Speeder
Special: Tow Cable Attack
Good Against: AT-ATs
Vulnerable To: AT-AAs, Anti-Air Turrets

Notes

Though this unit flies, it is used only during ground battles. The T-47 is a great unit to use against the Empire. It is especially good at attacking AT-ATs with the tow cable attack ability. An airspeeder wraps a cable around the legs of an AT-AT, forcing it to fall down and be destroyed. These units are also great for taking out turbolaser towers and power generators as well as other targets behind enemy lines. Airspeeders can be effectively attacked only by AT-AA units and anti-aircraft turrets. Therefore, if the enemy neglects to build these units, send your airspeeders scouting out the battlefield and attacking units and structures in advance of the rest of your force.

Space Units

Z-95 Headhunter

The Z-95 Headhunter is a ship design older than most of the pilots in the Rebel Alliance. Still considered maneuverable and durable, the Z-95 is a commonly used starfighter. The craft is used by planetary security and air defense units, as well as many pirate and outlaw groups and most notably, the Rebel Alliance. The original Mark I model was designed by Incom Industries and the Subpro Corporation as an atmospheric fighter that could be adapted to space travel.

Z-95 Headhunters typically have a set of triple-blasters on each wing. Rebel engineers have also outfitted the fighter with sophisticated sensor equipment, allowing the pilot to much more easily pinpoint and call out targets for other Rebel forces in the battle.

Stats

Primary Manufacturer: Incom Industries and the now-defunct Subpro Corporation
Unit Type: Fighter
Special: Hunt for Enemies
Good Against: TIE Bombers
Vulnerable To: Tartan Patrol Cruisers, TIE Fighters, Pirate Fighters

Notes

The Z-95 is the early fighter for the Rebellion. Don't even bother producing these once you have access to X-wings. You can order these fighters to go off and search for enemy fighters on their own. This can be great when you are trying to track down groups of enemy fighters during a battle. However, if the enemy has lots of capital ships, this order usually gets your squadron killed. Six Z-95s make up a squadron.

T-65 X-wing

The T-65 X-wing was the last starship designed by Incom Corporation before the company was nationalized by the Empire. Angry and frustrated over Incom's sudden seizure by Imperial forces, the company's senior design team plotted to defect. With the aid of a crack Rebel commando team, the X-wing's creators fled Incom and joined the Rebellion, bringing along the plans and prototypes for the new starfighter.

The X-wing takes its name from its double-layered wings, which separate into an X formation during combat to slow the fighter down to a comfortable attack speed and increase the pilot's field of fire. Along with four high-end laser cannons, the X-wing is equipped with deflector shields to protect the hull.

Stats

Primary Manufacturer: Incom Corporation
Unit Type: Fighter
Special: Lock Wings
Good Against: TIE Fighters, TIE Bombers, Darth Vader
Vulnerable To: Tartan Patrol Cruisers, Broadside Cruisers,
IPV-I Patrol Craft

Notes

Unlike Imperial fighters, Rebel fighters can jump to hyperspace and travel on their own rather than having to be carried by a capital ship. This lets the Rebels send fighters on raids and bring them into battle as reinforcements. The X-wing is the Rebels' main fighter, and it's best used for engaging enemy fighters. When you need to move them quickly across the battle area, at the cost of firepower, order them to lock their s-foils. When enemy cruisers approach, use this to make your getaway. There are five of these fighters per squadron.

Y-wing

Prior to the introduction of the X-wing starfighter, Y-wings were the signature fighters of the Rebel Alliance. The Y-wing is easily modified and can be reconfigured in countless variations. Rebel technicians often strip a Y-wing of bulky armor and generators before an assault on an Imperial convoy, or prepare the craft for bombing runs by adding more powerful shields and significantly increasing the vehicle's payload.

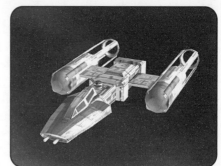

Y-wings can be outfitted with a variety of weapons and defensive systems. Many house a pair of laser cannons, proton torpedoes, and a rotating ion cannon. The Y-wing's ion cannon is often used to disable other ships, making it easier to conduct a raid or an assault on an Imperial convoy or outpost.

Stats

Primary Manufacturer: Koensayr
Unit Type: Bomber
Special: Ion Cannon Shot
Good Against: Acclamator Cruisers, Victory-Class Star Destroyers, Imperial Star Destroyers
Vulnerable To: TIE Fighters, Tartan Patrol Cruisers, Pirate Fighters

Notes

Y-wings are effective for attacking enemy capital ships. The proton torpedoes they fire can pass right through enemy shields. Therefore, use them to attack hard-points on an enemy ship before you have even lowered the shields. In addition, they can fire their ion cannon, which brings down an enemy's shields and disables it for a short time. Use this to give your Y-wings a better chance of surviving an attack. Always include at least one Y-wing squadron in the fleets you are using to land ground troops on a planet. Their presence allows you to call in bombing runs during land battles, which can quickly take out turrets and groups of enemies. There are three bombers per squadron.

A-wing

General Jan Dodonna joined forces with engineer Walex Blissex and secretly constructed and prototyped the A-wing early in the Galactic Civil War. The small wedge-shaped A-wing has become one of the Alliance's most daring innovations and is the Rebel Alliance's fastest fighter. The A-wing can outrun any ship in the Imperial Navy, which makes it perfect for hit-and-run missions.

The A-wing is equipped with two wing-mounted blaster cannons, but it has minimal deflector shields and is easily damaged by enemy fire. The A-wing also maintains a powerful set of avionic and jamming equipment, allowing the fighter to lure enemies away from combat or into an ambush.

Stats

Primary Manufacturer: Alliance Underground Engineering
Unit Type: Fighter
Special: Lure Enemy Fighters
Good Against: TIE Fighters, TIE Scouts, TIE Bombers
Vulnerable To: Tartan Class Patrol Cruisers

Notes

A-wings are dedicated fighters. They are faster than enemy units, including TIE fighters, and are great for taking on all types of TIE units. They can lure enemy fighters to their location. If TIE fighters are harassing your bombers and capital ships, move your A-wings off at a distance along with some Corellian corvettes. Then activate this ability and the TIE fighters will come to be ambushed by your fighters and corvettes.

Corellian Corvette

The Corellian corvette is a multipurpose ship produced by the Corellian Engineering Corporation for a wide variety of tasks, including passenger transport, cargo shipment, and military service. However, because the ships are fast, well-armed, and durable, the Rebel Alliance has a strong affinity for the vessels. The starships are commonly used as blockade runners because they can easily circumvent most obstacles.

The Corellian corvette is armed with laser cannons and over-sized drive engines for a ship of its scale. The engines can supply a large burst of power, boosting the ship's speed for a time and allowing the vessel to avoid a blockade or quickly enter a fight.

Stats

Primary Manufacturer: Corellian Engineering Corporation
Unit Type: Corvette
Special: Boost Engine Power
Good Against: TIE Fighters, TIE Bombers, Pirate Fighters
Vulnerable To: Acclamator Cruisers, Victory-Class Star Destroyers, Imperial Star Destroyers

Notes

The Corellian corvette is a fighter and bomber killer. It is essentially eight laser cannons attached to a large engine. When fighting against an enemy fleet, keep your corvettes close to your capital ships or space station to deal with enemy fighters and bombers, or use them to pursue and destroy fighters. Corvettes are also useful for taking out orbital defenses and making hit-and-run attacks. Move in and fire, then when your shields are nearly depleted, boost engine power and get away to let your shields recharge so you can repeat the tactic again. Corvettes work best in groups of four or five where their combined firepower can quickly destroy a single target before it can cause much damage in return.

Corellian Gunship

Produced by the Corellian Engineering Corporation, the Corellian gunship is a dedicated combat ship that has been around since the Clone Wars. The Rebel Alliance, in need of a small, fast attack vessel, decided to purchase a few of these starships after witnessing a group of pirates use them to successfully hijack an Imperial shipment guarded by several Imperial fighters and bombers.

Fast and deadly, the Corellian gunship boasts laser cannon batteries and concussion missile launchers that can bypass shields, damaging the hull directly. The ship's engines can supply a large burst of power, providing a speed boost and allowing the vessel to quickly engage in combat.

Stats

Primary Manufacturer: Corellian Engineering Corporation
Unit Type: Corvette
Special: Boost Engine Power
Good Against: Tartan Patrol Cruisers, TIE Bombers
Vulnerable To: Victory-Class Star Destroyers, Imperial Star Destroyers, Pirate Interceptors

Notes

The Corellian gunship is a great weapon for engaging Tartan patrol cruisers. Its concussion missiles penetrate the cruiser's shields, causing structural damage with each hit. However, avoid using the gunship against enemy capital ships, which will quickly destroy your gunships. Instead, move in to take out the Tartans, then use the boost engine power ability to quickly get away before the heavy guns come at you.

Rebel Cruiser (Nebulon-B Frigate)

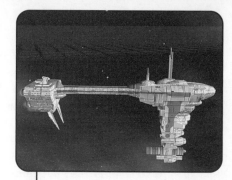

Nebulon-B frigates, also known as Rebel cruisers, are used by the Rebel Alliance to perform a host of duties including search and rescue operations. Many Nebulon-B frigates were stolen from the Empire, who originally commissioned the starships from Kuat Drive Yards to protect larger Imperial vessels during attacks. Some of the starships are converted into medical frigates devoted to caring for wounded soldiers and are staffed by medical droids and Rebel Alliance specialists.

Nebulon-B frigates house both laser cannons and turbolaser batteries in their weapons load-out. The Rebel cruisers also contain a deflector shield generator capable of sustaining large bursts of power that increase the shield strength for a time, allowing the ships to maintain a higher level of defense and stay in a fight for much longer.

Stats

Primary Manufacturer: Kuat Drive Yards
Unit Type: Frigate
Special: Boost Shield Strength
Good Against: Tartan Patrol Cruisers, IPV-I Patrol Craft
Vulnerable To: TIE Bombers, Imperial Star Destroyers,
Victory-Class Star Destroyers

Notes

The Nebulon-B is the standard Rebel capital ship. However, it is too weak to go up against Imperial Star Destroyers. Instead, use it against Tartan and Acclamator cruisers as well as Interdictors. When you come under heavy fire, activate the boost shield strength ability to increase the amount of damage your frigate can take from enemy laser fire.

Alliance Assault Frigate (Assault Frigate Mk. II)

Although few notable military contracts were signed with Rendili StarDrive, the company is constantly researching new technologies and designs. When the Rebel Alliance needed a starship that could pack more of an offensive punch at a cheap cost, they commissioned Rendili StarDrive. The end result was the assault frigate Mk II, which is based off of Rendili's Dreadnaught design.

Boasting complements of laser cannon and turbolaser batteries, the "Alliance assault frigate" can handle a variety of combat situations. Like the Mon Cal cruiser, this ship has a deflector shield generator capable of boosting shield strength when supplied with bursts of power, allowing the vessel to maintain a higher level of defense.

Stats

Primary Manufacturer: Rendili StarDrive
Unit Type: Frigate
Special: Boost Shield Strength
Good Against: Tartan Patrol Cruisers, Acclamator Cruisers, Broadside Cruisers
Vulnerable To: Imperial Star Destroyers, TIE Bombers

Notes

This capital ship is great for taking on Imperial capital ships with the exception of the Star Destroyer. While it has a lot of firepower, it is fairly weak when it comes to defenses. Use these frigates in groups and activate their shield ability to give them additional protection during the fight. When their ability wears off, withdraw them until it recharges and then move in again to attack.

Marauder Missile Cruiser

The Marauder missile cruiser is an Alliance refit of the Santhe/Sienar Systems *Marauder*-class corvette, many of which were purchased by the Corporate Sector Authority. The Authority lost many of these ships to smugglers and pirates in pitched battles, after which the smugglers sold them to the Rebel Alliance. Alliance engineers then redesigned the standard Marauder load-out to match firepower with the Empire's Broadside cruiser.

   The laser cannons were removed and the engines downsized to accommodate large, long-range concussion missile pods. The resulting ship is slower and less maneuverable than a standard Marauder but capable of much greater damage potential. The cruisers can barrage an area with missiles, creating heavy devastation in the process.

Stats

Primary Manufacturer: Santhe/Sienar Systems, Rebel Alliance
Unit Type: Corvette
Special: Barrage Area
Good Against: Imperial Space Stations, TIE Fighters,
TIE Bombers
Vulnerable To: Acclamator Cruisers, Victory-Class Star Destroyers,
Imperial Star Destroyers

Notes

The Marauder can be a very important part of your Rebel fleets. Their barrage ability allows them to attack at very long range— outside the range of most Imperial ships. Organize Marauders into groups of four or five and order all to barrage an area. Because it takes some time for the concussion missiles to travel, place the target where you expect the enemy to be in several seconds. For example, if a Star Destroyer is headed toward you, aim in front of it so that the missiles arrive at the same time as the Star Destroyer. Because the missiles pass right through the shields, a barrage by several Marauders can quickly eliminate Imperial capital ships. These cruisers are also great for attacking space stations that don't move, or capital ships disabled by ion cannon blasts or whose engines have been destroyed.

Mon Calamari Cruiser
(Mon Cal MC80 Star Cruiser)

The Mon Calamari take great pride in constructing their unique, handcrafted starships. Although their massive starships were originally designed for galactic exploration, the Mon Calamari quickly converted them into military vessels after clashes with the Empire. The ships were held in reserve to defend the Mon Calamari home-world, but eventually Commander Ackbar convinced his people to dedicate the cruisers to the Rebel Alliance.

Mon Cal cruisers are large, durable starships armed with ion cannons, turbolasers, and several deflector shield generators. The shield generators are designed to handle large bursts of power by increasing the shield strength, allowing the ships to maintain a higher level of defense and remain in combat much longer.

Stats

Primary Manufacturer: Mon Calamari
Unit Type: Capital Ship
Special: Boost Shield Strength
Good Against: Acclamator Cruisers, Tartan Patrol Cruisers,
Victory-Class Star Destroyers
Vulnerable To: TIE Bombers

Notes

Mon Calamari cruisers are the only Rebel capital ships that have a chance going toe-to-toe with large Imperial ships. Not only can you boost the shield strength of these cruisers, but their shield generators can never be destroyed. Therefore, enemies can't target your shields to knock them out so the cruiser is vulnerable. Because of their large size, these ships can be built only at the shipyards on Mon Calamari, Kuat, Sullust, or Fondor.

Rebel Structures

Alliance Barracks
(Delvin Constructs Model MilBar F-221)

The Alliance version of the Delvin Constructs Model MilBar F-221 troop barracks facility is designed to be constructed and deconstructed quickly at bases, and features more comfort and protection for the military personnel than the models used by the Empire. Though it cannot contain as many soldiers as the Imperial model, the supported soldiers have a great deal more room and privacy.

Notes

Rebel soldiers and Plex soldiers are produced here. The barracks is a requirement for construction of officer academies. It is a good idea for most of your planets to have barracks so they can produce their own defensive units.

Alliance Light Vehicle Factory
(Delvin Constructs Model Fac L-83)

Very similar to the Imperial light factory model, the Alliance version of the Delvin Constructs Model Fac L-83 light vehicle factory was modified to allow production of repulsorlift vehicles exclusively. The Rebel Alliance commissioned the use of a number of these factories throughout the galaxy in addition to the facilities they purchased for their hidden bases. The T2-B tank and assault speeder are both produced through this structure.

Notes

This factory produces T2-B repulsor tanks as well as the T-47 airspeeders. You need a light factory on a planet in order to build a heavy factory and turbolaser towers.

Alliance Heavy Vehicle Factory (Delvin Constructs Model Fac H-65)

The Alliance favored tracked vehicles over the walker technology of the Empire and their Delvin Constructs Model Fac H-65 heavy vehicle factory was designed accordingly. The Rebel Alliance purchased several of these facilities from Delvin Constructs and made arrangements with the manufacturers of their T4-B tanks and MPTL-2a artillery to produce the vehicles at multiple locations.

Notes

Because it requires a light factory to build a heavy factory, build these only on planets with enough slots to support lots of structures, then send the tanks and artillery units to where they are needed.

Alliance Officer Academy (Delvin Constructs Model Edu A-46)

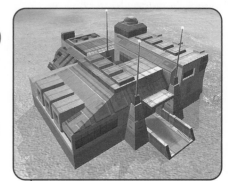

Many Rebel Alliance officers defected from the Empire or were promoted for their range of skills, but Rebel leaders still saw the need to train the new officers in their growing ranks. The Delvin Constructs Model Edu A-46 Alliance officer academy building suits that need. The officer academy building can be quickly constructed at any location to immediately begin training new officers.

Notes

You really only need one officer academy because you produce only a few officers during the course of a game. You can train both field commanders and fleet commanders here and need this structure in order to build an infiltrator training facility.

Infiltrator Training Facility (Delvin Constructs Model Edu I-73)

Rebel infiltrators come from the best of the best of the SpecForces. Their training grounds vary and are often set up on remote worlds. Every Model Edu I-73 infiltrator training facility follows a standard design and is constructed by the infiltrator trainees as part of their training. The building is built with prefabricated materials supplied by Delvin Constructs.

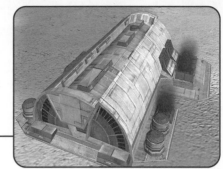

Notes

You usually only need one of these structures because you won't use a lot of infiltrators during a game. You need an officer academy in order to build one of these structures.

Alliance Command Center (Delvin Constructs Model Com C-52)

Rebel bases are often established very quickly. Often there are no available structures to convert into a Rebel base of operations. Once again filling the Alliance's need for cheap and fast, Delvin Constructs provides the Model Com C-52 Alliance command center building. Unfortunately this building is often left behind when Rebel bases are abandoned and are often later occupied by pirates looking to establish their own base of operations.

Notes

You do not build this structure. Instead, it is automatically included along with your other structures when a planet you control comes under attack by an invading army during a ground assault.

Ion Cannon (Planetary Ion Cannon)

This energy weapon is designed to overload a starship's electrical and computer systems, disabling the ship completely. A planetary ion cannon, such as the KDY v-150 Planet Defender, is protected by a spherical permacite shell and receives its power from a massive reactor normally buried about 40 meters below the ground. The cannon can emit a powerful ion pulse capable of streaking into low orbit and disabling huge starships.

Notes

Build these on planets at the border of your territory. The ion cannon, while a ground structure, is used during space battles. If you are invaded by an enemy fleet, use it as often as possible to disable enemy capital ships. This can give you a great advantage. As long as one of these remains operational on your planet during a ground battle, you can retreat from the planet without incurring any losses, even if there is an Imperial fleet in orbit.

Alliance Space Station

The Alliance space station serves as an orbital defense platform for a star system and manages the construction of ships. Space stations house a hangar, shields, communications array, multiple laser cannon and turbolaser cannon batteries, ion cannon batteries, proton torpedo launchers, and concussion missile launchers. Alliance space stations can be upgraded with up to four "arms" housing additional defenses.

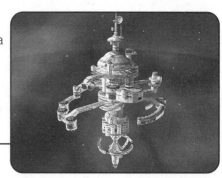

Notes

Build a space station in every system you control. Not only does it provide protection against enemy invasions, but it also increases the number of units you can support throughout the galaxy. Upgrade your stations to their maximum level for your border systems.

Rebel Build Pad Structures

Anti-Infantry Turret (Golan Arms DF.9 Anti-Infantry Battery)

Anti-infantry batteries serve as an early line of defense against hostile invasion by ground forces. Most models, including the Golan

Arms DF.9, utilize advanced precision targeting computers to decimate advancing infantry formations and destroy support equipment, including lightly armored vehicles. The weapons can be mounted in a variety of terrains and locales and often serve in conjunction with anti-vehicle batteries to protect strategic sites.

Notes

These are best built to help defend your base during defensive ground battles or your reinforcement points during offensive battles.

Anti-Vehicle Turret (Atgar 1.4 FD P-Tower Laser Cannon)

Anti-vehicle artillery units are fixed emplacements assigned to military installations, space stations, and other facilities. Like all anti-vehicle artilleries, the P-Tower is designed to target and destroy a variety of enemy craft, including landspeeders and repulsor tanks. Because the P-Tower's platform can rotate a full 360 degrees, the weapon has an impressive field of fire. It is also protected by light armor plating.

Notes

Build these in conjunction with anti-infantry turrets to help defend areas against vehicles.

Anti-Air Turret (Golan Arms FPC 6.7 Anti-Air Battery)

The Golan Arms FPC 6.7 anti-air battery is modeled after an Imperial design but further streamlines the base to allow for quick set up or break down at a moment's notice. The turret equips two rotating fire-linked flak pod cannons, allowing it to shoot at incoming air vehicles from any direction. The turret is designed to remove any threat from the air, primarily armed speeders or fighter/bombers.

Notes

As a Rebel, you only need to build these during defensive ground battles for protection against TIE bomber runs. Because the Imperials have no flying units during offensive battles, there is no need to build them in those circumstances.

The Galactic Empire has access to limitless resources as a result of its grasp on the galaxy. As such, it has powerful weapons and well-trained troops with battle experience ready to take on the Rebellion and bring it to its knees.

Heroes

Emperor Palpatine

Residing on Coruscant, Emperor Palpatine is the diabolical Sith Master who rules the galaxy through fear. Palpatine first rose to the position of Supreme Chancellor of the Republic before taking the title of Emperor. As Emperor, Palpatine promoted the doctrines of hatred, racism, and tyranny. He eliminated all opposition in violent fashion, forcing senators such as Mon Mothma and Bail Organa to withdraw from the Senate. He used his Sith Apprentice, Darth Vader, as his enforcer and hunted down the Jedi Knights, slaughtering the last of this noble sect to ensure that he would never be challenged. Meanwhile, he launched a massive military buildup and began constructing incredibly destructive starships, space stations, and weapons. During this dark time, hundreds of worlds were enslaved or ravaged, dissidents were murdered, and entire industries were nationalized.

Stats

Unit Type: Ground Hero
Special: Force Lightning, Force Corrupt
Good Against: Infantry
Vulnerable To: None

Notes

The Emperor is a powerful unit. He can be used during ground battles, but be careful with him. In some games, if he is killed, the game is over. His Force lightning ability can kill groups of infantry, while his Force corrupt power turns nearby enemy units to his side.

Both infantry and vehicles are then under your control. However, the power of the dark side causes these units to slowly lose health over time until they are destroyed—even if the enemy is not attacking them. When not using his abilities, the Emperor can still fight with his lightsaber and even regenerates health on his own over time.

Darth Vader

Born Anakin Skywalker, he was a spirited and talented child who exhibited strong Force potential. At an early age he became an expert pilot and a warrior of the Clone Wars, along with his mentor, Obi-Wan Kenobi. Obi-Wan trained Anakin in the ways of the Force, but Skywalker was impatient with the Jedi's painstaking methods. Skywalker let himself be embraced by the rapturous power of the dark side and was transformed into the Sith Lord, Darth Vader. Kenobi tried to draw him back to the light side, but they engaged in a duel on Mustafar that ultimately ended with Skywalker's body being consumed by flame. The shell of a man who emerged was sustained by specially built armor and a breathing apparatus. As a Dark Lord of the Sith, Darth Vader was key in helping the self-proclaimed Emperor Palpatine hunt down and exterminate the remaining Jedi Knights. Vader pilots a specially designed TIE Advanced x1 starfighter.

Stats

Unit Type: Space and Ground Hero
Special: Force Push, Force Crush, Call for Wingmen
Good Against: Infantry (Ground), Y-wings, Z-95 Headhunters (Space)
Vulnerable To: Corellian Corvettes, X-wings, A-wings,
Anti-Infantry Turrets

Notes

Vader is another hero unit who uses the power of the dark side of the Force. During ground battles, his Force push ability will kill nearby enemy infantry. He can even destroy vehicles with his Force crush ability. Vader is also great at destroying turrets. Order him to attack one from a distance and he uses the Force to eliminate the turret. When fighting in space, Darth Vader leads a squadron of TIE fighters. They protect him from damage until they are all destroyed. However, Vader can call for wingmen to replace those lost TIE fighters and gain more protection so he can remain in the fight.

Grand Moff Tarkin

Wilhuff Tarkin first entered galactic politics when he was appointed governor of the Seswenna sector of space. He fully supported Palpatine's bid to become Emperor and for this he was given the title of Moff of the Outer Rim Territories. His keen military mind and malevolence ensured his rapid advancement in rank until he became the first Grand Moff, the highest-ranking official beneath the Emperor. In this capacity, he commanded numerous sectors vital to the Empire and reported directly to the Emperor. During his reign, he advanced the "Tarkin Doctrine," which insisted that the galaxy should be ruled through fear and force. The Tarkin Doctrine culminated in the construction of the Death Star, the ultimate weapon of terror. As the Rebellion grew in strength, Tarkin devoted himself to completing construction of the Death Star and using it to root out the Rebel Alliance.

Stats
Unit Type: Fleet Commander
Special: Improves health and combat sight range of units in his fleet
Good Against: None
Vulnerable To: Unknown

Notes
Tarkin appears as a hero after the Death Star has been constructed. Though he is not a character that you can command directly in battle, his presence in a fleet will confer fleet commander bonuses to his units. When Tarkin is present in a fleet, retreat is not an option. Tarkin also offers a reduction in the cost of research facilities, but this isn't very useful because you need to tech all the way up to get him.

Boba Fett

Numerous tales have been told about Boba Fett's exploits as a bounty hunter, following in the footsteps of his "father" Jango Fett. His appearance has a striking resemblance to the armor worn by Jango, but it is clear that he has greatly modified the armored suit. Fett is a walking arsenal equipped with wrist blasters, a miniature flame thrower, and a fibercord whip. His helmet is now equipped with a macrobinocular viewplate, a broad-band antenna, motion and sound sensors, an infrared device, and an internal comlink connected to his ship, *Slave I*. The ship is a drastically altered *Firespray*-class patrol craft, rebuilt with holding cells, a dedicated tracking system, improved deflector shields, a massive hyperdrive engine, and numerous concealed weapons.

Stats

Unit Type: Space and Ground Hero
Special: Seismic Charge, Jet Pack, Flamethrower
Good Against: X-wing, Y-wing, Z-95 Headhunters
Vulnerable To: Corellian Corvette, Corellian Gunship, A-wing

Notes

Like Darth Vader, Boba Fett is both a space and ground hero. On the ground, he can use his flamethrower ability to unleash a vicious attack on enemy units. Then activate his jet pack to make a quick getaway. While in space, Fett pilots the *Slave I*, which comes equipped with seismic charges. When activated, the ship drops these explosives, which destroy all enemy fighter units in the area and damage larger ships.

Colonel Veers

Colonel Maximilian Veers is an autocratic and hardened commander of Imperial ground forces. Much speculation surrounds Colonel Veers's rise through the Imperial ranks and it has often been suggested that he murdered many of his competitors to achieve a place at Lord Vader's side. Whatever the case, it is clear that Veers is ruthless and aggressive, and he enjoys wreaking havoc with the destructive Imperial ground forces. Seeing a need for an intimidating, highly destructive ground vehicle, Colonel Veers resurrected the AT-AT concept from earlier Clone Wars–era walker designs and has been tasked with bringing the project to fruition. Veers conducts regular field tests with AT-AT walker prototypes at the Carida Military Academy. He pilots his own advanced AT-AT prototype named *Blizzard 1* and is recruiting candidates for an assault force of the mighty behemoths once full-scale production begins.

Stats

Unit Type: Ground Hero
Special: Deploy Stormtroopers, Maximum Firepower
Good Against: T4-B Tanks, T2-B Tanks, Anti-Vehicle Turrets
Vulnerable To: Airspeeders, Plex Soldiers

Notes

Colonel Veers fights on the ground in an AT-AT with the maximum firepower ability. When activated, it unleashes an attack on a target that causes increased damage. Also, he can deploy squads of stormtroopers from inside the AT-AT, which can be used to capture locations or other actions like regular squads.

Captain Piett

One of the few Imperial officers who hasn't incurred Darth Vader's wrath, Captain Firmus Piett received several promotions after his successors enraged Vader. Piett had several assignments patrolling backwater star systems under various commands and has extensive experience dealing with pirate groups, smugglers, and the Rebel Alliance. Like many of his contemporaries, Captain Piett worked his way up the Imperial ranks by carefully avoiding the ire of all his superiors. He is a confident and ruthless leader despite the demands of his position. Piett's current assignment is captain of the *Imperial I*-class Star Destroyer the *Accuser*, under Admiral Griff. The *Accuser* has been modified over other ships of the same class by Piett and contains a powerful proton beam capable of causing massive amounts of destruction to other vessels.

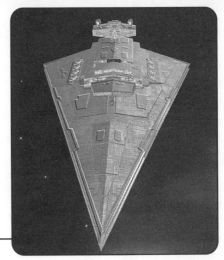

Stats

Unit Type: Space Hero
Special: Tractor Beam, Proton Beam
Good Against: Corellian Corvettes, Corellian Gunboats,
Marauder Missile Cruisers
Vulnerable To: Y-wings

Notes

Captain Piett fights during space battles aboard his Star Destroyer. A tractor beam can hold an enemy ship to prevent it from escaping or moving away, and the proton beam is a powerful attack that penetrates shields to cause a lot of structural damage to targeted ships.

Mara Jade

Mara Jade, a beautiful woman with green eyes and red-gold hair, is known as the "Emperor's Hand." She is virtually an extension of the Emperor's will, and she will go anywhere in the galaxy to carry out his orders, including assassinations. Her missions are so secret that not even the Emperor's closest aides know of her and she communicates directly with the Emperor himself. Mara Jade's strength in the Force is weak in comparison to trained Jedi and Sith, but it has been amplified directly by the Emperor on several of her missions. Although not a front-line combatant, she is light and fast on her feet and has extensive training in weapon use and tactics. At her private quarters on Coruscant, she has a droid assistant named Kaythree, a lanvarok for left-handers (although Mara herself is right-handed), a sleeve gun, and a lightsaber, among many other items in her personal weapons collection.

Stats

Unit Type: Ground Hero
Special: Thermal Detonator, Force Corrupt
Good Against: Turrets, Infantry
Vulnerable To: None

Notes

Mara Jade is a ground hero who has the same Force corrupt power as the Emperor, allowing her to turn nearby enemies to her side so she can take control of them until they eventually die. She can also throw thermal detonators, which work well against turrets, groups of infantry, and vehicles, as long as they don't move away before it explodes.

Ground Units

Stormtroopers

These are shock troops fanatically loyal to the Empire and impossible to sway from the Imperial cause. They wear imposing white armor, which offers a wide range of survival equipment and temperature controls to allow the soldiers to survive in almost any environment. Stormtroopers wield many weapons with great skill and attack in hordes to overwhelm their enemies. The Empire has also organized several specialized units, including snowtroopers and scout troopers.

Most stormtroopers carry the E-11 blaster rifle as standard equipment, save for a few specialized units such as the scout troopers. All stormtroopers are trained to fight using a variety of weapons and tactics in a variety of situations and environments, allowing them to take cover and maintain a position in combat.

Stats

Primary Manufacturer: Cloned at Various Locations
Unit Type: Infantry
Special: Take Cover
Good Against: Rebel Soldiers, Plex Soldiers
Vulnerable To: MPTL-2a Artillery, Anti-Infantry Turrets, Rebel Infiltrators

Notes

Stormtroopers are the Empire's only infantry unit. They are best used for taking control of locations and then defending them. To decrease the damage they take from enemy fire, order them to take cover. This reduces their movement speed as well. There are two squads of nine stormtroopers each in a company.

Scout Trooper (Speeder Bike)

Lightly armored but highly mobile Imperial stormtroopers usually assigned to planetary garrisons, scout troopers rely upon speeder bikes to patrol perimeters, perform reconnaissance missions, and scout enemy locations. Scout troopers wear specialized helmets equipped with built-in macrobinocular viewplates and sensor arrays. These devices feed into a small computer capable of instantaneously analyzing the surrounding terrain to aid the trooper in navigation.

Scout troopers rely on their lightly armored Aratech 74-Z speeder bikes to travel across battlefields quickly. A speeder bike is equipped with a single blaster cannon capable of defending the vehicle as it makes a fast getaway. Scout troopers often carry thermal detonators that they use to take down lightly defended or undefended targets. There are two scout troopers per company.

Stats

Primary Manufacturer: Aratech
Unit Type: Infantry
Special: Drop Thermal Detonator
Good Against: Rebel Soldiers, MPTL-2a Artillery
Vulnerable To: T4-B Tanks, T2-B Tanks, Anti-Vehicle Turrets

Notes

Scout troopers are very fast units, so you can move them around a battlefield very quickly. They can also drop a thermal detonator at their location and then speed away before it detonates. While this can be useful at times, during a ground invasion, when you have a limited number of units you can bring down to the surface, a company of AT-STs would be a better choice.

TIE Mauler (Imperial TIE ap-1)

The TIE ap-I or TIE mauler was developed by Santhe/Sienar Technologies to fulfill the Empire's need for a light, fast, and cheap ground vehicle to combat the increasing threat of the Rebellion. To keep costs down, TIE maulers are built with a standard TIE fighter cockpit that is suspended between two massive tank treads, much like the more advanced TIE crawler. The first units were field tested early in the Galactic Civil War and used throughout the conflict.

The TIE mauler sacrifices armor for its speed and maneuverability. It is armed with rapid-fire laser cannons and can use its tank treads to convince enemy troops to get out of its way as it races across the battlefield. TIE maulers are also equipped with a highly explosive self-destruct device that can be activated in an emergency.

Stats

Primary Manufacturer: Santhe/Sienar Technologies
Unit Type: Light Vehicle
Special: Self-Destruct
Good Against: Rebel Soldiers, Plex Soldiers
Vulnerable To: T2-B Tanks, Plex Soldiers, Anti-Vehicle Turrets

Notes

The TIE mauler is the ultimate anti-infantry vehicle. Its laser cannons quickly take out all types of infantry. However, you can eliminate infantry even quicker by running them over. Never send a TIE mauler off by itself. Instead, keep the platoon of five maulers together so they can cut a wider swath as they run over enemy infantry. Their combined firepower can chew through squads you can't get to. When a mauler's health is about half of maximum, run it next to an enemy unit or structure and use the self destruct ability. This takes a couple seconds. When it explodes, it causes a lot of damage to its surroundings.

AT-ST (All Terrain Scout Transport)

Developed by the Imperial Department of Military Research, the AT-ST is a reconnaissance and ground support vehicle used by the Empire in most conflicts. The AT-ST has two flexible legs that allow it to move quickly across the battlefield. Each scout walker is manned by a pilot and a gunner. Together, the two-man crew uses the vehicle to protect ground troops and guard the flanks and vulnerable under-belly of AT-AT walkers.

The AT-ST's highly maneuverable armored "head" is adorned with twin blaster cannons that can provide covering fire for ground troops or can barrage an area. The vehicles also maintain an array of sophisticated sensing equipment that the pilot uses to spot and call out targets for other Imperial ground troops.

Stats

Primary Manufacturer: Imperial Department of Military Research
Unit Type: Light Vehicle
Special: Barrage Area
Good Against: Anti-Infantry Turrets
Vulnerable To: T4-B Tanks, T2-B Tanks, Plex Soldiers

Notes

The AT-ST is the Imperials' standard ground combat workhorse. It is good against infantry as well as vehicles and structures. It can also walk over and destroy enemy infantry. It is extremely devastating when it is using its barrage area ability. This allows you to target an area into which all selected AT-STs rapidly fire their laser cannons. This quickly takes out enemy units and turrets. Always keep a company of four AT-STs together to maximize their firepower and for mutual support.

2-M Repulsor Tank

After suffering multiple defeats at the hands of Rebel T2-B tanks, tank brigade commanders called upon Rothana Heavy Engineering to develop a more powerful version of the IFT-T hover tank. The 2-M repulsor tank answered that need and proved superior even to Rebel T2-B tanks in initial field tests. Unfortunately the 2-M tanks were expensive and hard to maintain, and saw only limited use throughout the Galactic Civil War.

2-M repulsor tanks come equipped with shields, repulsor lifts, and a rotating laser cannon. They also contain additional power boosters in case the main repulsorlift battery fails. Tank commanders have found an additional use for the power boosters: They use them to supply additional power to the guns, increasing the tank's damage output for periods of time.

Stats

Primary Manufacturer: Rothana Heavy Engineering
Unit Type: Tank
Special: Boost Weapon Power
Good Against: T2-B Tanks, MPTL-2a Artillery, AT-APs
Vulnerable To: T4-B Tanks, Anti-Vehicle Turrets, Plex Soldiers

Notes

The 2-M repulsor tank is similar to the Rebel T2-B. It can move across all types of terrain, including water. Its shields allow it to last longer on the battlefield, and you can increase the damage it causes for a limited time by using its boost weapon power ability. This type of unit is good for moving ahead of your attack force to scout out enemy positions or to hit them in the flanks. As the tanks begin to have their shields lowered by enemy fire, pull them back so the shields can recharge. There are five tanks per company.

AT-AT (All Terrain Armored Transport)

Resurrected by Colonel Veers, the AT-AT concept originated during the Clone Wars with the successes of earlier walker designs. The AT-AT is encased in a heavy armor shell and is almost impossible to damage with conventional weapons. Components for these vehicles originated with numerous companies, but the vehicles were assembled at secret Kuat Drive Yards factories. Their unceasing approach causes fear in even the most hardened Rebel soldiers.

AT-ATs function well as combat vehicles, employing a set of four powerful head-mounted laser cannons. The AT-AT's heavy feet can crush walls and convince enemy troops to get out of the way. The transports also carry a complement of stormtroopers that can be deployed via rappel lines dropped from the vehicle's belly.

Stats

Primary Manufacturer: Kuat Drive Yards
Unit Type: Heavy Vehicle
Special: Deploy Stormtroopers
Good Against: T4-B Tanks, T2-B Tanks, Anti-Vehicle Turrets
Vulnerable To: Airspeeders, Plex Soldiers

Notes

This is the ultimate ground weapon. Its heavy firepower can take on vehicles and turrets alike. As it clears a reinforcement point or build pad, deploy a squad of stormtroopers from this walker to take control of the location and to help fight off attacks by Plex soldiers. This ability recharges over time, allowing you to bring in many squads without tapping into your reinforcement pool. Once you can build the AT-AT, all of your invasion forces should land some of these. Because they are vulnerable to airspeeders, it's a good idea to bring along an AT-AA to deal with that threat.

SPMA-T (Self-Propelled Medium Artillery Turbolaser)

The Self-Propelled Medium Artillery Turbolaser is based on the original Rothana Heavy Engineering SPHA-T model used in the Clone Wars. Due to the slow speed of the original, the design was lightened using more recent turbolaser designs and walker engineering. While the SPMA-T is smaller than the SPHA-T, it is a little faster and more maneuverable than its predecessor. The power system re-routes when deployed, while the main cannon readies itself for firing.

SPMA-Ts are artillery units by every definition and must deploy before they can fire their main cannons. The main cannons have a frighteningly long range and require targets to be painted in order to hit them. These vehicles are slow moving and not heavily armored, requiring an escort.

Stats

Primary Manufacturer: Rothana Heavy Engineering
Unit Type: Artillery
Special: Deploy/Undeploy
Good Against: Anti-Vehicle Turrets, Anti-Infantry Turrets
Vulnerable To: T4-B Tanks, T2-B Tanks, Plex Soldiers

Notes

This artillery unit is great for attacking enemy bases as well as infantry. Before it can fire, it must deploy, and then to move, it must undeploy. Therefore, the SPMA-T is tough to use in a maneuvering fight. Keep them at your landing zone with spotter units, such as stormtroopers, at the access points so the artillery can fire at enemies as they approach. Then move it up for the assault on the enemy base. There are three SPMA-Ts per company.

AT-AA (All Terrain Anti Aircraft)

Early in the Galactic Civil War, the Rebellion employed many tactics against the Empire, including the use of starfighters and airspeeders as land assault craft to plaster Imperial ground troops and vehicles. The Empire contracted with many corporations, including Rothana Heavy Engineering, to develop anti-air vehicles to keep these Rebel air assaults at bay. The All Terrain Anti Aircraft, or AT-AA, is one of these vehicles.

The AT-AA has a flak pod that sits on a walking shell. It can traverse a variety of battlefield terrain to get into position and stop air assaults. The vehicle also houses an array of sensing equipment that can be used to scramble missile guidance systems, lowering the risk of rocket attacks on Imperial troops.

Stats

Primary Manufacturer: Rothana Heavy Engineering
Unit Type: Light Vehicle
Special: Missile Jamming Field
Good Against: Air Speeders, Y-wings
Vulnerable To: T4-B Tanks, MPTL-2a Artillery

Notes

This walker is designed to shoot down airspeeders and Y-wings during bombing runs. If your opponent is using these units, be sure to bring along an AT-AA. It is also useful for decreasing the accuracy of missile units, such as Plex soldiers and T4-B tanks, by using its missile jamming field. This ability alone makes it worthwhile for escorting AT-ATs and other Imperial vehicles. There are three of these vehicles in a company.

Space Units

TIE Fighter

Developed by Sienar Fleet Systems, the TIE/Ln space superiority starfighter was used by the Empire during most of the Galactic Civil War. It is an agile single-pilot starfighter with a small, spherical cockpit suspended between a pair of immense solar array wings. The TIE fighter, which utilizes advanced twin ion engines, was designed primarily for speed. It does not contain a hyperdrive and must be transported aboard larger capital ships.

To decrease the vehicle's weight, it has not been equipped with life support systems, deflector shields, or hyperdrive engines. Armed with only a pair of standard laser cannons, the mass-produced TIE fighters must rely on their greater numbers to overwhelm enemy forces.

Stats

Primary Manufacturer: Sienar Fleet Systems
Unit Type: Fighter
Special: Hunt for Enemies
Good Against: Y-wings, Z-95 Headhunters
Vulnerable To: Corellian Corvettes, X-wings, A-wings

Notes

TIE fighters never operate on their own. Instead, they are carried into battle by capital ships or are garrison forces for space stations. They are inferior to Rebel fighters when matched one-on-one, but are great for attacking bombers or in large groups. When a TIE fighter squadron is destroyed, it respawns over time at the ship from where it launched as long as that ship still has an operational hangar. You can order your TIE fighters to go off on their own and search for enemy units to engage. However, that often results in your squadron being destroyed. A squadron contains seven fighters.

TIE Bomber

This heavy Imperial assault ship was designed by Sienar Fleet Systems and used for strategic strikes against surface and deep space targets. While slower and less maneuverable than standard TIE fighters, TIE bombers carry incredibly destructive payloads. TIE bombers are also manufactured with onboard life support systems, which all other TIE starfighters lack. Like standard TIE fighters, TIE bombers can be found aboard almost every Imperial space station and capital ship.

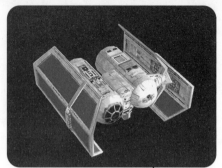

Although payload can vary depending upon mission profiles, a typical TIE bomber can carry dozens of missiles, bombs, mines, and thermal detonators for attack runs. The bombers can plaster an area on the ground or use their precise targeting computers to disable vital areas of capital ships such as shield generators and engines.

Stats

Primary Manufacturer: Sienar Fleet Systems
Unit Type: Fighter
Special: None
Good Against: Mon Cal Cruisers, Alliance Assault Frigates, Nebulon-B Frigates
Vulnerable To: Corellian Corvettes, X-wings, A-wings

Notes

TIE bombers, like TIE fighters, are deployed from capital ships and space stations. They are best used against capital ships. Their weapons can penetrate the shields of a target ship and cause structural damage. Therefore, use them to target vital systems such as shields or engines to make it easier for other units in your fleet to damage the enemy ship. Always include an Imperial capital ship with a hangar in your invasion fleets so you can use TIE bombers for bombing runs during ground battles. There are four bombers per squadron.

TIE Scout

A limited production, light reconnaissance starfighter developed by
Sienar Fleet Systems, the TIE scout was used mostly in the Outer
Rim territories as a scout fighter to scan locations for reconnaissance,
and to spot minefields or potential ambushes prior to fleet arrivals.
The fighter proved to be too expensive for the Empire to put into a
more widescale use. This kept the TIE scouts that were available
assigned to the most needed areas.

TIE scouts have hyperdrives and do not require a capital ship
hangar for transport. These fast fighters are equipped only with a set
of laser cannons. Their speed and advanced sensing equipment
allows the fighters to quickly spot targets and report fleet locations
to other Imperial ships in the battle.

Stats

Primary Manufacturer: Sienar Fleet Systems
Unit Type: Fighter
Special: Sensor Ping
Good Against: Y-wings, Z-95 Headhunters
Vulnerable To: A-wings

Notes

TIE scouts can be useful with their sensor ping ability. When this is
activated, you can select an area of the map and use the TIE scouts'
sensors to temporarily lift the fog of war for that area. However, in
most space battles, the enemy comes at you and you need all the
firepower you can get, rather than the weak weapons of the TIE
scouts. There are three scouts to a squadron.

Tartan Patrol Cruiser (*Tartan*-class Patrol Cruiser)

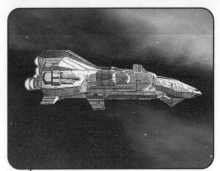

After an increasing number of pirate and Rebel attacks throughout the galaxy, the Empire commissioned the *Tartan*-class patrol cruiser from Damorian Manufacturing Corporation to combat the increasing threat. Field tests on earlier models showed that large groups of fighters were effective against the ships, due to an inability to track the targets. Later models were fit with improved tracking systems, allowing the ships to track multiple fast-moving targets at once.

Tartan patrol cruisers are fast and maneuverable and equipped with laser cannon batteries and shields. The ships also contain power boosters for the weapons and can sustain a brief period of increased firepower, allowing the ships to be effective during larger conflicts.

Stats

Primary Manufacturer: Damorian Manufacturing Corporation
Unit Type: Corvette
Special: Boost Weapon Power
Good Against: X-wings, Y-wings, A-wings
Vulnerable To: Mon Cal Cruisers, Alliance Assault Frigates, Nebulon-B Frigates

Notes

The Tartan patrol cruiser is the Empire's main weapon for taking out enemy fighters and bombers. Position them as a pickets in front of your capital ships to take out fighters headed toward your larger ships. You can also use these cruisers to help in attacking capital ships. Be sure to boost weapon power so that the Tartans cause enough damage to make up for the damage they will take.

Acclamator (*Acclamator*-class Cruiser)

While the Kaminoans labored to perfect an indomitable clone army, the neighboring shipyards of Rothana Heavy Engineering were subcontracted to develop the hardware, armor, and transports for the new infantry. The bold lines and stark silhouettes of the resulting craft were departures from the polished craftsmanship of personalized styles that marked the final Republic era. Instead, the wedge-shaped assault ships were foreboding harbingers of the new era to come.

Although designed to be a troop transport, *Acclamator*-class cruisers boast laser cannon and turbolaser batteries, a concussion missile launcher, a proton torpedo launcher, shields, and complements of TIE fighter and TIE bomber squadrons. The vessels can also maintain a period of increased firepower when bursts of power are supplied to the weapon batteries.

Stats

Primary Manufacturer: Rothana Heavy Engineering
Unit Type: Frigate
Special: Boost Weapon Power
Good Against: Corellian Corvettes, Marauder Missile Cruisers
Vulnerable To: Y-wings, Mon Cal Cruisers, Alliance Assault Frigates

Notes

The Acclamators are great for taking on smaller Rebel ships that do not have a lot of defenses. However, keep them away from capital ships such as frigates and cruisers. When attacking enemy ships, activate the boost weapon power ability to increase your damage. Acclamators carry four squadrons of TIE fighters and two squadrons of TIE bombers.

Victory-class Star Destroyer

Designed during the Clone Wars by Walex Blissex, a Republic engineer, the *Victory*-class Star Destroyer was considered the ultimate combat starship design when first launched. As larger, more-advanced Star Destroyers were built, *Victory*-class ships were reassigned to planetary defense roles. A number have been decommissioned and sold off to planetary defense forces, including the Corporate Sector Authority.

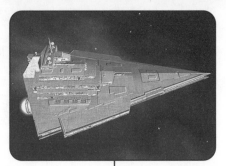

   Victory-class Star Destroyers may be old, but they still pack a powerful punch. The vessels house turbolaser and ion cannon batteries, a deflector shield generator, and complements of TIE fighter and TIE bomber squadrons. The ships can also maintain a period of increased firepower when bursts of power are supplied to the weapon batteries.

Stats

Primary Manufacturer: Rendili StarDrive
Unit Type: Frigate
Special: Boost Weapon Power
Good Against: Corellian Corvettes, Corellian Gunboats,
Nebulon-B Frigates
Vulnerable To: Y-wings, Mon Cal Cruisers

Notes

This Star Destroyer is capable of taking on the entire Rebel fleet with the exception of the Mon Calamari cruisers. Its ion cannon can quickly take down a target's shields, making the target vulnerable to laser fire from this ship as well as others in your fleet. Like many Imperial ships, the Victory can boost weapon power. Carried aboard are six squadrons of TIE fighters and three of TIE bombers.

Imperial Star Destroyer

A mammoth starship that forms the core of the Imperial Navy, the Imperial Star Destroyer is the most prominent symbol of the Empire's military might, and is an engineering marvel.

   These vessels are built for combat. Imperial Star Destroyers are armed to the teeth with turbolaser and ion cannon batteries, a deflector shield generator, and complements of TIE fighter and TIE bomber squadrons. The mighty vessels also boast a tractor beam useful for pulling ships into gun range or keeping them from escaping.

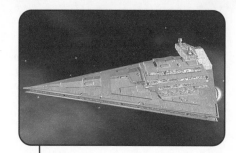

Stats

Primary Manufacturer: Kuat Drive Yards
Unit Type: Capital Ship
Special: Tractor Beam
Good Against: Corellian Corvettes, Corellian Gunboats, Nebulon-B Frigates
Vulnerable To: Y-wings, Mon Cal Cruisers

Notes

This is the ultimate Imperial starship. Use the tractor beam to hold an enemy ship in place so your fleet can more accurately target it and prevent it from escaping. It carries 10 TIE fighter squadrons and five TIE bomber squadrons. Due to its large size, Imperial Star Destroyers can be built only at Kuat, Sullust, Fondor, and Mon Calamari.

Interdictor Cruiser (Immobilizer 418 Cruiser)

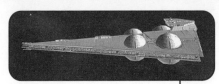

A valuable addition to the Imperial Navy's fleet, the Immobilizer 418 Interdictor cruiser is built on a standard heavy cruiser hull but is customized with hardware that prevents nearby ships from escaping into hyperspace. Interdictor cruisers, or Immobilizer 418 cruisers, at first appearance look like small Star Destroyers, but they're recognizable because of four large globes that house gravity well projectors that mimic a mass in space and thus prohibit hyperspace travel.

Interdictor cruisers are armed primarily with laser cannons, shields, and gravity well generators. Imperial strategy is to place Interdictors on the perimeter of a battle area to prevent Rebel ships from escaping. The ships also contain a sophisticated sensor array that can jam missile guidance systems.

Stats

Primary Manufacturer: Sienar Fleet Systems
Unit Type: Frigate
Special: Gravity Well Generator, Missile Jamming Field
Good Against: Marauder Missile Cruiser
Vulnerable To: Y-wings, Mon Cal Cruisers

Notes

The Interdictor is a good ship to have in your fleet. By activating the gravity well generator, you can prevent those pesky Rebel fleets from hitting you and then running away. In addition, its missile jamming field makes missile and torpedo attacks by the enemy much less effective.

Broadside Missile Cruiser (*Broadside*-class Cruiser kdb-1)

The *Broadside*-class cruiser was produced in the early days of the Galactic Civil war by Kuat Drive Yards. It was designed for the Imperial Navy to use as a long-range missile ship. Most models of the Broadside were lightly armored and ran with a small crew. Early models carried a payload of expensive diamond-boron missiles; their high-yield area effect detonations proved useful against tightly packed ship formations. However later models were fitted with cheaper concussion missiles.

KDY engineers decided that speed and maneuverability were unnecessary for this ship; as a result the Broadside is almost never encountered without an escort of some kind. *Broadside*-class cruisers house concussion missile launchers and shields. The ships can also barrage an area with missiles, causing a massive amount of damage.

Stats

Primary Manufacturer: Kuat Drive Yards
Unit Type: Corvette
Special: Barrage Area
Good Against: Rebel Space Stations, X-wings, Y-wings
Vulnerable To: Mon Cal Cruisers, Assault Frigates, Corellian Gunboats

Notes

Broadside cruisers are great for long-range attacks against space stations and capital ships. Use their barrage area to fire a massive number of concussion missiles at an area of space. Because space stations do not move, they make great targets. However, when firing at a moving capital ship, you have to target an area ahead of the ship so that the missiles arrive at the same time as the ship. After a bit of practice, you can be pretty accurate. Because the missiles penetrate the enemy's shields, they cause structural damage. Group your Broadsides together for barrages and you can take out even a Mon Calamari cruiser in short order.

The Death Star

Conceived by Grand Moff Tarkin and constructed in secret, the Death Star is a battle station of immense proportions. Tarkin developed a prototype at his secret Maw Installation, a research facility that even the Emperor knew nothing about. The Death Star is 120 kilometers in diameter, roughly the size of a small moon, and is the largest starship ever built, boasting an insanely destructive super laser designed to destroy planets. The Death Star houses more than a million individuals, including troopers, officers, gunners, pilots, and support personnel of every variety. The Death Star houses weapons in the form of thousands of turbolasers and ion cannons, bristled across the space station's surface, while the numerous hangars hold hordes of TIE fighters and other ships. The Death Star's main weapon is a super laser that is capable of destroying an entire planet.

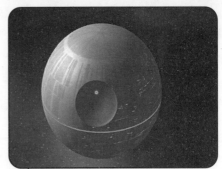

Stats

Unit Type: Battle Station
Special: Super Laser
Good Against: Planets
Vulnerable To: Red Squadron

Notes

This unit must be built after completing all of the technology upgrades and research. It does not function like a normal unit. Instead, you send it by itself or as part of a fleet. When it enters an enemy system, a countdown begins, showing the time until the Death Star is in range. Once the timer reaches zero, a button appears in the command bar allowing you to fire the super laser and destroy the planet. Before firing, you must use your escorting fleet to eliminate Red Squadron if it is in the system, or Luke Skywalker will destroy the Death Star.

Imperial Structures

Imperial Command Center
(Delvin Constructs Model Com C-38)

Imperial bases are models of form and function. Delvin Constructs created the Model Com C-38 Imperial command center with that in mind. Imperial officers use the building as one centralized location to direct all base and ground force operations on a planet. Enemies will know when there is an Imperial base in their midst when they see the command center off in the distance.

Notes

This structure is included automatically when you take control of a planet.

Imperial Barracks
(Delvin Constructs Model MilBar C-427)

The Imperial version of the Delvin Constructs Model MilBar C-427 troop barracks facility is a standard military housing facility, modeled for functionality and defensibility like much of their permanent structures. Unlike the Rebel Alliance barracks model, this version can be constructed quickly at bases and can house several companies of stormtroopers and scout troopers at the expense of luxury.

Notes

You can recruit stormtroopers and scout troopers at the barracks.

Imperial Light Vehicle Factory
(Delvin Constructs Model Fac L-113)

The Delvin Constructs Model Fac L-113 Imperial light vehicle factory is modeled after a typical AT-ST manufacturing plant in Balmorra. This version of the light vehicle factory is easily constructed and can be set up quickly at any location to immediately begin producing new vehicles for Imperial ground forces. The factories can be retrofitted to handle the production of TIE maulers.

Notes

Build the light vehicle factory on several of the planets you take control of so that you can create your own garrison forces. You can build AT-STs and TIE maulers here. You must have one of these structures on a planet before you can build turbolaser towers.

Imperial Heavy Vehicle Factory (Delvin Constructs Model Fac H-121)

With the Imperial tendency to produce large, intimidating ground units, the Delvin Constructs Model Fac H-121 Imperial heavy vehicle factory was designed to construct the middle-range ground units including the SPMA-T and the 2-M repulsor tanks. There was an attempt to allow for the construction of AT-ATs as well, but it was found that the larger walker required individual attention that the heavy factory could not provide.

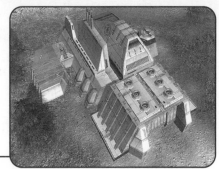

Notes

You must have a light vehicle factory on the planet to build this structure. Once you have a heavy vehicle factory, you can construct the hypervelocity gun.

Imperial Advanced Factory (Delvin Constructs Model A-Fac 333)

The Delvin Constructs Model A-Fac 333 Imperial advanced factory can handle the largest of vehicles the Imperial Army requires. Though tooled to allow the construction of any large vehicle, the Empire uses the advanced factory almost exclusively for the construction of the AT-AT and AT-AA walkers. This is one of the largest and most expensive models that Delvin Constructs produced, and the Empire uses them sparingly throughout the galaxy.

Notes

You need a heavy vehicle factory on a planet to build one of these structures. Build them on planets that are secure because you do not want to lose such an investment to a Rebel raid.

Imperial Officer Academy (Delvin Constructs Model Edu-A-34)

Delvin Constructs modeled the Edu-A-34 Imperial officer academy after one of the classrooms in the education building at the Imperial Academy on Carida. The facility can be constructed easily at any location, providing Imperial commanders with the ability to promote and train new officers anywhere in the galaxy before sending them off to one of the military training academies in the Core Worlds for more formalized training.

Notes

You need only one of these structures, so build it on Coruscant or another base planet. A barracks is required on the planet to build this structure. It trains both fleet and field commanders for your fleets and armies.

Hypervelocity Gun (Imperial Department of Military Research/Taim & Bak HVs-2 Hypervelocity Gun)

This planetary defense weapon, designed by the Imperial Department of Military Research along with the newly formed Taim & Bak, takes on a more serious threat than weapons such as the planetary ion cannon can handle. The HVs-2 hypervelocity gun is designed to fire at ships in orbit by projecting metal slugs at high rates of speed via a magnetic field. It has its own ray shield and auto-loader in a protected underground facility.

Notes

This is a good structure to build on all of your border systems to help defend them during space battles. Use it as often as it is available during such fights. For land battles, it is only a target and can't be used. You need a heavy vehicle factory on a planet to build one of these structures.

Magnapulse Cannon (Kuat Drive Yards KDY m-68 Planetary Magnapulse Cannon)

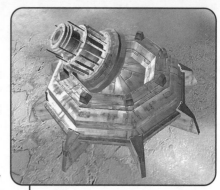

The KDY m-68 planetary magnapulse cannon is a planetary weapon built with an underground generator and a large rotating plasma cannon above the surface. The cannon lobs plasma balls outward at enemy vehicles, causing massive electrical disturbances that disable the target for a time. The cannon was originally designed as a surface-to-space weapon, but it turned out to be more effective at surface-to-surface combat, unlike later models such as the planetary turbolaser.

Notes

Build these on border planets where you expect the Rebels may try to invade. Use it to target groups of vehicles and disable them so your units can then attack without fear of taking damage during the process.

Imperial Space Station

The Imperial space station serves as an orbital defense platform for a star system and manages the construction of ships at Imperial orbital shipyards. Space stations house a hangar, shields, communications array, multiple laser cannon and turbolaser cannon batteries, ion cannon batteries, proton torpedo launchers, and concussion missile launchers. Imperial space stations can be easily fit with up to four "extensions" housing additional defenses.

Notes

Build a space station in each system you control and upgrade it as much as possible. This increases the number of units you can support during a game and also offers protection against enemy incursions into your space. During space battles, you can order upgrades to armor and firepower at a space station.

Research Facility (Corporate Sector Authority Res-a Technology Center)

Provided they continue to funnel funds and resources to the Empire, the Corporate Sector Authority has complete independence from Imperial rule. The CSA provides resources to the Empire at a substantial gain. The Res-a technology center or research facility can be used by the Empire to develop new technologies supporting the war effort as long as the CSA gets full rights to produce the technology for their own use afterward.

Notes

For the Imperials, to increase your technology level, you must first construct a research facility on one of your planets—you only need one. When it is built, you can then spend credits to research a new technology level. After the research is completed, you gain access to all units and structures for the level. The sooner you can do research, the sooner you have access to more powerful units.

Imperial Build Pad Structures

Anti-Infantry Turret (Taim & Bak Bp.2 Anti-Infantry Turret)

In an effort to become an industry leader in weapons technology, newly formed Taim & Bak developed the Bp series of turrets under contract for the Empire. Each turret in the series is designed with simplicity in mind and can be set up at a base to provide protection. The Bp.2 anti-infantry turret houses a rotating blaster cannon that can quickly target and fire upon enemy troops.

Notes

Build these structures on build pads near your bases and reinforcement points to protect these locations.

Anti-Vehicle Turret (Taim & Bak Bp.4 Anti-Vehicle Turret)

In an effort to become an industry leader in weapons technology, newly formed Taim & Bak developed the Bp series of turrets under contract for the Empire. Each turret in the series is designed with simplicity in mind and can be set up at a base to provide protection. The Bp.4 anti-vehicle turret houses a powerful rotating blaster cannon that can target and fire upon enemy vehicles.

Notes

These turrets are very effective if you are having trouble with enemy vehicles moving through your territory.

Anti-Air Turret (Taim & Bak Bp.5 Anti-Air Turret)

In an effort to become an industry leader in weapons technology, newly formed Taim & Bak developed the Bp series of turrets under contract for the Empire. Each turret in the series is designed with simplicity in mind and can be set up at a base to provide protection. The Bp.5 anti-air turret houses rotating twin light flak pod cannons that can fire at incoming air vehicles from any direction.

Notes

If the Rebels are using airspeeders and Y-wing bombing runs, build a few of these around your base to protect your structures against enemy flying units.

The galaxy is not all either Imperial or Rebel. There are pirates and inhabitants of systems who would rather just be left alone and not involved in the conflict. Some individuals and corporations make a profit off of both sides, offering services and products to both the Empire and the Rebel Alliance.

Common Units

These units are available to both the Empire and the Rebel Alliance.

Bounty Hunter

Bounty hunters capitalize on the vendettas of others, tracking down fugitives for their enemies, for their masters, or simply for justice. Many bounty hunters belong to a loose organization referred to as the Bounty Hunter's Guild, but there are a few who choose to operate outside of the group. Find bounty hunters looking for contracts in places run by villainous types such as the Hutts.

Notes

Bounty hunters can travel around the galaxy alone without being detected by enemy units. Use this ability to scout out systems to see what is in orbit. However, their main job is to eliminate heroes. Send them to a planet to neutralize an enemy hero such as a smuggler or other character. You have to pay a fee for this service, and the more valuable the target, the higher the bounty. If you can afford it, send out several bounty hunters at one time to eliminate a number of the enemy's heroes simultaneously. This can really cause some problems, especially if the enemy was relying on the abilities of those heroes.

Field Commander

Culled from the best recruits in the galaxy, field commanders are trained at one of the Imperial military academies located throughout the Core Worlds. Or in the Rebellion's case, they were trained at one of the Imperial academies and later defected or came from elsewhere and were promoted. Field commanders offer the benefit of their training to any ground force they are assigned to by improving the combat effectiveness of all of the troops under their command.

Notes

When a field commander is present on the battlefield, the sight range of all your ground units is increased and your units also receive a 25 percent health bonus. Therefore, when you have room to land a field commander, do so to give your force an advantage.

Fleet Commander

Culled from the best recruits in the galaxy, fleet commanders are trained at one of the Imperial military academies located throughout the Core Worlds. Or in the Rebellion's case, they were trained at one of the Imperial academies and later defected or came from elsewhere and were promoted. Fleet commanders offer the benefit of their training to any fleets they are assigned to by improving the combat effectiveness of all of the ships in the fleet.

Notes

The fleet commander takes up station on one of the ships in your fleet. When he is in a space battle, all your units receive a 25 percent health bonus and can see farther through the fog of war. It is a good idea to have a fleet commander in each of your main fleets.

Smuggler

Smugglers are always looking to profit at someone else's expense and can quickly diminish the income of any business or government through their illegal activities. All smugglers put a price on the jobs they do and that fee must be paid up front, followed by a percentage of the take from the haul. They are always willing to bargain and can be found in any local cantina along with other unscrupulous types.

Notes

Send smugglers to enemy-controlled systems to steal credits. This can be doubly effective because you gain credits while your opponent is losing credits he or she might spend on units to fight against you. You can tell if a smuggler is stealing at a system because a "minus" sign appears next the system name. You can also use smugglers to scout out systems for you to see what the enemy has in orbit, because smugglers can move across the galaxy stealthily.

Common Structures

These structures can be built by both the Empire and the Rebel Alliance.

Cantina

Cantinas are wretched hives of scum and villainy, perfect for those looking to work with unscrupulous types. Deals of all kinds are made in the cantinas, most of them dangerous and highly illegal. Just about anything goes in this place, save for one standing condition: If you've got a dispute, leave blasters out of it. Smugglers of all kinds visit cantinas and are often found here.

Notes

Cantinas can be built only on Abregado-Rae, Atzerri, Corellia, Nal Hutta, Ryloth, and Tatooine. You only need to build one because you do not need a large force of smugglers. However, if you can afford it, send out a lot of smugglers all at once to the planets under the enemy's control. This forces the enemy to spend a lot of credits on bounty hunters to eliminate all of your smugglers. Meanwhile, you are earning money from their stealing.

Mining Facility (CMC-22 Mining Facility)

The CMC-22 mining facility is a product of the Corellia Mining Corporation. It is almost entirely automated and you can construct it anywhere mining facilities are needed. You can modify the mining facility to mine almost any precious resource that both the Empire and Rebellion use for raw materials or to sell off for credits. The Corellia Mining Corporation sells these facilities to anyone who wishes to purchase one, in exchange for a share of the profits.

Notes

This is your main money maker during a game. When taking control of planets, build mines on any slot you do not need for other structures. Some planets away from the front lines should have all mines. If you look at an economic summary of your income during a game, you should see at least three-quarters of your income derived from mines.

Shield Generator (CoMar Weapons SLD-14 Shield Generator

Bases equipped with CoMar Weapons SLD-14 shield generators can prevent orbital bombardments and energy attacks directly on the base itself. The shield generator does not prevent troops and vehicles from landing beyond the field radius or from entering the field radius. Shield generators require a lot of power and rely on a standard base power generator. The shield will fail if the power runs out.

Notes

While active, a shield generator creates a protective umbrella over the surrounding area. Units outside the shield can't fire lasers through it and if they move through the shield, their speed is seriously reduced until they are all the way through. However, units within the shield can fire out.

Hutt Palace

Expansive fortresses located anywhere a Hutt resides, Hutt palaces offer many opportunities for work of a criminal nature. Bounty hunters are often found here looking for contracts from the Hutts or anyone else willing to pay. The towering palaces are places of terrible violence and debauchery where unwanted guests are likely to be imprisoned in one of the citadel's many cells or murdered by belligerent guards.

Notes

A Hutt palace can be built only on Atzerri, Nal Hutta, Ryloth, and Tatooine. You only need one because you won't be producing a lot of bounty hunters.

Communications Array (MicroThrust Processors Communications Array)

Field commanders rely on good communications in order to win battles. The MicroThrust Processors communications array transmits all battlefield information and radar locations to the troops in the field. The building uses a substantial amount of power and requires a standard base power generator to function. Losing power is just as bad for field commanders as losing the communications array itself.

Notes

This is not a structure you can build, but is often part of a base during ground battles. It lowers the fog of war for the defender while it is functioning.

Power Generator

Power generators are used throughout the galaxy to supply large amounts of power to cities, bases, factories, and planetary weapons. Both the Empire and the Rebellion use power generators at their bases to keep their communications arrays, base shields, turbolaser towers, and mining facilities functioning at peak levels. Generators need to be protected by troops and perimeter defenses.

Notes

If the enemy has a lot of defenses, locate and take out the power generator. That makes your assault a lot easier. You do not build power generators. Instead, they are automatically built when you build a structure that requires power on a planet.

Turbolaser Tower (Taim & Bak XX-10 Turbolaser Tower)

A variant of the Taim & Bak XX-9 turbolaser tower used aboard space stations and capital ships, the XX-10 is a planetary surface weapon with a rotating turbolaser turret that can track and fire upon enemy troops and vehicles. Turbolasers require an enormous amount of power, which is supplied by standard base power generators. A loss of power to the turbolaser causes the weapon to be utterly useless during an assault.

Notes

These can be built from the galactic view and cause a lot of damage to enemy units. If you are attacking against these defenses, take out the power generator first or use artillery or air units to destroy these defenses.

Common Build Pad Structures

These structures can be built by both the Empire and the Rebels on controlled build pads.

Repair Station (Loratus Manufacturing Automated Repair Droid)

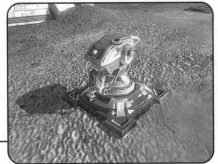

The Loratus Manufacturing automated repair droid is an on-the-spot repair facility for combat situations. The droid is equipped with a variety of tools to allow repairs of nearly any vehicle. While engineers and droids are commonly used for vehicle repairs, the ARD or repair station can be placed strategically on the battlefield and provide patch jobs for vehicles that only have time for a quick fix.

Notes

Vehicles can take a lot of damage during combat. With a repair station, you can fix them up and keep them in action much longer.

Sensor Node (MicroThrust Processors X2-a Series Sensor Node)

Specializing in communication equipment, MicroThrust Processors provides another piece of equipment for the battlefield, the X2-a series sensor node. Sensor nodes can be placed throughout the battlefield to collect and monitor specific locations for any kind of activity and transmit the data back to field troops. Individual sensor node range is small, but a network of nodes placed throughout a battlefield can provide field commanders with a lot of valuable information.

Notes

Sensor nodes can be built on build pads. Use them along routes to your base or reinforcement points to monitor enemy movements. They can also serve as spotting units for artillery and bombing runs.

Bacta Healing Station (Zaltin Bacta Corporation Field Bacta Tank)

Bacta, a synthetic chemical developed from an ancient remedy to heal all but the most serious of wounds, is the primary source of income for Zaltin Bacta Corporation. The company has developed a variety of delivery systems for bacta, including the field bacta tank, or bacta healing station as it is commonly called. It is designed for easy transportability in field combat situations and is used throughout the galaxy.

Notes

Build one of these at your base or near a reinforcement point so you can pull back your infantry to heal them. Some players like to place them near the front and position their infantry within its healing radius so they can be healed while engaged in combat.

Existing Structures

Many maps contain structures left behind from before the Galactic Civil war. You can't build these structures from the galactic mode. However, you can take control of them during a battle by moving an infantry unit adjacent to them.

Abandoned Heavy Factory

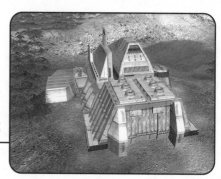

For years Delvin Constructs has been a supplier of cheap and easily constructed prefabricated building designs throughout the galaxy. Often the owners of these buildings abandon them when they vacate a facility and buy a new one to use at their new location. It is common for field commanders to come across buildings such as an abandoned heavy factory that require only a bit of retooling to bring them back online once claimed.

Notes

When you find these structures, you can purchase units that you can use during the ground battle. As the attacker, this is the only way you can get new units that are not already in your fleet up in orbit.

Abandoned Sensor Array

Sensor arrays have been used throughout the galaxy to help provide advance warning of an attack or monitor enemy activity on the battlefield. These buildings have proven to be useful targets and are often captured rather than destroyed during battles. Sometimes when a base is abandoned, these buildings are left behind by their previous owners and require only a few simple repairs to bring them back online once claimed.

Notes

You can come across these during a ground battle. Move infantry next to one to take control of it. It eliminates the fog of war and allows you to see where all enemy units and structures are located.

Resource Pad (Corellia Mining Corporation CMC-RP05 Resource Pad)

The CMC-RP05 resource pad is a scaled down version of the CMC-22 mining facility developed by the Corellia Mining Corporation. The resource pad mines and processes raw materials with a high rate of loss and is often used at resource-rich locations that can be strip-mined. Both the Rebellion and the Empire use resource pads to quickly mine raw materials to sell off for credits, giving a share of the profits to the Corellia Mining Corporation in return for its use.

Notes

By taking control of resource pads during a ground battle or skirmish, you receive credits to your account. Grab these and hold them during a battle so you get credits and your opponent does not.

Orbital Structures

In addition to space stations which you build in the galactic mode, some orbital maps have abandoned facilities or satellite build pads where you can build orbital structures.

Asteroid Mining Facility (Corellia Mining Corporation CMC-A14 Mining Facility)

The CMC-A14 mining facility or asteroid mining facility is another product of the Corellia Mining Corporation. It can be constructed anywhere asteroid-based mining facilities are needed. The mining facility can be modified to mine almost any precious resource that both the Empire and Rebellion use for raw materials or to sell off for credits. The Corellia Mining Corporation sells these facilities to anyone who wishes to purchase one, in exchange for a share of the profits.

Notes

Need some credits during a space battle? Take control of an asteroid and build one of these mines on it to start bringing in some credits, which you can use for upgrades.

Laser Defense Satellite (Corporate Sector Authority Md-12 Satellite Platform)

Continuing to seek personal gain from any conflict, the Corporate Sector Authority has developed an easily modifiable satellite platform for use as a perimeter space defense weapon. The Ld-12 or laser defense satellite is a platform that has been modified to house laser cannons capable of tracking and firing upon fighters and smaller ships, causing a considerable amount of damage.

Notes

As with the missile defense satellite, take this out as the attacker. During a battle, you can also build defense satellites on orbital build pads after destroying the enemy's satellite.

Missile Defense Satellite (Corporate Sector Authority Md-12 Satellite Platform)

Continuing to seek personal gain from any conflict, the Corporate Sector Authority has developed an easily modifiable satellite platform for use as a perimeter space defense weapon. The Md-12 or missile defense satellite is a platform that has been modified to house missile launchers capable of tracking and firing upon mid-sized ships, causing a considerable amount of damage.

Notes

These defenses, often in orbit around a space station, can cause a lot of damage to an invading fleet. Therefore, target and destroy them as you approach.

Orbital Long Range Scanner (Loronar Corporation OLR Scanner)

Seeing conflict as good for profits, Loronar Corporation develops a multitude of military hardware and other equipment that it sells to anyone looking to buy. The orbital long range scanner is one of the many technologies they sell. The orbital long range scanner detects ships in hyperspace over many light years' distance, providing advance warning of approaching enemy fleets.

Notes

This is a structure you can build in orbit from the galactic view. It is great for seeing the movement of enemy fleets in nearby systems.

Mercenaries and Pirates

The galaxy covers a large amount of space, and it is difficult for the Empire to patrol all of it. Hostile pirate forces have appeared in numerous locations, causing a lot of trouble in the infested star systems. Pirates are often found piloting a variety of ships and vehicles such as frigates, fighters, and skiffs in addition to fighting as foot soldiers. They occasionally take control of planets and establish asteroid bases and land bases on these planets. Mercenaries, on the other hand, are found during battles on planets and in space, selling their services to whichever side can afford it.

Mercenary and Pirate Units

Pirates come armed with blasters as well as Plex missiles.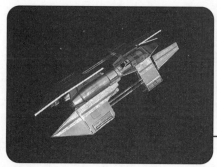

 Pirates also fight in space with their fighters.

Pod Walker (All Terrain Attack Pod)

The All Terrain Attack Pod, or AT-AP walker, is essentially a piece of mobile artillery. A three-legged walker with a closed canopy, the AT-AP walks in a two-legged configuration but has a third leg that lowers for stability as a gunnery platform. Rothana Heavy Engineering produced them for the Republic during the Clone Wars, but they are now used by mercenaries.

Notes

Pirates usually put these vehicles to good use on planets they control. Take them out or you will receive a lot of damage to your unit.

Swamp Speeder (Infantry Support Platform Speeder)

The infantry support platform speeder or swamp speeder is a repulsorlift vehicle powered by a large turbofan and armed with a pair of twin blaster cannons lethal to enemy infantry. Precise, controlled vectoring of the turbofan's thrust makes the swamp speeder a highly maneuverable vehicle. Uulshos Manufacturing produced them for the Republic during the Clone Wars, but they are now used by mercenaries looking for work in local cantinas.

Notes

You will face these vehicles when you fight to take control of a pirate planet.

IPV (IPV 1 Imperial Patrol Vessel)

These smaller patrol ships are used mostly by Imperial and local security forces, merchants, and mercenary captains. Sienar Fleet System's IPV 1 Imperial Patrol Vessels are excellent local defense ships, frequently used against pirates, smugglers, and hostile forces. System patrol craft usually have powerful sublight engines but no hyperdrives. Local mercenary captains piloting these ships can be found frequenting merchant space docks.

Notes

These are smaller ships you can hire. They're useful for taking on enemy fighters and bombers.

Mercenary and Pirate Structures

Merchant Space Dock

Independent ship captains are often looking for places to pick up additional work, whether it be transporting cargo or supporting local security forces. The merchant space dock is an orbital gathering place that serves this purpose. These small independent orbital stations provide a place for ship captains to gather and an opportunity for fleet commanders to recruit them into their local defense forces for additional support.

Notes

When you come across one of these during a space battle, you can purchase mercenary units to help in your fight.

Mercenary Outfitter

Conflict often provides good business, and many have sought all kinds of opportunities. One of those ventures is the mercenary outfitter. These small, independent businesses have sprung up throughout the galaxy in an effort to provide and profit from the sale of the latest military equipment produced by a variety of corporations. Field commanders in need of an edge can purchase any equipment upgrades available at these facilities.

Notes

When you are the attacker during a ground battle, if you find one of these structures, you can purchase upgrades for your units to increase defense and firepower.

Indigenous Forces

Many planets throughout the galaxy have various sentient species inhabiting them. The local inhabitants such as the Wookiees, Ewoks, Geonosians, Mon Calamari, Humans, Twi'leks, Jawas, Tusken Raiders, and others may decide to aid your forces in combat depending on their predisposition toward you. Others may aid your enemies and some may attack or ignore any intruders.

These indigenous forces maintain local habitats where they live. Troops stationed at these planets have reported a variety of unique structures that they have come across on inhabited planets such as the Ewok village; Wookiee trees, houses; Tusken Raider villages; Geonosian spires, Sandcrawlers; and other types of cities and living quarters.

Tusken Raiders live on Tatooine and fight against anybody who comes near them.

Jawas spawn in Sandcrawlers and fight against the Imperials. They can be found on Tatooine.

These are Ewoks and their tree huts on Endor. They often fight on the side of the Rebellion.

Creatures

The galaxy is teeming with life, some friendly and some very hostile. Creatures such as wampas, the Sarlacc, rancors, banthas, tauntauns, and others can live on a variety of worlds and may interact with troops or may ignore troops. It is best to be wary of them because some of the larger creatures such as the rancor have been known to eat troopers and smash vehicles when encountered.

Rancors are large, vicious beasts that can kill infantry and destroy vehicles. Stay at a distance and kill them before they hurt you.

The Sarlacc lives in the desert in pits. Its arms can reach out and grab infantry that come too near.

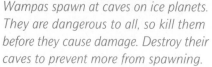

Wampas spawn at caves on ice planets. They are dangerous to all, so kill them before they cause damage. Destroy their caves to prevent more from spawning.

Some creatures, such as the tauntaun and the bantha, are docile and will not attack at all.

Abregado-Rae

A manufacturing and trade-oriented planet located in the Abregado system of the Core Worlds, Abregado-Rae is a temperate planet with rolling hills, lakes, and rivers. The planet's spaceport seems safe, at least to the untrained eye. Beneath the spit-shine and polish lies the heart of a smuggler's paradise, a spaceport where the galaxy's uncounted species mingle briefly, have wild and sometimes fatal flings, and then head off again for parts unknown. The smuggling community maintains a rather large underground information network on this planet.

Stats

Climate: Temperate

Terrain: Hills, rivers, lakes

Average Weather: Clear, rain

Diameter: 12,000 km

Sentient Species: Human

Population: 40 million

Wildlife: Gados

System/Star: Abregado

Tactical Information: The cost of producing AT-STs is reduced.

Maps

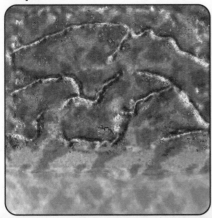 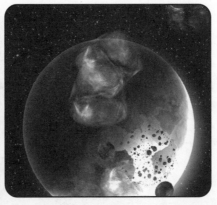

NOTE

When Pirates control the orbit over a system, they can exist nested within asteroid fields. The Empire and Rebellion, on the other hand, require room for Starbase expansion, so space debris is removed.

Aeten II

Located in the Outer Rim and plagued by volcanic activity, Aeten II is known for its deposits of rare stygium crystals, which are used in the construction of cloaking devices. Because stygium crystals are extremely valuable, a number of unscrupulous prospectors descended upon Aeten II, where they competed for the rare crystals with deadly abandon. As a result, Aeten II became one of the most dangerous planets in the Outer Rim territories. By the rise of the Empire, Aeten II's cache of crystals had been all but depleted, making the manufacture of new stygium-based cloaking devices a near impossibility. Prospectors looking to retool old mining facilities here have since found other valuable resources to mine.

Stats

Climate: Volcanic

Terrain: Lava rivers, volcanoes

Average Weather: Hot, ash fall

Diameter: 4,900 km

Sentient Species: Human

Population: 18,490

Wildlife: None

System/Star: Aeten

Tactical Information: Additional income is provided by mining facilities located throughout the planet.

Maps

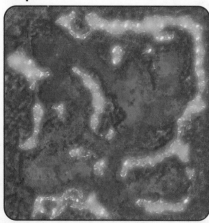

Alderaan

A peaceful, utopian Core World that serves as the spiritual heart of the galaxy, Alderaan boasts vast skies and plains that support more than 8,000 subspecies of grass, numerous wildflowers, and a wealth of unique species. The people of Alderaan love the land and work with it, rather than destroy it. Their society is immersed in high culture and education, and is founded on ecological principles that protect the planet's natural beauty. The horrors of the Clone Wars were taken to heart and the people of Alderaan adopted pacifism, banning all weapons from the planet's surface. However the rise of the Emperor has caused a growing opposition to Imperial rule and increased support for the Rebellion.

Stats

Climate: Temperate

Terrain: Grasslands

Average Weather: Clear, rain

Diameter: 12,500 km

Sentient Species: Human

Population: 2 billion

Wildlife: Thranta, nerf

System/Star: Alderaan

Tactical Information: Imperial base size is restricted due to Alderaan's opposition of the Emperor. Rebel soldiers receive a reduction to the damage they receive.

Maps

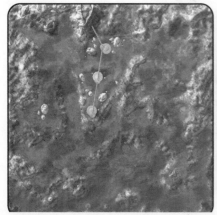

Alzoc III

A frozen planet in the Alzoc system in the Outer Rim, the moonless planet is covered with desolate, frozen plains, and its powerful sun glares harshly off the reflective snow. Wildlife on Alzoc III is almost nonexistent with only snow slugs and the Talz readily visible on the planet's surface. The Talz are the only sentient species on the planet and are native to Alzoc III. They conduct mining operations underground with exports such as the valuable Alzoc pearl. Talz mining operations have proven to be a profitable source of income.

Stats

Climate: Frozen

Terrain: Frozen tundra

Average Weather: Clear, snow

Diameter: 16,431 km

Sentient Species: Talz

Population: 500 million

Wildlife: Snow slug

System/Star: Alzoc

Tactical Information: Additional income is provided by Talz mining.

Maps

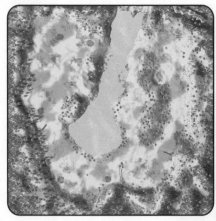 

Anaxes

A Core World, also known as the Defender of the Core, Anaxes has enjoyed naval prestige for millennia. Among Anaxes's plains, mountains, and forests sits a large establishment called the Anaxes Citadel. The citadel is a massive complex of training schools, research labs, intelligence centers, offices, archives, and parade grounds. The people of Anaxes refer to themselves as Anaxsi and carry much pride in their naval history. The terraced hills above the citadel are dotted with estates held by families that may not be Old Anaxsi, but whose names are synonymous with naval service.

The people of Anaxes fully support the Imperial Navy and will not tolerate dissent. The cost of producing Victory Star Destroyers is reduced.

Stats

Climate: Temperate

Terrain: Plains, forests, mountains

Average Weather: Clear, rain

Diameter: 16,100 km

Sentient Species: Anaxsi (Human)

Population: 512 million

Wildlife: None

System/Star: Axum/Solis Axum

Tactical Information: Hostility exists toward Rebel forces due to Anaxsi Imperial loyalty.

Maps

Atzerri

A temperate Free Trader world located in the Inner Rim, it has the most minimal government necessary to stave off complete chaos. Atzerri's terrain consists primarily of marshes and cities where almost anything, legal or illegal, can be had for a price. The Trader's Coalition charges a hefty fee for every service. Ships control their own entry and departure and must negotiate with independently owned spaceports to land. Arriving visitors run a gauntlet of gaudily lit stores known as Trader's Plaza, designed to hook new arrivals and separate them from their credits as soon as possible. Many of these stores get their wares from the local black market.

Stats

Climate: Temperate

Terrain: Cities, marshes

Average Weather: Clear, rain

Diameter: 14,000 km

Sentient Species: Human

Population: 4 billion

Wildlife: Atzerrian meek

System/Star: Atzerri

Tactical Information: Planetary income fluctuates due to the presence of the black market.

Maps

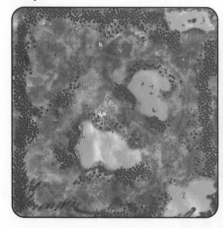

Bespin

Located in the Anoat sector of the Outer Rim, Bespin is a large gas giant that has no landmasses, but its upper atmosphere of billowing clouds hosts an envelope of breathable air called the "Life Zone" where a variety of life forms have evolved. Local inhabitants have established floating colonies here such as Cloud City, a popular resort and mining town. The Cloud City Wing Guard handles security, police, and emergency duties for Cloud City while the Baron Administrator runs the city's day to day and mining operations. Bespin's chief and most profitable export is the precious Tibanna gas that is used to power blasters and other energy weapons.

Stats

Climate: Layer of breathable atmosphere

Terrain: Gas

Average Weather: Wind storms

Diameter: 118,000 km

Sentient Species: Human, Ugnaught

Population: 6 million

Wildlife: Velker, beldon

System/Star: Bespin

Tactical Information: Additional income is provided by Tibanna gas mining.

Maps

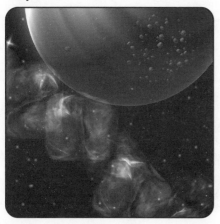

Bestine IV

A planet in the Bestine system of the Inner Rim, Bestine IV is a temperate planet with many rocky islands among its vast oceanic landscape. Weather on Bestine IV is generally known to be mild with occasional hurricanes sweeping across the planet's surface. The planet's population has struggled for years to establish their settlements atop the planet's island spires to create an island paradise. More recently the planet has become increasingly attractive due to Bestine's small but growing ship repair and construction industry, which can be credited to the planet's unique oceanic-based shipyards that are designed primarily to quickly produce frigate-sized vessels.

Stats

Climate: Temperate

Terrain: Rocky islands, oceans

Average Weather: Clear, rain

Diameter: 6,400 km

Sentient Species: Human

Population: 62 million

Wildlife: Sink crab

System/Star: Bestine

Tactical Information: The cost of producing Acclamator cruisers is reduced.

Maps

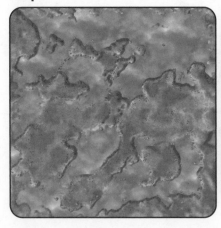
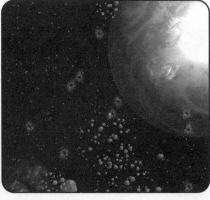

Bonadan

This planet has long been one of the Outer Rim Corporate Sector Authority's most important factory worlds and busiest ports. Bonadan is a parched yellow sphere crisscrossed by rust stripes because of heavy soil erosion. Bonadan industry has thrived at the expense of ecology, because any plant life on the surface that wasn't intentionally destroyed has disappeared due to overmining, pollution, and neglect. A densely populated planet, Bonadan houses many sentient species from all over the galaxy. The world is covered with factories, refineries, docks, and shipbuilding facilities in 10 spaceports. Bonadan's diverse economy is considered the most lucrative of any planet in the Corporate Sector.

Stats

Climate: Polluted

Terrain: Eroded wastes, industrial centers

Average Weather: Clear, smog

Diameter: 13,100 km

Sentient Species: Human, alien

Population: 12 billion

Wildlife: Tortapo

System/Star: Bonadan

Tactical Information: Additional income is provided by Bonadan's diverse economy.

Maps

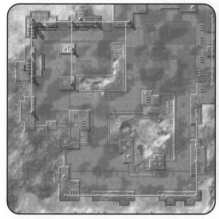

Bothawui

Bothawui is a neutral Mid Rim world that is the base of the Bothan spynet. Bothawui is a clean, mountainous, forested, and cosmopolitan planet. Streets in the major cities are clean and wide, and lined with tall buildings built of a natural glittering stone. This well-organized world has always been considered neutral territory, because it has been an active hub for operatives of every stripe. Although they have much to offer the galaxy, Bothans are probably best-known for their intrepid spies. The Bothan spynet is among the largest intelligence organizations, with operatives stationed throughout the galaxy.

Stats

Climate: Temperate

Terrain: Mountains, valleys, forest

Average Weather: Clear, rain

Diameter: 9,000 km

Sentient Species: Bothan

Population: 2.5 billion

Wildlife: Kra'jya, ganjuko, halkra, krak'jya, skar'kla, rals

System/Star: Both

Tactical Information: Tactical information for nearby systems is available due to the Bothan spynet.

Maps

Byss

The mysterious planet Byss lies at the heart of the Imperial holdings in the Deep Core. An eerie blue-green sunlight bathes everything on the planet in an unusual glow, contributing to the overwhelming strangeness of the world. The planet itself is something of a myth, built up to pique the curiosity of those who have heard of a mysterious paradise planet ruled by the Empire. With tranquil scenery, low geological activity, exceedingly mild seasons, and the feel of a luxury resort, the planet appears to be the perfect place to live, which is exactly what Emperor Palpatine wants people to believe. The Emperor's dark side energies corrupted the world and its inhabitants, allowing the planet to be quickly built up.

Stats

Climate: Temperate

Terrain: Lakes, plateaus, urban sprawls

Average Weather: Clear, rain

Diameter: 21,600 km

Sentient Species: Human

Population: 19.7 billion

Wildlife: None

System/Star: Beshqek

Tactical Information: AT-ATs receive a boost to speed and firepower.

Maps

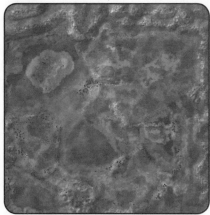 

Carida

One of several planets in the Caridan system of the Colonies region, Carida is a large, high-gravity world with a wide variety of terrain. The planet's varied surface—with rocky mountains, frozen ice fields, jungles filled with carnivorous plants, and arid deserts—provided perfect training for combat in harsh environments. The planet is populated by humans and humanoids that have thin limbs and heavy, barrel chests. Representatives of the Caridan government joined the campaigning for the Military Creation Act, offering their renowned academic institutions for Republic use at the start of the Clone Wars. Carida has since become the site of the Empire's most important stormtrooper training center.

Stats

Climate: Temperate

Terrain: Jungles, deserts, oceans, arctic tundra

Average Weather: Clear, rain

Diameter: 18,324 km

Sentient Species: Caridan, human

Population: 25 million

Wildlife: Combat arachnid

System/Star: Caridan

Tactical Information: The cost of producing infantry units is reduced.

Maps

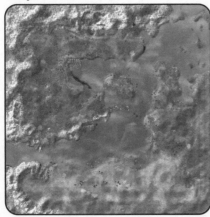 

Corellia

The Core World system of Corellia is home to five inhabited planets: Corellia, Drall, Selonia, Talus, and Tralus. Corellia is a temperate planet covered by rolling hills, thick forests, lush fields, and large seas. Wildlife includes the dangerous sand panther, grass snakes, and the slice hound. Although Corellia is regarded as an industrialized world, the majority of the planet's inhabitants occupy small towns or farms. The galaxy's most prolific starship manufacturing company, Corellian Engineering Corporation, maintains orbital shipyards at Corellia, allowing the planet to remain largely rural. Corvette-sized ships produced at Corellia are cheaper due to the abundance of resources and talented individuals available from CEC.

Stats

Climate: Temperate

Terrain: Forest, jungles, hills, fields, seas

Average Weather: Clear, rain

Diameter: 11,000 km

Sentient Species: Human, Selonian, Drall

Population: 3 billion

Wildlife: Sand panther, grass snake, slice hound

System/Star: Corellia

Tactical Information: Cost of Corellian corvettes is reduced due to the presence of the Corellian Engineering Corporation.

Maps

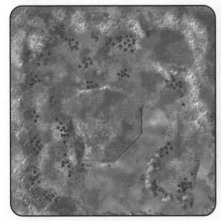 

Corulag

A planet of 15 billion citizens, it is in the Bormea sector of the Core Worlds, along the Perlemian Trade Route. The planet boasts vast urban sprawls with the underdeveloped areas covered in forests of sturdy bamboo. The planet's population is devoted to Emperor Palpatine and is viewed as a "model" world of proper Imperial behavior. The capital city of Curamelle was the site of Corulag Academy, a branch of the Empire-wide military school. New troops are sent to the academy to learn the finer points of galactic warfare before being sent off world to continue training at other branches of the military school.

Stats

Climate: Temperate

Terrain: Urban sprawls, oceans, forest

Average Weather: Clear, rain

Diameter: 12,749 km

Sentient Species: Sullustan

Population: 15 billion

Wildlife: Bulfusi

System/Star: Corula

Tactical Information: Cost of training for infantry is reduced due to the Corulag Academy.

Maps

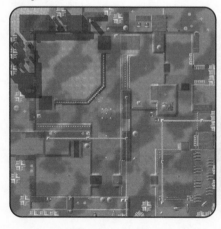

Coruscant

Sometimes referred to as the jewel of the Core Worlds, Coruscant is known as the center of the universe and the seat of government since the earliest days of the Republic. The planet's surface is essentially a single, enormous multilevel city with buildings that extend as much as 6,000 meters into the atmosphere and can be several blocks wide. The skies of Coruscant are a constant hive of activity that is crowded with starships from around the galaxy traveling the planet in tightly controlled sky lanes. The Emperor directly controls the Imperial Navy and Galactic Senate from here.

Stats

Climate: Temperate and controlled

Terrain: Urban

Average Weather: Clear

Diameter: 12,240 km

Sentient Species: Human

Population: 1 trillion

Wildlife: Hawk-bat, spider-roach, duracrete worm, sewer rat

System/Star: Coruscant

Tactical Information: Additional income is provided by the Imperial government.

Maps

Dagobah

Dagobah is a mysterious swamp planet located in the far reaches of the galaxy. Dagobah's landscape is covered with giant gnarltree forests, twisting waterways, and a shroud of mist. Free of technology and overrun by foliage and wild beasts, Dagobah is a tumultuous and primeval world. Dagobah is probably most notable for its sheer diversity of life including the voracious swamp slug, the predatory dragonsnake, and flying bogwings. Searching for anything in Dagobah's swamps would yield little gain, but those with something to hide would benefit greatly.

Stats

Climate: Murky

Terrain: Swamp

Average Weather: Clear, rain

Diameter: 8,900 km

Sentient Species: None

Population: 0

Wildlife: Dragonsnake, giant swamp slug, bogwing

System/Star: Dagobah

Tactical Information: Ground bases are undetectable due to the planet's natural environment and terrain.

Maps

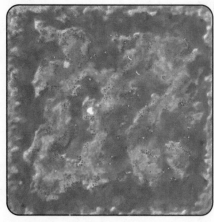

Dantooine

An olive, blue, and brown world, Dantooine is far removed from the bustle of the galactic trade routes deep in the Outer Rim. Dantooine is an isolated, unspoiled world covered by sprawling grasslands and oceans. Two moons float in the skies above, while herds of livestock roam empty steppes and savannas of lavender grasses. Dantooine is largely uninhabited save for a small human population and a few tribes of the nomadic Dantari that can be found wandering the coastlines. Separated by forests of spiky blba trees, colonists maintain individual family estates largely isolated from each other. Dantooine's distance from trade routes is often overlooked as a military benefit.

Stats

Climate: Temperate

Terrain: Grasslands, steppes, savannahs, mountains

Average Weather: Clear, rain

Diameter: 9,830 km

Sentient Species: Human, Dantari

Population: 334,000

Wildlife: Stalker lizard

System/Star: Dantooine

Tactical Information: Ground bases are undetectable due to Dantooine's isolated location.

Maps

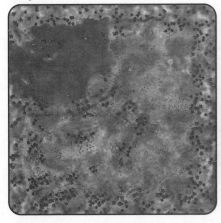

Endor

Located in the Moddell sector of the Outer Rim, this silvery gas giant plane is orbited by nine moons. The largest moon is the size of a small planet and is known as the forest moon or simply Endor. It is covered by savannas, mountains, and woodlands with trees that reach thousands of meters in height. A wide range of intelligent creatures inhabit Endor, from the vicious and towering Gorax to the courageous Ewoks. The Ewoks build their sprawling villages in Endor's trees that are connected by suspended bridges, ropes, and wooden platforms. Ewoks are deceptively innocuous, but they are keen warriors and hunters capable of using their ingenuity and natural surroundings to their advantage.

Stats

Climate: Temperate	
Terrain: Forest, savannas, mountains	
Average Weather: Clear, rain	
Diameter: 4,900 km	
Sentient Species: Ewok, Gorax	
Population: 30 million Ewoks	
Wildlife: Blurrg, condor dragon	
System/Star: Endor	
Tactical Information: Ewoks may aid friendly forces. TIE mauler, AT-ST, and AT-AA units gain a defense bonus against blaster fire.	

Maps

Eriadu

A polluted factory planet in the Seswenna sector, Eriadu is a trading and governmental hub in the Outer Rim. It is a slate-gray world of rugged landmasses and toxic slender seas. Industry holds sway over all Eriadu, fouling air, land, and sea with unrelenting outpourings of toxic by-products. The primary city, Eriadu City, is in the southern hemisphere. A thriving seaport that had grown up around the mouth of a major river, it spread almost one hundred kilometers inland. The Eriaduians are some of the finest weapons developers in the known galaxy, capable of quickly filling any contract they get.

Stats

Climate: Polluted

Terrain: Polluted urban sprawls, toxic seas

Average Weather: Clear, smog

Diameter: 13,490 km

Sentient Species: Human (Eriaduian)

Population: 22 billion

Wildlife: Eriaduian rat

System/Star: Eriadu

Tactical Information: The cost for T4-B units is reduced.

Maps

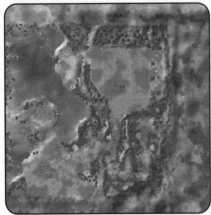 

Fondor

An industrial Colonies World in the system of the same name, Fondor is densely populated and has sprawling urban centers, factories, and junkyards across the entire planet. Fondor is in the Tapani sector in an area designated as a manufacturing and shipbuilding center precisely because of resource-rich asteroids, moons, and other worlds ripe for abuse. The planet boasts huge orbital starship construction facilities that provide an abundant feeding ground for mynocks, flying parasites that feed on energy. They are often found chewing on exposed power cables of ships in construction. Fondor's orbital starship construction facilities cater to frigate-sized starships, reducing their cost.

Stats

Climate: Temperate

Terrain: Urban sprawl

Average Weather: Clear, rain

Diameter: 9,100 km

Sentient Species: Human

Population: 5 billion

Wildlife: Mynock

System/Star: Fondor

Tactical Information: Cost of assault frigates is reduced due to Fondor's orbital construction facilities.

Maps

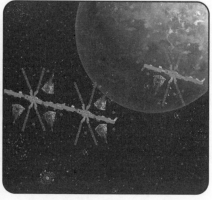

Fresia

Located in the Core Worlds, Fresia is a small planet of rocky islands and fractured archipelagos. The planet's population is relatively small at only 2.3 million and is one of the core's least populated planets. Fresia is the home of Incom Industries, a large starship manufacturer known most notably for their fighter craft and personal transports. Design fabrication research at Incom's headquarters on Coromon Island has found ways to reduce the time needed to prototype and construct fighter craft at the corporation's construction facilities.

Stats

Climate: Temperate

Terrain: Islands, oceans

Average Weather: Clear, rain

Diameter: 10,308 km

Sentient Species: Human

Population: 2.3 million

Wildlife: None

System/Star: Fre'ji

Tactical Information: Cost of A-wing squadrons is reduced due to Incom Corporation's development capabilities.

Maps

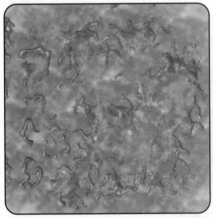

Geonosis

Less than a parsec away from Tatooine in the Outer Rim, Geonosis is a ringed and harsh rocky world. Geonosis has a red-tinted sky and its surface is marked by mesas, buttes, and barren stretches of parched desert hardpan. Radiation and asteroid storms occasionally blast the surface, driving life forms underground for protection. Geonosian fauna has adapted for such circumstances, and the planet is seemingly devoid of life. The dominant species are Geonosians, sentient insectoids that inhabit towering spire-hives. The Geonosians typically keep to themselves, but they maintain large factories for the production of a variety of ground units and weaponry for clients looking to do business.

Stats

Climate: Arid

Terrain: Desert, barren

Average Weather: Clear

Diameter: 11,370 km

Sentient Species: Geonosian

Population: 100 billion

Wildlife: Sand snake, picador, acklay, nexu, reek

System/Star: Geonosis

Tactical Information: Cost of MPTL-2a units is decreased due to Geonosian·production facilities.

Maps

Hoth

An isolated, barren ice planet located in the outer reaches of the known galaxy, Hoth is a dangerous world where the elements are a constant threat. The entire planet is blanketed in snow and ice, with evening temperatures dipping well below the freezing point. Meteors also crash against Hoth's surface with frightening regularity. Hoth is inhabited by few species save the savage wampa ice creature and the docile tauntaun. The planet is often overlooked as having any value for settlements, military, or mining operations, making it ideal for a smuggling base or secret installation.

Stats

Climate: Frozen

Terrain: Ice caves, frozen plains, mountain ranges

Average Weather: Clear, snow, blizzard

Diameter: 12,875 km

Sentient Species: None

Population: 0

Wildlife: Tauntaun, wampa

System/Star: Hoth

Tactical Information: Ground bases are undetectable due to Hoth's distant location.

Maps

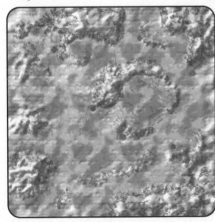 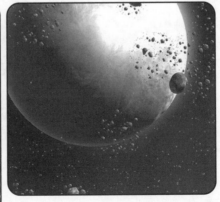

Ilum

A mountainous planet located in the Outer Rim, Ilum is a cold, icy world with no known settlements. Ilum crystals used in the building of Jedi lightsabers can be found in Ilum's Crystal Cave. The crystals grow in intricate formations and glow in the dark cave. Unlike lightsaber crystals found elsewhere, Ilum crystals produce only blue and green blades. Force-sensitive individuals can feel vibrations emanating from them, creating a sense of power.

Stats

Climate: Frozen

Terrain: Mountains, ice

Average Weather: Clear, snow

Diameter: 5,870 km

Sentient Species: None

Population: 0

Wildlife: Gorgodon

System/Star: Ilum

Tactical Information: Cost of SPMA-T production is reduced.

Maps

Jabiim

Located in the Outer Rim, Jabiim is a storm-drenched world with mineral wealth. After years of exploitation, the world that was once famed for its endless rains is now becoming a desert. The moisture that is left in the atmosphere has become terminally polluted, causing sporadic storms of violent electricity and deadly acid rain. All that's beautiful has been decimated. Vast strip mines now scar its surface, and its seas and rivers run black with ash and slag. Huge digging and boring machines continue to cut ever deeper into the surface of the dying planet. Jabiim's harsh atmospheric conditions cause repulsorlift vehicles to break down quickly.

Stats

Climate: Temperate

Terrain: Desert, seas, rivers

Average Weather: Clear, acid rain

Diameter: 10,700 km

Sentient Species: Human, Jabiimite

Population: 100 million

Wildlife: None

System/Star: Jabiim

Tactical Information: Repulsorlift vehicles are inoperable due to electrical storms, acid rain, and mud, including: 2-M tanks, T2-B tanks, scout troopers.

Maps

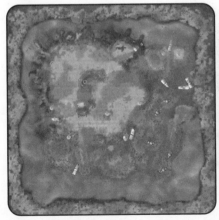

Kashyyyk

Located in the Mid Rim, Kashyyyk is a green-and-brown jungle planet covered with kilometers-high wroshyr trees. It is the homeworld of the fierce but loyal Wookiees. The Wookiees inhabit the wroshyr trees in huge cities that are naturally supported by the thick wroshyr tree branches. The wroshyr tree canopies provide a natural cover and lower aerial visibility into the Wookiee cites. Despite this, Trandoshan slavers routinely land and operate on the planet to capture Wookiees for slave labor. Anyone who can provide aid to the enslaved Wookiees may be granted a Wookiee life debt.

Stats

Climate: Temperate

Terrain: Forest, jungle

Average Weather: Clear, rain

Diameter: 12,765 km

Sentient Species: Wookiee

Population: 45 million

Wildlife: Kinrath, katarn, terentatek

System/Star: Kashyyyk

Tactical Information: Ground bases are undetectable due to wroshyr tree canopies. Wookiee warriors may aid Rebel forces.

Maps

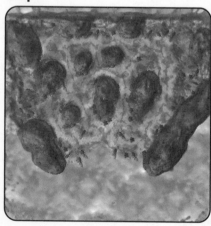 

Kessel

A largely inhospitable and desolate Outer Rim world, Kessel has an abundance of profitable and unique glitterstim spice. In order to support life on Kessel, mining operations have established air-producing factories capable of creating a thin atmosphere. The mines themselves are located far below Kessel's barren surface. Prisoners are often forced to labor ceaselessly in the dark mines, where they can fall prey to energy spiders and other dangers. Automated workers have recently begun replacing the prison labor force. Smugglers participating in the Kessel Run provide additional income in order to avoid unnecessary Imperial entanglements.

Stats

Climate: Barren with thin atmosphere

Terrain: Alkali flats and barren, rocky mountains

Average Weather: Cold and dry

Diameter: 6,632–7,980 km (non-spherical)

Sentient Species: Human, many alien species

Population: 700 (military and administrative), 10,400 (prisoners)

Wildlife: Energy spider

System/Star: Kessel

Tactical Information: Additional income is provided by spice running.

Maps

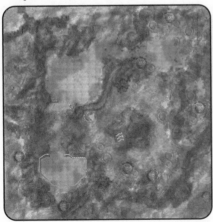 

Korriban

A hidden Outer Rim world in the Horuset system that has served as a Sith burial planet for several millennia, Korriban is a mountainous planet littered with dry river beds, canyons, tombs, and ruins. Korriban is the ancient homeworld of the Sith, and now a haunting ground for the fallen Sith Lords. The Sith Lords are interred within great temples located in the Valley of the Dark Lords on Korriban. The tombs are designed to focus and amplify dark-side energy, which permeates the entire valley. Each temple is guarded by strange and brutal dark side beasts and human skeletons that are activated through a combination of machinery and Sith magic. It is said that Korriban is a great source of power.

Stats

Climate: Cold and dry

Terrain: Mountains, canyons, dry riverbeds, tombs, ruins

Average Weather: Dry

Diameter: 16,890 km

Sentient Species: None

Population: 0

Wildlife: Sith Lord spirits, guardian tuk'ata

System/Star: Horuset

Tactical Information: The cost of 2-M tank production is reduced.

Maps

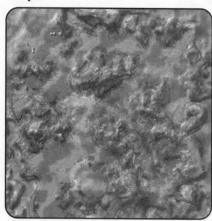 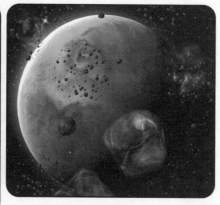

Kuat

A temperate Core World that is the site of the massive Kuat Drive Yards starship construction facility, Kuat is located in the Kuat sector in the most densely populated section of the galaxy. The planet is covered in expansive forests and plains and has generally mild weather. Kuat society is structured by class, where the lower and middle classes are often considered not worthy of notice by the elite. Kuat's upper classes are the families of the legendary Kuat merchant houses, including Kuat Drive Yards (KDY). KDY's efficient construction processes have increased the speed at which starships are produced and they have become a well-known producer of warships throughout the galaxy.

Stats

Climate: Temperate

Terrain: Forest, plains

Average Weather: Clear, rain

Diameter: 10,000 km

Sentient Species: Human

Population: 3.6 billion

Wildlife: Drebin

System/Star: Kuat

Tactical Information: Cost of Imperial Star Destroyer production is reduced due to Kuat Drive Yards construction processes.

Maps

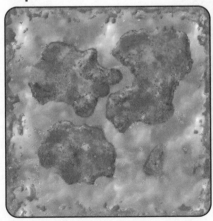 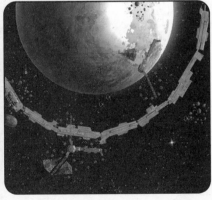

Manaan

A small Mid Rim planet in an insignificant system, Manaan's most remarkable feature is the calm, azure ocean that completely covers its surface. To accommodate off-world visitors, the amphibious Selkath have constructed Ahto City, a bustling spaceport floating on the endless ocean's waves. Manaan is known throughout the galaxy for one thing: being the sole producer of kolto, a powerful healing agent harvested from the ocean surface. This one export is so valuable that it has made the tiny world into one of the most influential independent planets in the galaxy. Many a battle has been won or lost due to the size of an army's kolto reserves.

Stats

Climate: Temperate

Terrain: Ocean

Average Weather: Clear, rain

Diameter: 14,220 km

Sentient Species: Selkath

Population: 500,000 Selkath (estimated); 2,000 foreigners

Wildlife: None

System/Star: Pyrshak

Tactical Information: Infantry auto heals due to kolto healing agent reserves.

Maps

Mon Calamari

This Outer Rim world is almost completely covered with water. The surface of the planet Mon Calamari (sometimes called simply Calamari) is covered with small marshy islands and enormous floating cities. The architecture and design of the floating cities have an organic appearance, with rounded edges and irregular surfaces, demonstrating the inhabitants' love for the natural beauty of their world. Mon Calamari is home to more than 27 billion inhabitants: the peace-loving Mon Calamari and the cautious Quarren. Raw materials from the ocean depths are mined by the Quarren and used by the Mon Calamari for various construction projects throughout the floating cities and orbital shipyards.

Stats

Climate: Temperate

Terrain: Ocean, islands

Average Weather: Clear, rain

Diameter: 11,030 km

Sentient Species: Mon Calamari, Quarren

Population: 27 billion

Wildlife: Krakana, sea slug, choarn, lampfish, whaladon

System/Star: Calamari

Tactical Information: Cost of Mon Calamari cruisers is reduced due to Mon Calamari's access to raw materials and orbital shipyards.

Maps

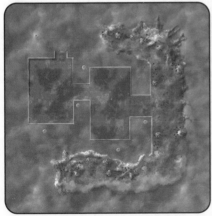 

Naboo

A temperate planet in the Chommell sector of the Mid Rim, Naboo is covered by thick swamps, rolling plains, and green hills. Unlike many other planets, Naboo lacks a molten core. Instead, the planet's innards are composed of a massive honeycomb structure filled with water. The planet is also home to numerous animal species and is inhabited by the peaceful Naboo and the more warlike Gungans. The Naboo typically populate striking cities such as Theed, while the Gungans dwell in exotic bubble cities hidden in lakes and swamps. Both the Naboo and the Gungans oppose the Emperor.

Stats

Climate: Temperate

Terrain: Grassland, swamp

Average Weather: Clear, rain

Diameter: 12,120 km

Sentient Species: Naboo, Gungan

Population: 600 million

Wildlife: Kaadu, falumpaset, fambaa, shaak, colo claw fish, tusk cat

System/Star: Naboo

Tactical Information: Imperial base size is limited due to Naboo's opposition toward the Emperor. T4-B tanks gain a damage bonus.

Maps

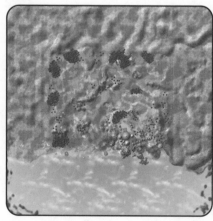 

Nal Hutta

A bruised-looking green, blue, and brown planet in the Y'Toub system of the Mid Rim, Nal Hutta's name means "glorious jewel" in Huttese. The planet was once a pleasant world of mountainous rain forests and home to the Evocii. After the Hutts arrived here from Varl, they forced the Evocii off the planet and transformed it into a gloomy planet of stinking bogs, stagnant scum-covered puddles, and patches of sickly marsh grass inhabited by insects and spiders. Strip mining has polluted the atmosphere and a greasy rain drizzles on its squatters' villages and ghettos. The Hutts engage in criminal activities of all kinds throughout the galaxy.

Stats

Climate: Temperate

Terrain: Swamp, decaying urban zones

Average Weather: Polluted, rain

Diameter: 26,100 km

Sentient Species: Hutt, various aliens

Population: 7 billion

Wildlife: T'landa Til, various aliens

System/Star: Y'Toub

Tactical Information: Planetary income fluctuates due to Hutt criminal activities.

Maps

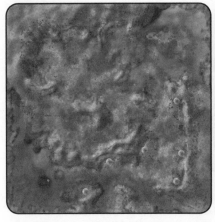

Polus

Humbly orbiting the binary star Avindia in the Outer Rim, Polus is an arctic, mostly mountainous planet with one massive frozen ocean. The average daytime temperature is 50 below freezing with frequent blizzards and ice storms and the brief but seasonal warming period when the planet is hit by light from both suns. Polus is inhabited by the Pyn'gani, who are masters of thermal dynamics. Their cities and habitats are shielded by a network of heat generators protecting them from the extreme cold. The Pyn'gani played a major role in developing the carbonite freezing process used to store goods for long-term shipment, and mining the valuable metal continues to be major source of income.

Stats

Climate: Arctic

Terrain: Mountainous, scattered cities

Average Weather: Blizzards, ice storms

Diameter: 9,562 km

Sentient Species: Pyn'gani

Population: 600,000

Wildlife: Dral'k ice worms, various aquatic life forms

System/Star: Avindia system

Tactical information: Additional income is provided by carbonite mining.

Maps

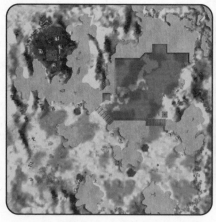

Ryloth

Located in the Outer Rim near Tatooine and home to the Twi'leks, Ryloth is the principal planet in the Ryloth system. Mountainous Ryloth rotates so slowly that its rotation is equal to the length of its orbit around the sun. One side of the planet always faces the sun and the only habitable areas are in the band of twilight separating the two sides. Heat storms in Ryloth's thin atmosphere help to distribute warmth throughout the twilight zone, where the Twi'leks live in a network of mountain catacombs. Twi'leks are a humanoid species with two large, fleshy head-tails growing from their skulls. Twi'lek culture is very social with information about everyone and everything on the planet changing hands constantly.

Stats

Climate: Arid

Terrain: Mountains, deserts, tundra

Average Weather: Clear, heat storms

Diameter: 10,600 km

Sentient Species: Twi'lek

Population: 1.5 billion

Wildlife: Lylek

System/Star: Ryloth

Tactical Information: Stormtroopers receive a health bonus.

Maps

Shola

Located in the Magatesso system, Shola is a barren, volcanic planet with a dense atmosphere and heavy magma flows littering the landscape. Massive ruins and deep crevasses are scattered throughout the planet but remain largely unexplored due to the volatile atmosphere, ground quakes, and heavy magma flows. Deep scans of the planet also show mining tunnel systems that lead almost to the planet's core and support the theory that the alien species that once existed here may have destroyed themselves in a massive cataclysm that left the planet in its current state. Long-term exposure to Shola's environment can be extremely harmful to those trying to take refuge here.

Stats

Climate: Volcanic

Terrain: Desolate, mostly flat, magma rivers

Average Weather: Ash storms, dust storms

Diameter: 13,296 km

Sentient Species: None, unknown (extinct)

Population: 0

Wildlife: Magma snake

System/Star: Magatesso system

Tactical information: Infantry slowly take damage from exposure to the environment.

Maps

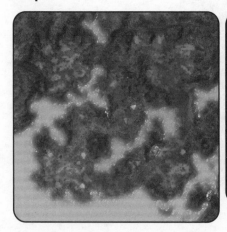

Sullust

A volcanic Outer Rim world in the Sullust system, Sullust is covered with thick clouds of hot, barely breathable gases. Sullust is inhabited through its vast networks of underground caves where native Sullustans, jowled, mouse-eared humanoids with large round eyes, have built beautiful underground cities that draw large crowds of tourists. Piringiisi, one popular resort, is known for its hot springs and green mud. The massive SoroSuub Corporation is based on Sullust and employs nearly half the population in its mining, energy, packaging, and production divisions. SoroSuub produces a variety of ships, vehicles, and weaponry, but its facilities are equipped to cheaply produce smaller corvette-sized ships.

Stats

Climate: Volcanic

Terrain: Lava rivers, volcanoes, underground caves

Average Weather: Hot, barely breathable, ash fall

Diameter: 12,780 km

Sentient Species: Sullustan

Population: 18.5 billion

Wildlife: Drutash grub

System/Star: Sullust

Tactical Information: Cost is reduced for Tartan patrol cruisers due to the presence of the SoroSuub Corporation.

Maps

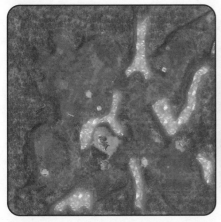

Taris

An urban Outer Rim world, Taris was once a gigantic city planet rivaling Coruscant, but thousands of years ago, the planet's population of 6 billion was utterly destroyed during a massive conflict between Jedi and Sith forces. In the millennia since, the planet has been resettled. Inhabitants have rebuilt some cities, although much of the planet still lies in ruin. Historians believe the swoop bike originated here and continue to excavate the ruins all over the planet in search of proof. Materials processing centers throughout the planet provide the abundance of raw materials used to support the thriving ship industry.

Stats

Climate: Temperate

Terrain: Urban

Average Weather: Clear

Diameter: 12,200 km

Sentient Species: Human

Population: 1 billion

Wildlife: None

System/Star: Taris

Tactical Information: Cost of T2-B tanks is reduced.

Maps

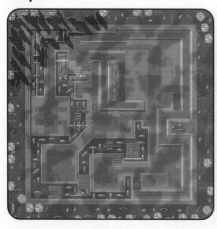 

Tatooine

Along the Outer Rim, the harsh desert world of Tatooine orbits the twin suns of the Tatoo system. Tatooine is marked by mesas, canyons, and expansive desert seas. Most settlers operate moisture farms in the desert, but cities such as Mos Eisley attract a wide range of criminals and rogues. Tatooine's many dangers include bands of roving Tusken Raiders, carnivorous krayt dragons, and sudden sandstorms. Tatooine is controlled by the Hutts, powerful gangsters and crime lords who have made the desert world into a hub of criminal activity including gambling, smuggling, and slavery. Stealth operators often find it to be a more profitable venture to work for the Hutts than to risk spying on them.

Stats

Climate: Arid

Terrain: Desert, mesas, canyons

Average Weather: Clear, sandstorms

Diameter: 10,465 km

Sentient Species: Human, Hutt, Jawa, Tusken Raider

Population: 200,000

Wildlife: Dewback, bantha, ronto, eopie, rancor, womp rat, Sarlacc, krayt dragon

System/Star: Tatoo

Tactical Information: T2-B tanks and assault speeders gain a bonus to their armor.

Maps

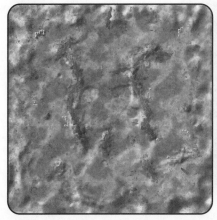

Thyferra

The Inner Rim homeworld of the mantis-like Vratix and located in the Polith system, Thyferra is a green-and-white world covered with rain forests; it has little axial tilt and is unbearably humid. It has two airless, uninhabited moons and orbits a yellow star. Although the Vratix already had colonized other bodies in their system, contact with the Republic ushered in a technological revolution. The Vratix soon invented the healing fluid called bacta by growing alazhi and mixing it with the chemical kavam. The remarkable fluid was extremely profitable, and powerful Vratix operations spread across many worlds. Thyferra is the center of the galaxy's bacta industry and has excellent medical facilities and aid stations.

Stats

Climate: Tropical

Terrain: Jungles, cave networks, mountains

Average Weather: Clear, rain, hurricane

Diameter: 10,221 km

Sentient Species: Humans, Vratix

Population: 117 million

Wildlife: Knytix

System/Star: Polith

Tactical Information: Infantry auto heals due to the abundance of Thyferran bacta.

Maps

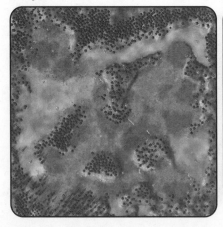

Vergesso Asteroids

These asteroids are located in the Lybeya system of the Bajic sector in the Outer Rim. The Tenloss Syndicate built a hidden shipyard in a nickel-iron asteroid referred to as the Vergesso Asteroid. The asteroid was the size of a small moon and had a surface pockmarked with craters. The asteroid field is one of the less violent asteroid fields in the galaxy and is easier to navigate than most others. Scanners have difficulty penetrating the asteroid field, which the Tenloss Syndicate uses as an advantage to keeping the base a secret.

Stats

Climate: None

Terrain: None (asteroid field)

Average Weather: None

Diameter: 250,000 km (asteroid field diameter)

Sentient Species: Humans, assorted aliens

Population: 85,000

Wildlife: Dianoga

System/Star: Lybeya

Tactical Information: X-wing, Y-wing, A-wing, and Z-95 fighters all gain a damage bonus.

Maps

Wayland

A simple clerical error in the Old Republic planetary registry lost the Outer Rim planet Wayland from all known charts, and doomed the expeditionary vessel seeking to settle a colony there. The planet is covered in lush forests and mountains with two native species, the Psadans and the Myneyrsh. Without support from the Republic, the human colonists regressed technologically, discarding their blasters for bows and arrows, their modern fabrics for furs and hides. The colonists continue to clash with the two native intelligent species on Wayland, despite being forgotten by the galaxy at large.

Stats

Climate: Temperate

Terrain: Forests, mountains

Average Weather: Clear, rain

Diameter: 6,500 km

Sentient Species: Human, Psadan, Myneyrsh

Population: 28 million

Wildlife: Clawbird, vine snake, garral

System/Star: Wayland

Tactical Information: T4-B and MPTL-2a units receive a speed boost.

Maps

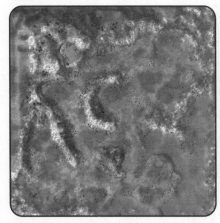

Yavin 4

In the Gordian Reach sector of the Outer Rim lies the monstrous orange gas giant Yavin. The moon Yavin 4 is a hot jungle world with four main continents separated by six oceans. Volcanic mountain ranges and wide rivers can be found amid the thick jungles. The moon has both a wet and dry season, and chaotic storms whip across its surface every few months. Yavin 4 was settled by a Dark Lord of the Sith, Naga Sadow, and his minions. Over time, survivors of Sadow's people evolved into the deadly Massassi Warriors, who built dramatic temples throughout the jungles before they vanished into legend. Massassi temples can be used as ship hangers, allowing for cheaper production of fighter craft.

Stats

Climate: Temperate

Terrain: Rain forest

Average Weather: Clear, rain

Diameter: 10,200 km

Sentient Species: Human, Massassi (Extinct)

Population: Varies (0–1,000)

Wildlife: Piranha beetle, stinger lizard, bellybird, crystal snake, howler

System/Star: Yavin

Tactical Information: X-wing, Y-wing, A-wing, and Z-95 fighters all gain a boost to shield strength.

Maps

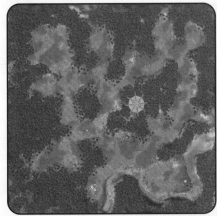

Rebellion! From scattered pockets of resistance across the galaxy, a group of freedom fighters known as the Rebel Alliance forms to challenge the awesome power of the Galactic Empire.

Relying on cunning and strategy to strike at Imperial targets, the Rebels have located prototypes of the devastating new X-wing fighter, and plan a bold raid to acquire them.

A ragtag fleet of Rebel starships, led by Captain Raymus Antilles in his specially designed flagship, the Sundered Heart, moves into formation for the assault....

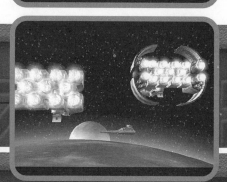

The Rebellion campaign gets started right away with action. As Captain Antilles and his fleet arrive at Fresia, they find an Imperial fleet blockading the system. Because Antilles's Rebel fleet is no match for this massive armada, they must find some way to get the Imperials to leave.

Shipyard Diversion

BRIEFING

The Rebel plan to steal the X-wing prototypes and rescue the defecting scientists has been rendered impossible due to a change of plans by the Empire. An Imperial armada is blockading the planet of Fresia, to serve as security for the upcoming Incom nationalization ceremony.

TASK

Take a fleet to Kuat and attack the shipyard to create a diversion.

Space Battle at Kuat

OBJECTIVES

1. Destroy the six Imperial shipyards.
2. The Sundered Heart must survive.

LEGEND

SY Shipyard

Captain Antilles's fleet arrives at Kuat and prepares to attack.

For this mission, you begin with four Corellian corvettes as well as Antilles's modified corvette. With these five ships, you must destroy the Kuat shipyards. Your fleet begins in the map's southeast corner, with the six shipyards near the center. There are Orbital Resource Containers surrounding each shipyard, which are easily destroyed, and almost instantly take out the shipyards when they explode. All of your corvettes have the boost engine power special ability. This redirects power to your engines, increasing the speed of your corvettes—at the cost of reducing your firepower. Therefore, use this only when you want to run from enemies. If you use it to get to enemies, you will arrive with less firepower than normal.

The *Sundered Heart* also has the weaken enemy ability. By clicking on this, the cursor changes to a targeting reticle with a green range circle around it. Position it so a group of enemies is within the circle and then click to decrease the amount of damage these enemies can inflict on your units. This lasts a short time, even if the enemy ships leave the area where they were targeted.

Enemy cruisers offer your biggest threat, so target them whenever they appear.

Your main threats during this mission are TIE fighters that arrive on the scene, as well as *Tartan*-class patrol cruisers and defense satellites. Assign your four corvettes to one group and the *Sundered Heart* to its own group. Order all of your ships to head for the closest shipyard and begin attacking it. It does not matter where you start. As soon as an enemy cruiser appears, order all your ships to fire on it to destroy it quickly before it can cause much damage. When TIE fighters arrive, let Antilles take them on himself while the other corvettes work over the shipyards.

If you get swarmed by TIE fighters, use the boost engine power ability to move your ships away from the action and then engage the enemy squadrons one at a time as they pursue.

During the fighting, your ships take hits. It's important to monitor their status. Keep all of your ships selected so that you can see their blue shield and green health bars. As long as you have some blue, your ships will not take physical damage. However, if a cruiser's shields are close to down, select it and use the boost engine power ability to move it away from the enemies until its shields return to near maximum. This prevents you from actually losing one of your ships. Also be sure to use Antilles's weaken enemy ability when a group of TIE fighters and cruisers all come at you. This ability takes some time to recharge after use, so save it for clusters of enemies to maximize it.

The shipyards can take a lot of damage, so once you have eliminated the defenses around them, order all of your ships to fire together before more enemies arrive.

After you destroy the first shipyard, continue to the next. If necessary, pull your entire fleet back. This may be due to heavy attacks by TIE fighters as well as defense satellites. Once the enemy ships are destroyed, and your shields are back up, then move in to continue your attack on the shipyards. The enemy fleet from Fresia does not arrive until you have destroyed all of the shipyards, so don't feel rushed. Don't risk your ships so you can hurry. Keep a close eye on the *Sundered Heart* because you lose the mission if it is destroyed. Your fleet automatically jumps to hyperspace when the Imperial fleet arrives. The diversion is a success.

Interpreting the Network

BRIEFING

With sensor drones deployed around Fresia, the Alliance is once again thwarted from stealing the X-wing fighters. The Imperial's reliance on a relatively unguarded network uplink on Wayland may be the key to getting past the sensors undetected.

TASK

Take R2-D2 with a ground assault force to Wayland and have him steal codes from the Imperial network.

Now that you have completed your first mission, Antilles and his fleet have returned to Alderaan. You now have the galactic view of the game. The Rebel Alliance controls only three planets—Alderaan, Dantooine, and Yavin 4. R2-D2 and C-3PO are also on Alderaan while your third hero unit, Mon Mothma, is on Dantooine. Before you send the droids to steal the codes, you need to build up your forces. Highlight Mon Mothma, the leader of the Rebel Alliance, and you see that she reduces production cost by 25 percent at her current location. Because you have only three planets, she can shuttle between them to save you some credits as you build up your strength.

Mon Mothma on Dantooine gives you a discount on purchasing units and structures. Move her to each of your planets before placing an order.

Start off by zooming in on Dantooine. The planet begins with a barracks, some infantry units, and a level-1 space station. While Mon Mothma is still there, recruit two Rebel soldier platoons and two Plex soldier platoons, construct a mine to help bring in more credits, and upgrade your space station to level 2. Now send Mon Mothma to Yavin 4. This planet has a light vehicle factory where you can produce T2-B repulsor tanks. With Mon Mothma's discount, order four of these units as well as a mine, plus upgrade your space station here to level 2. Finally, send Mon Mothma to Alderaan and build a mine, an officer academy, and some infantry troops, plus upgrade your space station.

Once your space stations are at level 2, you can then produce Y-wing bombers as well as Corellian corvettes and Nebulon-B frigates. Build a few Y-wing bombers, and some of the larger ships as well if you want. However, don't worry about producing any more Z-95 Headhunters. You gain access to X-wings before you need fighters, so hold off.

Assemble your assault force on Yavin 4. Don't forget to bring along a Y-wing squadron for bombing runs.

Now assemble your ground assault force at Yavin 4. You must have R2-D2 and C-3PO to complete this mission. You also need four platoons of Rebel soldiers, four platoons of Plex soldiers, and three platoons of T2-B repulsor tanks. Also bring a squadron of Y-wings so you have bomber support. Drag all of these units into the same fleet spot on the zoomed-in view of Yavin 4. Then zoom out and drag this fleet to an orbital slot over Wayland. Once in orbit, drag your fleet to the surface of Wayland to begin the ground battle.

Ground Battle on Wayland

OBJECTIVES

1. *The droids must survive.*
2. *Escort Artoo to the uplink station.*

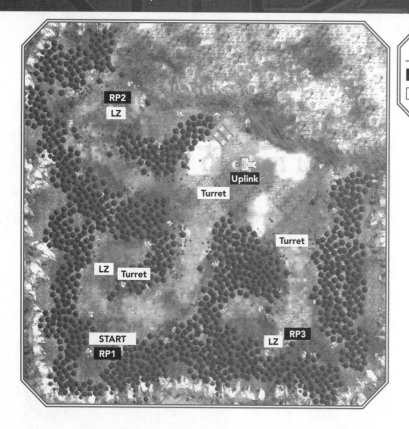

LEGEND

RP **Reinforcement Point**
LZ **Landing Zone**

When the mission begins, you have a platoon of Rebel soldiers on the planet along with the droids. First, bring down some reinforcements. Click on the reinforcements button and then drag units from the window to the area around the reinforcement point. Start off with two platoons of T2-B tanks, two more platoons of Rebel soldiers, and two platoons of Plex soldiers. Leave one of each platoon behind at the reinforcement point while you send the rest, along with the droids, along the path to the northwest.

The Imperial turret is the first enemy you run into. Use the droids to take control of it instead of destroying it.

Not far from your reinforcement point, you discover an Imperial anti-infantry turret. While you could just send your T2-B tanks to blast it, instead use R2-D2's special ability to take control of enemy turrets. This gives you some additional firepower when the Imperials attack from the north. Order your infantry to take cover while your Rebel soldiers fire on the stormtroopers, and your tanks and Plex soldiers attack the AT-ST walkers. You can even call in a bombing run on the enemy if needed. Once these enemies have been dealt with, lead your force north toward the uplink station. Either take control of or destroy another turret. Then send the droids to the uplink. The process takes a few minutes. However, the Imperials are not going to let you do it without a fight.

The Imperials land three groups of units to try to stop you from getting the codes. Don't let them destroy the droids or the mission will be a failure.

TIP

Be sure to bring in reinforcements as the Imperials begin attacking from all sides. Hold on to your initial reinforcement point so you can replace your losses. You definitely want to bring down another platoon of T2-B tanks.

Position your northern troops so they protect the droids against Imperial attacks from the west. If you destroyed the turret, build a bacta healing station on the build pad for healing your infantry. Watch the minimap to see when the reinforcement point in the northwest turns red. That warns you that enemy troops are landing there. Before long, Imperial stormtroopers and AT-ST walkers attack from the west. As before, use your Plex soldiers and tanks against the walkers. Next, you receive word that Imperial shuttles are landing forces in the southwest. The troops you left back at the reinforcement point can move west a bit and fire at the shuttles as the enemy unloads. Call in a bombing run right on the shuttles and you may take out some of the enemy units while they are vulnerable.

Don't forget to call in bombing runs. They wipe out stormtroopers and really damage enemy vehicles.

The final attack against your force comes from the southeast reinforcement point. Position your tanks in a line to the west of the uplink station with your infantry behind them. The Imperials send TIE maulers, which try to run over and kill your infantry. Focus on the maulers first and then deal with the stormtroopers and AT-STs.

OBJECTIVE

3. Escort the droids to a friendly reinforcement point.

By this time, R2-D2 should have completed his assignment. It is now time to get off of Wayland. Send the two droids back to your initial reinforcement point along with some protection, just in case any Imperials are still around on the map. Once the droids arrive at the reinforcement point, the mission ends and you can now go after those X-wing fighters.

The transports arrive to take R2-D2 and C-3PO to safety.

Theft of the X-wing

BRIEFING

Now that all obstacles have been cleared from space, the final assault on Fresia can begin. The target is Incom's prototype X-wing fighters. The Alliance has put together a crack team of pilots ready to fly them back to the Rebel base. Now it's up to the landing forces to get the pilots safely to the ships.

TASK

Take a ground assault force to Fresia and capture the X-wing fighters.

While you have retreated your forces from the surface of Wayland, you should also have defeated all of the Imperial troops on the planet. Send your ground troops that are still in orbit over Wayland down to the surface to take control of the planet. Not only do you add the planet to your side, you are also rewarded with a good number of credits. Use them to build a space station at Wayland as well as a mine so you can start using the planet. Leave some infantry and a platoon of tanks behind for now and take the rest of your force, including the droids, back to Yavin 4.

Wayland is ripe for the taking. Grab it now before the Imperials can build more troops to defend it.

At the other planets, continue to build up your forces. Remember to send Mon Mothma to each planet to purchase units and structures at a discount. Upgrade your space stations at Alderaan and Yavin 4 to level 3 and start putting together an assault force for your attack on Fresia. Because you won't encounter any Imperial space units, you don't need any space units of your own except for a Y-wing squadron. Recruit a field commander on Alderaan where you have your officer academy. This unit makes your troops more effective in battle.

Your assault force should consist of at least four platoons each of T2-B repulsor tanks, Rebel soldiers, and Plex soldiers as well as a field commander and a Y-wing squadron. You may want to take five of each platoon to be on the safe side. When your assault force is ready, put it all in the same fleet slot over Yavin 4, then send it to Fresia. After it arrives in orbit, drag your fleet down to the surface to start the battle.

Fight for the X-wings on Fresia

OBJECTIUES

1. Escort the pilots to the X-wings.
2. At least one pilot must survive.
3. Destroy the power generator to disable the turbolaser towers.

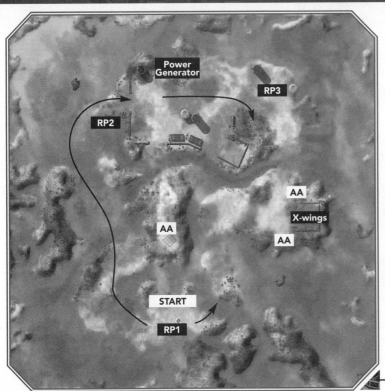

Power Generator

RP3

RP2

AA

X-wings

AA

AA

START

RP1

LEGEND

AA	Anti-Aircraft
←→	Path
RP	Reinforcement Point

Protect your pilots so they can fly the X-wings off of Fresia.

Your troops begin landing in the south. The pilots land with your starting force, but keep them as far south as possible and away from the enemies. Quickly order down a couple platoons each of T2-B tanks, Rebel soldiers, and Plex soldiers, plus your field commander. Your reinforcement point comes under attack quickly, so you have to get ready. Position a line of tanks along the shore of the stream to the east backed up by a platoon of each type of infantry. Position the rest of your combat troops to the east. Expect Imperial attacks from both directions.

NOTE

The smallest unit of Rebel infantry is a squad. Three squads of Rebel soldiers make up a platoon while only two squads of Plex soldiers make up a platoon. Five T2-B tanks form a platoon as well.

The X-wings are to the northeast. However, the eastern route is protected by turbolaser towers that will chew up your forces. Therefore, you need to take out the power generator in the north. Your strategy for this battle is to hold to the east of your reinforcement point while advancing along the western side of the map. Your attack force consists of a platoon each of tanks, soldiers, and Plex soldiers. Leave a platoon of each type of infantry and your field commander to cover the western side of the reinforcement point in case Imperials get past your attack force.

Concentrate all of the fire of your attack force on a single AT-ST at a time to quickly destroy it—then have all your units attack the next one.

As your attack force advances north, you first run into stormtroopers. Order your infantry to take cover, then attack the enemy. As you cross the second stream about halfway across the map, you run into several AT-STs. Call in a bombing run to damage them and then finish them off with your tanks and Plex soldiers. There is also a reinforcement point in the northwest. Take control of it and you can land reinforcements right where you need them.

Call in a bombing run right here to hit both turrets—even if you can't see them both.

Continue north with your troops. There are no build pads in this mission, so you can't build a bacta healing station to heal your troops. Therefore, if they start getting low on health, bring down some reinforcements. Near the power generator, you find a wall with an opening into the Imperial base. There are two turrets by the opening, so call in a bombing run right at the middle of the opening to damage or destroy the turrets before you approach. Don't enter the base right away. Instead, wait for your bombing run to recharge.

Once you enter, you face stormtroopers, AT-STs, and TIE maulers. Form a line at the entrance with your tanks while you call in Y-wings to bomb the concentrated enemy units. Once the TIE maulers are destroyed, move your infantry into the base to help fight. After the Imperial units are eliminated, target the power generator.

While not required, it is a good idea to lay waste to the Imperial base in the north. You can destroy several structures. Just watch out for turrets that can ruin your day. When you have eliminated all of the units and structures in the base, move out with your units back at the reinforcement point. Send them northeast to destroy the turbolaser turrets and other enemy units guarding the fighters, then bring the pilots to the X-wings to complete your objectives.

Deliver the pilots to the X-wings.

OBJECTIVE

4. Destroy all anti-aircraft turrets.

Before your pilots can take off in the X-wings, you now have to destroy the anti-aircraft turrets. There are eight total—four near the X-wings and four more in the map's center. The turrets near the X-wings are easy to take out because you have troops right there. However, the others in the center are tougher to get to because the Imperials land many units at that point to try to prevent you from stealing the fighters. Send your western attack force south from the base to the central turrets. While you can try to call in bombing runs, they will probably be shot down by the anti-aircraft turrets. Therefore, you have to use your ground units to fight past the enemies. Concentrate your fire on the four central turrets. Once they are destroyed, the mission is complete and you do not have to worry about the other enemy units that remain on the map.

The Rebel attack force battles to destroy the central anti-aircraft turrets.

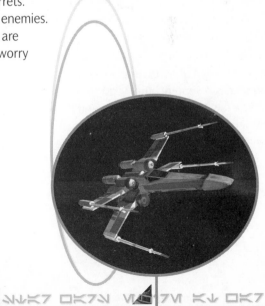

Kessel Rescue

BRIEFING

During the Fresia crackdown after the Alliance theft of the X-wings, many Incom scientists were captured. The prisoners are being transported in Imperial shuttles as part of a convoy headed for Kessel. They have to go slowly to navigate an asteroid field in the area, and they won't want to risk damaging the larger capital ships—this makes them vulnerable. The infamous spice mines of Kessel are death sentences to any Empire prisoners sent to work there, and the Alliance wastes no time staging a rescue before the prisoners can reach the mines.

TASK

Use the Y-wing fighters' ion cannon special ability to immobilize the convoy's shuttles, then rescue the prisoners with the *Sundered Heart*.

You have a space battle coming up. Therefore, you need to build up a fleet of space units. If you have not done so already, upgrade your space stations on Yavin 4 and Alderaan to level 3. If he is not already there, send Captain Antilles to Alderaan where the fleet will assemble. Start producing some Nebulon-B frigates, Corellian corvettes, Y-wings, and X-wings.

Imperial shuttles are carrying the prisoners to the spice mines of Kessel.

While your fleet is building, take control of Fresia. You have a fleet already in orbit. Just send your ground forces down to the planet's surface and you automatically take control of the planet. Build a space station and upgrade it to level 3. Also build some mines there to increase your income. Leave a few units on the surface to guard, and a few ships in orbit, then send the rest of your fleet back to Alderaan. The Kuat shipyards are an inviting target. While it is not that tough to take control of this planet, the Imperials will come at you with a vengeance.

Your fleet assembling at Alderaan for the rescue mission at Kessel must include Captain Antilles's *Sundered Heart*. In addition, take along a couple frigates, four corvettes, all of your T-95 Headhunters, six squadrons of X-wings, and at least six squadrons of Y-wing fighters. When the fleet is ready, drag it into an orbit slot over Kessel and get ready for a fight.

Put together a fleet for the rescue at Kessel. Be sure to bring along plenty of Y-wings.

Space Battle in the Kessel Asteroid Field

OBJECTIVES

1. Use Y-wings to disable the six shuttles and the *Sundered Heart* to rescue all of the prisoners.
2. The *Sundered Heart* must survive.
3. All transport shuttles must survive.

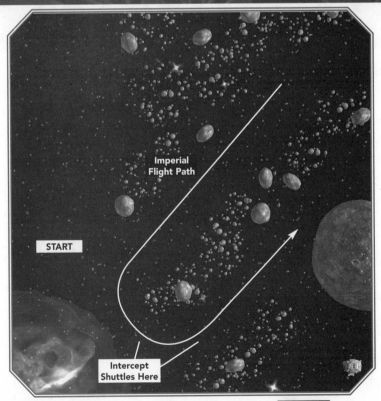

Your fleet arrives in the map's southwestern part. The Imperial space units head southwest along the central corridor in the asteroid field, turn east, then follow the eastern corridor back up toward the north. Because you know where they must go, you can set up an ambush. The shuttles continue on their course while the enemy combat units can maneuver to engage you.

Your fleet jumps into the Kessel system along the path the Imperials take to the prison.

The main strategy for this mission is to thin out the shuttles from the rest of the Imperial fleet. To do this, first send all of your Y-wings and the *Sundered Heart* to the southern edge of the turn the Imperials will make. Then position the rest of your fleet across the corridor before the turn.

TIP

Pay close attention to your Y-wing bombers. They will want to go into action against the Acclamators. However, you can't afford to lose them. Keep them away from the fight—have them lie in wait for the shuttles. Also, be sure to select only one squadron before you use the ion cannon ability or all selected squadrons will use their ability—and all will have to wait for it to recharge.

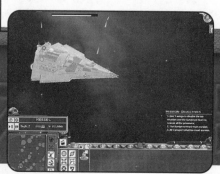

The lead Acclamator is your primary target. Knock out its shields and then its engines to stop it from escorting the first group of shuttles.

The Imperial fleet is led by an Acclamator cruiser. Order your frigates and X-wings to attack the cruiser, focusing on the shields and engines, while your corvettes and T-95s take on the TIE fighters and TIE bombers. A group of three shuttles follows the first cruiser. As the shuttles make the turn, order individual squadrons of Y-wings to use their ion cannon ability on each of the shuttles to disable them and leave them floating in space. Once they're disabled, move the *Sundered Heart* next to each to rescue the prisoners aboard. While you could rescue them later, get them now so that you have half of your objectives accomplished.

The second group of shuttles is preceded by another Acclamator and other smaller ships. Use the same tactics as before. However, you need to be a bit quicker because the Imperials send in reinforcements—more cruisers—to prevent you from getting the prisoners. Therefore, once you have cleared away the enemies from this second group of shuttles, move your attacking units west past your start point. The Y-wings can then disable the shuttles as they turn the corner. Quickly pick up the prisoners with the *Sundered Heart*.

While the attack group fights off the Imperial combat vessels, the Sundered Heart *moves in to pick up the prisoners from the disabled shuttles.*

After you have rescued the prisoners from all six shuttles, your fleet automatically jumps to hyperspace to complete the mission.

Stealing from the Rich

BRIEFING

Hearing rumors of an Imperial superweapon in the works, the Alliance decides to use its most unlikely heroes—a pair of droids—to intercept Empire communications and learn more about what they're up to.

The Alliance charges the droids with eluding the local system defenses and landing on the planet, then tapping into the network at the nearest available terminal. The presence of a few droids on a maintenance errand shouldn't be much of a concern of the Empire....

TASK

Drag the droids into the steal action on an Imperial planet to steal technology.

To accomplish your new mission, you first need to make sure that the R2-D2 and C-3PO unit is in an orbital slot by itself. When you click on the droids, steal slots appear at all Imperial controlled planets you can access. It does not matter which planet they choose to go to—the technology available will be the same. Drag the droids to Mon Calamari or Kuat. When the droids arrive at the system, a steal technology window opens.

R2-D2 and C-3PO steal some technology from Mon Calamari. Get the T4-B tanks to begin with, then come back for more later.

You can choose from three items. To get more information about each, place the cursor over the technology icon and wait for an information window to pop up. Below each icon is the cost in credits to acquire that technology. You can choose from T4-B tanks, assault frigate MK. II, and the infiltrator training facility. Because your next mission will be a ground battle, go for the T4-B tanks—they increase your ground firepower quite a bit. After stealing the technology, the droids are unavailable for a short time. Their hero icon in the screen's upper right corner shows a timer letting you know approximately how long you must wait. Once they return to the galactic view, use them again until you have the other two technologies.

TIP

While waiting for the droids to make their next theft of technology, build up your infrastructure. Click on the holocron button and select summary to see your galactic economy. As you see, mines make up a big chunk of income. It is a good idea to build mines on empty building slots that you don't plan on using in the near future. You can always sell the mine later to open up a slot for another structure.

During a game, it is always a good idea to steal as much technology as you can. When the droids are not being used for something else, order them to steal. Because R2-D2 and C-3PO travel in a stealthy space ship, they can move around the galaxy undetected by the Imperials. Because of this ability, send them to systems as spies to determine who controls a planet and get an idea of what size of force they have on the surface and in orbit.

Imperial Liberation

BRIEFING

The news of a prison break on Kashyyyk is causing the Empire a great deal of grief. A lone rogue has taken it upon himself to liberate the prisoners from their containment and help them fight off the Empire's slavers.

Although this lone crusader's motives are unknown, the act of liberating the Wookiees is one that the Rebels cannot ignore. Injustice at the hands of the Empire cannot be tolerated! Therefore, the Rebel Alliance will help free the Wookiees from their enslavement.

TASK

Send a ground assault force to Kashyyyk and assist this crusader in liberating as many Wookiees as possible.

THE REBEL ARMY

You will be performing a lot more ground invasions during the next few missions. These are to accomplish objectives, but also to take control of planets so you can use them as bases and for the credits they provide to the Rebel Alliance. Therefore, you need to assemble a ground invasion fleet. With R2-D2 and C-3PO stealing new technology, you can build a more powerful army to take on the Imperial ground forces. By this time, you can construct the heavy vehicle factory. With this, you can produce two of the most powerful Rebel land units—the T4-B tanks and the MPTL-2a artillery. Build some heavy vehicle factories at two or more of your planets and start producing these vehicles.

The Rebel invasion army is stationed at one of the original planets, such as Alderaan, where it will be safe from enemy attacks. This army's variety and depth of units allows it to take on whatever the enemy has waiting for you down on the surface of the planets you are invading.

You really only need one invasion army. Once you take a planet, leave some units behind to garrison it, then replace your losses with units you produce throughout the galaxy. It is a good idea to keep your army in a separate fleet from your main space fleet. That way, when you get into a space battle, your army's weak transports are not vulnerable to enemy space units. Park your army fleet in orbit over a safe planet such as Alderaan or Yavin 4. Then just send it to the planet you need to invade, returning to the home base when the task is complete. While this takes a bit more time than keeping your army fleet at the front lines, it's much safer.

While you can land only up to 10 units during a land battle, your army fleet should be overstocked with a variety of units so you can send down reinforcements for your losses and also for flexibility on the battlefield. Following is a suggested list of units for your army fleet. It is a bit on the heavy side, but it allows you to take on a large enemy ground force and still be able to seize control of the planet.

- Field commander
- 4 Rebel solider platoons
- 4 Plex soldier platoons
- 4 T2-B repulsor tank platoons
- 3 T4-B tank platoons
- 2 MPTL-2a artillery platoons
- 1 Y-wing squadron (bombing runs)

With this setup, one of your T2-B tank platoons usually lands first. Depending on the reinforcement point where you land, you can bring down only two to four more units. Start by landing a Rebel soldier platoon for capturing another reinforcement point as well as a T-4B tank platoon for firepower. If possible, also land an artillery platoon. Their long-range firepower can really help you take on the enemy, and you can use the spotter droids that come with them to scout out enemy locations anywhere on the map and call in bombing runs while your units are still at a distance.

To get to Kashyyyk, you have to go through Kessel or Kuat. Because you recently fought in orbit over Kessel, that is usually the best place to start. Send in a fleet to take control of the space around Kessel, then move in your ground troops. You should have no trouble taking this planet. Build up a level-3 space station and leave some troops behind as a garrison. Then send R2-D2 and C-3PO to Kuat to spy for you. If it doesn't look too bad, take in a large space fleet and capture this planet as well. Build the highest level space station on Kuat and leave a big space fleet there for when the Imperials try to take it back. Just be sure to get your army fleet away to safety as soon as you take control of the planet. Now head for Kashyyyk. Have R2-D2 and C-3PO scout ahead. There usually isn't an enemy fleet in orbit. If there is, you need to send a space fleet. Otherwise, just send your army fleet to invade.

Prison Break on Kashyyyk

OBJECTIVES

1. Han Solo must survive.
2. Destroy five prisons.

RP3

Prison 4

Imperial
Base

Prison 5

LEGEND

RP Reinforcement Point

RP2   Wookiee
        Dwelling

Prison 3

Prison 1

RP1

Wookiee
Dwelling   Prison 2

Wookiee
Dwelling

Han Solo helps out during this mission. Use his special abilities and then keep him out of the way.

Your army lands at reinforcement point 1. The Imperial base is directly north—however, you don't need to worry about attacking the base. The mission ends when all prisons are destroyed. Because your T-2B repulsor tanks land at the start, bring down a platoon each of Rebel soldiers, Plex soldiers, T4-B tanks, MPTL-2a artillery, and a field commander. While you could bring down more, you don't need it right now. As soon as your artillery hits the ground, order it to deploy. The Imperials are east of your location. Lead with your T2-B tanks to find them, then bring in your T4-B tanks to hit them. Order your T4-Bs to use their rocket ability. This causes more damage to vehicles, and the splash damage quickly wipes out squads of stormtroopers.

The T4-B tanks and MPTL-2a artillery provide a lot of firepower to your ground forces, letting you blow the enemy away.

Use the spotter droids' sensor ping ability to see what is around the area between prisons 1 and 2. Call in bombing runs on the turrets and advance your army to this area. You will probably have to move your artillery closer to support your other units as they clear the enemy force from around the two prisons. After the enemy units have been neutralized, fire on and destroy the two prisons. Squads of Wookiee prisoners are released from each prison once it is destroyed. Select them and send them to a Wookiee dwelling and they will pick up their bowcasters and be ready to help you fight against the Imperials.

The Wookiees, after visiting a dwelling, are armed and ready to take on the Empire.

TIP

Han Solo can be a lot of help during this battle. Just be sure to keep him safe because the mission will end in failure if he is eliminated. His EMP burst ability disables all nearby vehicles. Use his spring ability to rush up to some enemy vehicles, then use the EMP burst to disable them. Quickly move Han Solo back to a safe spot while his abilities recharge, and destroy the units he disabled before they come back online.

As you are attacking the prisons, enemy units come at you from across the river to the north. Set up your T2-B tanks along the river-bank to act as a warning and first line of defense. When you are ready to advance, use a scout droid's ability to see the area around prison 3. Bomb enemy concentrations and turrets, then send in your force to finish off the defenders and destroy the third prison.

Reinforcement point 2 is just northwest of prison 3. While taking control of it does not increase the maximum number of units you can have on the planet, it does provide a location for bringing in more units close to the fight. Use your Wookiee squads, after they have been armed, to take control of reinforcement point 2 as well as to see what lies ahead.

Use the same tactics as before to attack prison 4. The entrance to the Imperial base is northwest of this prison, so be ready for enemy units to come at you here. Land a second platoon of T4-B tanks at reinforcement point 2 and order them to help cover the entrance to the base. Once prison 4 is destroyed, go to work on prison 5. After this last prison is a smoldering ruin, the mission immediately ends with you as the victor. Han Solo has saved the Wookiee, and the two will help you from time to time in your battle against the Empire.

With the Wookiee safe, Han Solo returns to the Millennium Falcon and takes off from Kashyyyk.

Highest Bidder

BRIEFING

In contacting some of the underworld's more questionable sources of information, Mon Mothma has inadvertently put the Alliance at risk. A pirate associate of one of the contacts has obtained data on the locations of Alliance sympathizers and facilities. If this data were to fall into the Empire's hands, the Alliance would be in great jeopardy.

The pirate has set up a meeting with the Empire in neutral territory near Atzerri, hoping to cash in on this sensitive data.

TASK

Build a fleet. Escort Captain Antilles to Atzerri and recover the data.

If you do not have control of Kashyyyk after the last mission, send your army fleet back down to the surface to take control of this planet. As usual, build up a space station and garrison the surface with some troops.

Meanwhile, there is new technology for you to steal. Send R2-D2 and C-3PO to an Imperial-controlled planet to steal some for you. You have two options. Go for the T-47 airspeeders first. These craft are great for your invasion army. They are excellent for taking on the Imperial AT-ATs, they can take out turbolaser towers and other defenses, plus they can scout around the battlefield to locate the

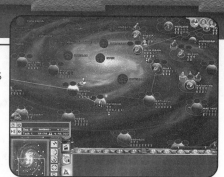

To get to Atzerri, you have to take control of several planets to create a safe route to this distant planet.

enemy units and structures. Once the droids are back, send them to Bothawui to see what the Imperials have positioned there. Then order the droids to steal the technology for the A-wing fighters.

Atzerri is at the galaxy's western end. Though you only need a space fleet to complete your objective, you have to travel through several hostile, enemy-controlled systems. Therefore, invade your way west across the galaxy. Not only will this provide a safe route to send reinforcements to your space fleet, it also adds to your economy and cuts off the Imperial planets to the south from those in the north.

Bothawui is your first target. Make sure your space fleet is loaded with the newest and most powerful ships, and then send it into orbit at Bothawui. You have to fight a pretty serious space battle to clear the space around the planet. Then send in your invasion army to fight a land battle and take control of the planet. The Bothan civilians are your allies and will fight with you against the Imperials.

On Bothawui, you begin in the east and can have only three units. Quickly fight west to a second reinforcement point, which lets you bring down two more units. The key on this planet is to build bacta healing stations and repair stations to keep your units at their best. Proceed counterclockwise from the start until you have eliminated all of the enemy. Take care of Bothawui by building a space station and structures. █████

Fight both a space and land battle for control of Bothawui as you head to Atzerri and increase your galactic economy.

Eriadu is your next target. Replace your losses to both your space and army fleets and then head there. Eriadu has only one reinforcement point and it allows you to land up to 10 units. A few turbolaser towers cover your routes to the Imperial base in the north, so use airspeeders to take them out before advancing your land units. While not necessary, it is also a good idea to take control of Tatooine. Use the same strategy and tactics as you have during past planetary invasions. You begin in the south and can pick up a second reinforcement point in the west soon after the battle starts. Be sure to garrison the planet with both space and ground defense before sending your fleets away.

The path to Atzerri is now clear. Send your invasion army back to Alderaan. Then make sure your space fleet is strong and contains Captain Antilles. Move it to Atzerri to begin the next campaign mission. █████

The airspeeders work well for attacking turbolaser towers and other structures or units behind enemy lines on Eriadu and Tatooine. Just watch for AA units.

Capture the Pirate at Atzerri

OBJECTIVES

1. *The* Sundered Heart *must survive the battle.*
2. *Disable the pirate's frigate by damaging it.*
3. *Recover the stolen data by moving a ship close to the disabled pirate.*
4. *Destroy the remaining Interdictor cruisers.*

You must get to the pirate before the Imperials can catch him.

Your fleet enters orbit at the map's northern part. After you arrive, an Imperial fleet jumps into the system to the south, with the pirate's ship between you and the Imperial fleet. Your main task is to get the pirate. You do not need to take out the Imperial star destroyer or cruisers. Instead, focus on the pirate.

To avoid the Imperial capital ships, the pirate follows a course into the asteroid fields. He then follows the fields to the south where the pirate's ship attacks the Interdictors. These Imperial cruisers have gravity well generators that prevent enemy space vessels from escaping the system by jumping into hyperspace.

Order your entire fleet to move east and follow the asteroids south. Your smaller vessels can move through the asteroids while frigates are best kept to the eastern side of the asteroids. Send your corvettes south past the pirate using their boost engine power ability so they can attack the pirate from the front while the rest of your fleets hits the ship from the side and rear.

Disable the pirate's ship and then move in to take the pirate off the ship before the Imperials can get him.

TIP

By the time the pirate gets to the southern part of the map, you can bring in some reinforcements to the space nearby. Bring in frigates or corvettes to quickly disable the pirate and then attack the Interdictors.

There is no reason to disable the pirate ship right away. In fact, concentrate on getting your fleet to the area near the Interdictors and avoiding the rest of the Imperial fleet. This gives the pirate some time to attack the Interdictors before you disable his ship, making your final objective easier. Move all of your ships in to attack the pirate cruiser in the south. After receiving a lot of damage, the pirate's ship is disabled. Order your fleet to then attack the Interdictors so you have a way to escape. While this engagement is taking place, order the *Sundered Heart* to move next to the pirate's ship to retrieve the data. Finish off the remaining Interdictors, and once they are all eliminated, the Rebel fleet automatically jumps into hyperspace to make its getaway, thus ending the mission.

To make the jump to hyperspace and escape, you have to destroy the four Interdictor cruisers in the south.

Rescue the *Millennium Falcon*

BRIEFING

As fate would have it, when the Alliance suddenly finds itself in need of a smuggler's assistance, one they've had past dealings with volunteers—albeit unintentionally. Han Solo seems to have run afoul of the Empire yet again. This time, he's caught in a tractor beam of an Imperial Star Destroyer, more than likely looking for illegitimate cargo that he's carrying. In return for saving his neck, the Alliance will certainly be able to persuade him to assist in future operations.

TASK

Take a fleet to Corellia and rescue Han Solo.

After the Rebels get the pirate away from the Imperials, the enemy leaves Atzerri. Move your army fleet to this planet and take control without a fight. As usual, garrison it with space and land defenses. Nearby Bespin is a prize you can't pass up. Replace the losses to your space fleet, then send it to engage the Imperials there.

You have to attack a space station. Marauder missile cruisers work really well for this type of attack. Use their barrage area ability to fire massive numbers of concussion missiles at the space station or in the path of Imperial capital ships. Target the station's shield generator, then the hangar to prevent it from spawning more garrison ships.

Once you have beaten the enemy, you gain control of Bespin. Because it is a gas giant, there is no land to fight for. Bespin also adds a lot of credits to your coffers each galactic day. The fight for Bespin probably cost you some losses. Replace them, then send your space fleet to Bothawui to stage your next attack.

To rescue Han Solo, you need speed more than firepower. Therefore, from your main space fleet, create a raid fleet composed of the *Sundered Heart* plus Corellian corvettes and gunships and X-wing fighters. Then send this raid fleet to Corellia.

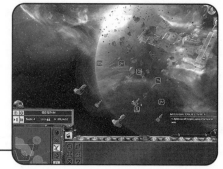

The battle in space over Bespin can be tough. However, it is worth it in the long run.

Raid above Corellia

OBJECTIVES

1. *The* Millennium Falcon *must survive.*
2. *Disable the tractor beam holding the* Millennium Falcon.

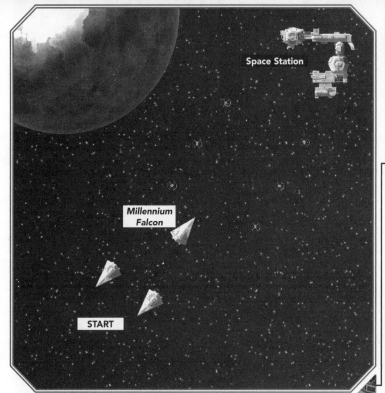

An Imperial Star Destroyer has Han Solo and Chewbacca in tow.

The important thing to realize about this mission is that it's not a battle. It's more like a raid.

You begin in the map's southwest corner. The Imperial space station is in the northeast corner. The Star Destroyer holding the *Millennium Falcon* is headed to the space station. Two additional Star Destroyers try to stop you.

Target only the tractor beam hard-point when you catch up to the Star Destroyer.

You don't have a lot of time before the Star Destroyer takes the *Millennium Falcon* to the space station. Therefore, you have to ignore the two defending Star Destroyers. Order your corvettes and gunships to use their boost engine power ability and your X-wings to lock their s-foils so that all of your ships can move faster than normal. After selecting the ability, order them to move to the space station. As they approach the central Star Destroyer, order all of your units to fire on the tractor beam hard-point. Once this hard-point is destroyed, the *Millennium Falcon* is free to jump into hyperspace and escape—quickly followed by your fleet to end the mission.

Han Solo escapes from the Empire's clutches. Maybe next time he'll jettison his illegal cargo before his ship can be boarded.

Needle in a Haystack

BRIEFING

Now that the Alliance knows the location of one of Grand Moff Tarkin's research facilities, it is imperative to retrieve additional information on this superweapon. The station is heavily defended, so Han Solo has been tasked with infiltrating an Imperial cargo facility and attaching an EMP device to a container bound for Tarkin's station. This mission must be covert, as any attention will cause greater scrutiny on the cargo, and our bomb may not reach its target.

TASK

Take Han Solo to Vergesso, find the cargo container bound for the research facility, and attach the EMP device to it.

Because you already control the space above Corellia, you might as well land on the surface and take complete control of the planet.

You have a new mission. However, before you rush to send Han Solo to Vergesso, you might as well take over another planet. Your space fleet is already in orbit over Corellia. Therefore, bring in your invasion ground fleet to land units on the surface of the planet and add it to the Rebel Alliance. It is lightly defended, but bring your entire invasion fleet just in case the fight turns out a bit tougher than expected. Also take your fleets to Naboo to secure it for your side. The biggest threats to the ground battle on Naboo are the turbolaser turrets that block your access from the beach where you land to the rest of the map. Use airspeeders to attack and take these defenses out, then advance northeast to take control of the other two reinforcement points. Garrison the two planets you just captured, then send Han Solo to the Vergesso Asteroids to perform his task.

If you want to take Naboo, bring some airspeeders to deal with the turbolaser turrets.

Scanning in the Vergesso Asteroids

OBJECTIVES

1. Scan the cargo containers until you find the one bound for Tarkin's station.
2. Plant the EMP device in the correct container.
3. The Millennium Falcon *must survive the mission.*

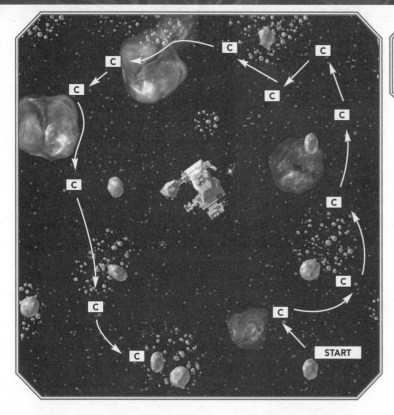

LEGEND

| C | Container |
| → | Path |

START

This mission is really quite easy—if you stay calm and do the right thing. Han Solo and Chewbacca enter this space in the southwest corner. The key to avoiding a lot of Imperial resistance is to move around counterclockwise. Fly to the first container near the small nebula. You have to stay near it for a few seconds to scan it. Then proceed around to each container in order as shown on the map. The container's location varies each time you play this mission and the right one is always found after you have already searched most of the others. Therefore, you can't take a quick shortcut straight to the correct container—you have to scan most of them.

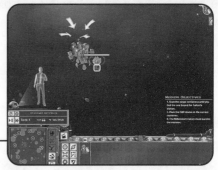

Fly up to the containers to scan them.

Stay near the edges of the map to avoid detection by the Imperials. You run into some TIE fighter squadrons, but as long as there are only one or two at a time, the *Millennium Falcon* has no trouble neutralizing them. If you see a Tartan cruiser headed your way, try to avoid it—especially if there are several. You can use the *Millennium Falcon*'s invulnerability special ability when under attack by a cruiser or larger vessel. This prevents the ship from taking damage from enemy fire for a short time—enough to get out of the area.

You need to stay next to each container for a few seconds while it is scanned.

About halfway through the mission, Boba Fett arrives on the scene and begins to look for you. Don't let this distract you. Stick to the containers so you can get out of this asteroid field as quickly as possible. If you follow the recommended order, you usually find the right container in the southwestern quadrant. When Han Solo identifies it, you have to stay near it for a bit longer while he plants the EMP device. That accomplished, Han and Chewie jump to hyperspace and escape to complete the mission.

The Tartan cruisers are a real threat. However, if you stay at the edges and move counterclockwise, you usually miss them.

Borrowed Time

BRIEFING

With the cargo container holding the EMP device delivered to the station, now is the time to launch our raid and secure the data on this Imperial superweapon. Once the fleet nears the system, the EMP will be detonated, granting us the most time possible to get to the station and search for the information. Several raiding parties are ready to board the station—we just have to make sure no other Imperials show up.

TASK

Build a fleet. Escort the *Sundered Heart* to Corulag and protect the shuttles while the soldiers search for the information.

After Han Solo plants the EMP device, the Imperials leave the Vergesso Asteroids. Move your fleet in and take control. Because there is no planetary surface, all you need to do is take control of the space and you earn some easy credits. While you have to get your fleet to Corulag, you might as well pick up some planets along the way. Nearby Dagobah is a great place to start. Follow that by invading the trio of planets consisting of Endor, Bestine IV, and Sullust. All of these have large space stations that you must first destroy. However, the ground battles are fairly easy. By taking these planets and garrisoning them, you have not only added to your power, but also deprived the Empire of them. Now with the space lanes in this part of the galaxy secure, make sure your space fleet has replaced any losses and then send it to Corulag.

Take control of the Imperial planets along your way to Corulag.

Raid over Corulag

OBJECTIVES

1. *Protect the troop transports until the search is complete.*
2. *The* Sundered Heart *must survive the mission.*
3. *At least one shuttle must survive the mission.*

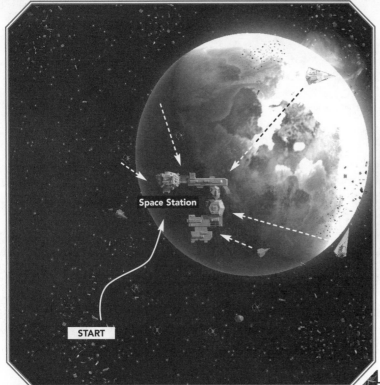

LEGEND

→ Rebel Path
--→ Imperial Path

Space Station

START

The troop transports carry the raiding parties to the space station. You do not control them, but you must protect them.

This space battle is a bit different than most. At the start, the space station and all of the Imperial space vessels around it are disabled due to the blast by the EMP device. However, the enemy starts attacking one by one as the effects wear off. There are four troop transports that you do not control. They automatically fly to the space station and unload the raiding parties who are looking for the data. Your job is to engage Imperial units as they appear and prevent them from attacking the transports.

TIP

Both your assault frigate MK. II and the Nebulon-B frigate have the boost shield strength ability. As they come under fire from the cruisers and capital ships, be sure to activate this ability. It will help them stay in the fight longer and allow them to help protect the troop transports.

As Imperial units get into action, the minimap shows them as green circles. That gives you an idea of which direction they are coming from. Use your frigates to attack the enemy Tartan cruisers while you save your missile cruisers for the Star Destroyers and other capital ships. Use the missile barrage area ability and target the space in front of the capital ships so that by the time the missiles arrive, the Imperials are in the barrage area. If you can take out the engines of these large enemy vessels, they are sitting ducks for your missile cruisers. Your fighters and Y-wing bombers should focus on the capital ships as well. As you lose units, be sure to bring in reinforcements to replace them. You usually need more frigates, because they move in close to attack and often take the brunt of the enemy fire.

While your frigates move in close, keep your missile cruisers at a distance so they don't get targeted by the enemy but can still make their long-range missile attacks.

TIP

Keep an eye on the *Sundered Heart* during this mission. If it starts taking damage, use its boost engine power ability to get away to a safe section of space while its shields recharge. If you lose this ship, the mission is a failure.

During the mission, you receive audio updates from the raiding parties on the space station. Once they get the data, they return to their transports. As soon as the raiding parties are clear of the space station, your entire fleet automatically jumps to hyperspace to conclude the mission.

Handle with Care!

BRIEFING

Mon Mothma has sent out the call for Han Solo and Chewbacca, asking them to perform a service in return for a surprisingly large fee. What the task is, only Mon Mothma can say.

TASK

Move the *Millennium Falcon* to Mon Mothma's location.

Once you have returned to the galactic view, you receive a message that Captain Antilles has been assigned to *Tantive IV* to take Princess Leia on a secret mission for the Rebel Alliance. R2-D2 and C-3PO went with them. As a result, you lose access to both of these heroes. If you do not already have a fleet commander, recruit one to take command of your space fleet.

The space around Corulag is clear after your last mission. It's a good idea to take control of the surface as well—however, this will be a tough battle. Corulag is very loyal to the Empire and the civilians fight against you rather than against the Imperials as the indigenous people on several other worlds have done during the campaign. The battlefield is a city and the Imperials have lots of turrets and a powerful force that includes AT-ATs. You definitely need airspeeders, T4-B tanks, and artillery. Your force lands in the southeast corner. Secure the southwest reinforcement point and then advance north along the eastern side to take out the power generator. Then just continue to destroy the Imperial base in the northwest.

If you invade Corulag, you will need some heavy firepower to defeat the Imperials and their civilian allies.

TIP

Before you move Han Solo and Chewbacca to Mon Mothma's location, it's time to make sure your planets are well defended. After this mission, the Imperials go on the attack. You need at least three strong fleets—four if possible. Position three of them at Kashyyyk, Kessel, and Kuat. If you have a fourth, or at least any space units you can put together, send those to Corellia. Build an ion cannon on each of these four planets as well—even if you have to sell an existing structure to open up a slot. Also, build ion cannons at Yavin 4, Dantooine, and Wayland in preparation for future battles.

That is all you need to do for know. Leave Geonosis alone because it usually has a very powerful Imperial fleet in orbit over it. Now select Han Solo and send him to the same system as Mon Mothma to begin the next mission.

Smuggler's Raid on Carida

OBJECTIVE

1. *Han Solo and Chewbacca must survive the mission.*
2. *Destroy the power source for the turbolaser towers.*
3. *Get Han and Chewie to the storage area and recover the schematics.*
4. *Get Han and Chewie to the shuttle landing area.*

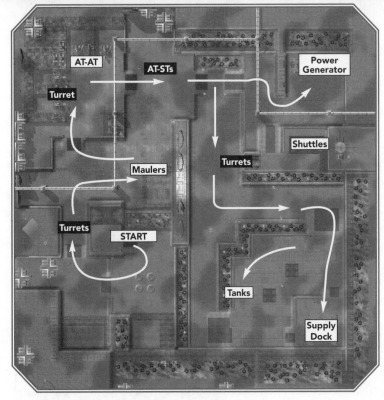

Han Solo and Chewbacca once again find themselves performing a dangerous assignment for the Alliance. This time, it's infiltrating a heavily fortified Imperial city...on foot. Their goal is to find the schematics that the Empire has annexed. Recovering these schematics may be just what the Alliance needs to get the Mon Calamari back into the fight. Han and Chewie must work together to navigate the city, avoid or neutralize the Imperials encountered, and reach the supply dock, where they can recover the plans and steal a ship to get them off-world.

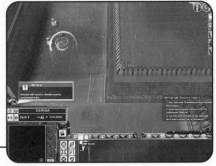

Han can disable the turrets with his EMP burst ability.

For this mission, you have only the two hero characters to control. While you are familiar with Han Solo from a previous mission, Chewbacca is new. He has the spring ability, just like Han Solo. However, Chewbacca also has the capture vehicle ability that lets him hijack an enemy vehicle. You need to use both Han and Chewie's abilities to get through this mission. The supply dock is in the map's southeast corner. However, because turbolaser towers guard it, you first need to take out the power generator in the northeast.

You begin on a landing platform. To complete your objectives, follow the route illustrated on the map. Head south and to the west. A couple of stormtrooper squads patrol around here. While you can try to time it to avoid them, they usually see you and attack. You have to fight it out there. Order both characters to attack the enemy troops. You'll take some damage but neutralize them in the end.

As you begin to head north, you find a couple of turrets along the path's western side. As they start to turn to fire, make sure you have both characters selected, order them to move to the turrets, and then click on the spring ability. When Han is near the turrets, click on the EMP burst ability to disable the towers. If you want to, attack the turrets and try to destroy them before they come back online. However, you can also just continue north out of their range.

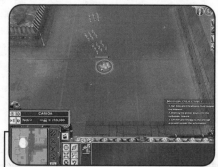

Continue to where a platoon of TIE maulers is parked. Order Chewie to capture one and use it to run over the squads of stormtroopers to the north and west. This is much quicker than using the laser cannons. To do this, just order the mauler to move past enemy infantry and it will run them down. Keep Han near the other maulers so he can use the EMP burst to disable them if they become active. Then move Han to the build pad to the south of the maulers to take control of it and build a bacta healing station there. If the mauler is destroyed, Chewie and Han can position themselves within the station's healing radius as they fight off the stormtroopers.

Once the troopers are eliminated and both characters are at full health and with their abilities recharged, send them west and then north up a ramp toward a single turret. Use Han's EMP burst to disable it and then order your characters to fire at and destroy the turret. Now Chewie can capture the AT-AT and use it. Wait for Han's EMP ability to recharge, then send the AT-AT east to engage the AT-STs near the bottom of the ramp. Han Solo should spring out and use the EMP to disable the group of walkers and then rush back up the ramp while Chewie in the AT-AT destroys the enemies.

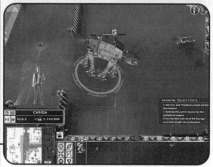

Chewie can hijack the TIE maulers as well at the AT-AT. If necessary, he can steal an AT-ST or any other enemy vehicle.

Continue east to the power generator. A turret and some stormtroopers are on guard, but they are little trouble for the AT-AT. Walk it over the enemy troops to eliminate them faster than shooting at them. Use another build pad in this area to build a repair station to fix the damage the AT-AT has taken.

Once you are repaired and ready to go, head back down to the road that leads south. There are three turrets along the eastern side as you advance. You also run into more AT-STs and stormtroopers. If necessary, retreat to the repair station to fix the AT-AT. After clearing out the road, follow the route on the map to the east where you run into more stormtroopers near the ramp. Clear them out and then get Han to the supply dock where he finds the schematic. More stormtroopers are west of the supply dock. If the AT-AT takes too much damage, Chewie should hop out. There are some 2-M repulsor tanks he can steal.

The schematics are in this supply dock.

All that remains is to get to the shuttles near the power generator. You run into more AT-STs and stormtroopers as you head north along the road. Han should EMP the walkers and then keep moving. Don't stay and fight. Keep Chewie in the tank as long as possible for firepower if needed, but keep Han moving and sprinting as much as possible. Once you get to the shuttles, Han and Chewie steal one and head off the planet.

The Defense of Mon Calamari

BRIEFING

Mon Calamari are a fierce and passionate people. With their spirit rekindled by the return of their enslaved people and the reclamation of their technology, they have revolted against the Imperials that subjugated them. They staged revolts all over the planet, and the Imperials stationed on Mon Calamari were easily overcome. Rapidly taking the battle into space, they made use of any ships they could to attack the Imperial vessels stationed above them. Finally liberated, they have quickly set about rebuilding their fleet and preparing for all-out war against the Empire.

Wasting no time, the Empire set a plan in motion to retake Mon Calamari and prevent its people from becoming a threat to Imperial domination. A massive fleet has been organized and will soon leave from Imperial controlled space. Their mission: retake the rebellious planet Mon Calamari.

TASK

Defeat the Imperial fleet before it can reach Mon Calamari.

As soon as you finish the previous mission with Han and Chewie, get ready for an attack. The Imperial fleet leaves Coruscant and heads to Corellia. If you have this planet under your control, be ready to defend. The enemy has a huge fleet that you probably cannot defeat at Corellia. If you followed the tip included before the previous mission, you already have fleets stationed at the three planets that provide access to Mon Calamari—Kashyyyk, Kessel, and Kuat. You also need ion cannons on each of these planets as well as Corellia. Place orders at all of these planets for additional ships as needed.

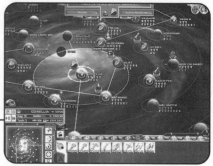

Corellia is the first target of the Imperial fleet on its way to Mon Calamari.

You also now have control of Mon Calamari. Select it and build an ion cannon on the surface and Mon Calamari cruisers in orbit after upgrading the space station if needed. If the Imperial fleet manages to get through your defenses to Mon Calamari, you have a fleet there for a final stand against the Imperial survivors.

TIP

If Mon Mothma is on Alderaan or one of the planets in the Imperial's path, move her to the safety of Yavin 4 or Dantooine.

Taking on the Imperial Fleet

OBJECTIVE

1. Kill the invading Imperial forces to preserve the space control of the system.

The first attack on Rebellion territory occurs at Corellia, if you invaded this planet. Because your strongest fleets are at the three planets bordering Mon Calamari, you have to make do with what you have at Corellia. Defend this planet's orbit to delay the Imperial fleet and to cause as much damage as possible. It is your Alamo. Your space station should be at level 5, providing the most defenses possible. Depending on what ships you have there, organize them into a group of missile cruisers and a group of everything else.

At Corellia, the Imperial fleet hits you with many Star Destroyers all at once.

TIP

During a space battle where you are defending a system, you can order a number of upgrades at your space station that increase firepower as well as your ships' defenses. You should have plenty of credits at this stage of the game, so order as many upgrades as you can into the production queue when you select the space station. This gives your fleet an edge over the enemy.

The key to defending a system from an enemy fleet is to use the planetary ion cannon. This operates much like a bombing run during ground battles. Click on the ion cannon icon near the minimap and then click on an Imperial ship. Target the closest Star Destroyer and fire. The ion cannon disables the ship for a time. Keep an eye on the ion cannon icon so you can fire it again as soon as the cannon recharges. If you use it as much as possible, you can disable three or more enemy ships at one time.

Order your missile cruisers to fire barrages at the disabled ships, while the rest of your fleet goes after the enemy ships closest to the space station. If you have reinforcements, bring them in as you take losses to keep your available firepower as high as possible. When things start to turn against you, pull back your fleets, especially the missile cruisers, so they are behind the space station. The station can take a lot of damage, so use it as a shield for your remaining ships. Keep fighting to the last ship and try to destroy as many Star Destroyers as possible to give your other fleets an advantage if you are unable to defeat the Imperials at Corellia.

If the Imperials prevail at Corellia, the fleet moves on to another system as they advance to Mon Calamari. Use the same tactics as you did at Corellia in order to defeat the Imperials. However, if the Imperials make it all the way to Mon Calamari, they should be so weakened that you can defeat them with the Mon Calamari cruisers stationed in orbit there along with Commander Ackbar's flagship, the *Home One*. This cruiser has the redirect-all-fire special ability, which orders all nearby cruisers to concentrate their fire on Ackbar's target. As before, remember your ion cannon. That alone can make or break a battle.

Before beginning a battle, zoom in on the planet so you can see what the enemy fleet contains. While the fight at Corellia weakened the Imperial fleet, it still has many capital ships.

After disabling a Star Destroyer, several Rebel missile cruisers fire a missile barrage at the ship to quickly reduce it to space debris.

While a ship is disabled, order your fleet to attack it. Target the engines to prevent it from moving when it comes back online, so it is a sitting duck for missile barrages.

The Final Battle

BRIEFING

The Empire's ultimate weapon, the Death Star, has been unleashed upon an unsuspecting galaxy. The planet Alderaan was the first to pay the price, with millions of deaths being the cost. The Rebel fleet is far too weak to confront the battle station head on, but with the aid of General Dodonna's military knowledge and courageous fighter pilots, the Rebellion may yet have a chance.

TASK

Confront the Death Star in a tactical battle that includes Red Squadron. If Red Squadron survives the battle, Luke can destroy the Death Star and win the game.

TASK

Do not allow Mon Mothma to be destroyed by the Death Star—her presence is vital to the Alliance, and the game is lost if she is destroyed.

TIP

Only Red Squadron can destroy the Death Star. Without Red Squadron you can destroy the accompanying fleet, but the Death Star itself is immune to all other attacks.

As soon as the Imperial fleet headed for Mon Calamari is defeated, Alderaan is destroyed by the Death Star. There is nothing you can do to prevent it. However, quickly get as many of your fleets to Wayland as possible. The Death Star moves much slower than the fleets, so you just might make it in time. If it doesn't look as if the fleets will arrive in time, and you do not have a decent fleet at Wayland, move Mon Mothma, Red Squadron, and any other heroes to Dantooine so they are not destroyed by the Death Star. If Wayland should be destroyed, wait to see where the Death Star will move next. Then send your fleet, along with Red Squadron, to that system to prepare for the fight against the Death Star.

The Death Star approaches a planet.

After Alderaan, the Death Star heads to Yavin 4.

Battle Against the Death Star

OBJECTIVES

1. Kill the invading Imperial forces to preserve the space control of the system.
2. Red Squadron must survive the battle.

Wherever you fight the Death Star, the tactics are the same. The Death Star appears in the background of the battle area, but you can't directly attack it. Therefore, this space battle is similar to the ones you fought defending Mon Calamari. Use your planetary ion cannon to disable the Imperial capital ships. However, you have to keep Red Squadron alive. Move it to a far, empty corner of the battle area while the rest of your fleet takes on the Imperial fleet. It is not quite as powerful as some of the fleets you fought against earlier because the Imperials are relying on the Death Star to win.

You must defeat the Imperial fleet before Red Squadron can make an attack run on the Death Star.

A timer at the top of the screen shows how long until the Death Star is in range to destroy the planet. However, you don't have to worry about that. The battle continues until you defeat the Imperial fleet—or are defeated by them. Once the tactical space battle is complete, the result depends on the status of Red Squadron. If you have kept it alive, then Luke can make his attack against the Death Star and destroy it. If not, then the Death Star destroys the planet. Red Squadron reappears on the galactic map after awhile, and you have to take on the Death Star once again. Once the Death Star is destroyed, the Rebel Campaign is a success.

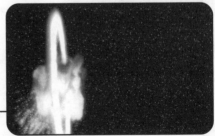

Red Five, better known as Luke Skywalker, uses the Force to aim his proton torpedoes at the Death Star's weak spot. The Death Star is destroyed and the Rebels are victorious...for now.

THE EMPIRE CAMPAIGN

The entire galaxy is under the rule of the tyrannical Galactic Empire. The only remaining resistance is the small Rebel Alliance that dares to challenge their military supremacy. The impending creation of the Empire's ultimate weapon, the Death Star, threatens to crush the Rebellion. Once operational, the Empire will have the power to destroy an entire planet. Threatening to turn the tide of this struggle is an unknown Imperial traitor who deals in military secrets. The Emperor has tasked his apprentice, Darth Vader, with tracking down and eliminating this double agent....

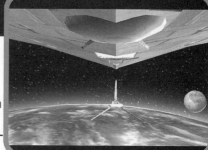

The Imperial campaign lets you play as the other side during the Galactic Civil War. You must put down the Rebellion as you work to build the ultimate superweapon—the Death Star. You should have already gone though the tutorials, and it's a good idea to play through the Rebellion Campaign first because the Imperial Campaign is a bit more difficult and assumes you are already familiar with the Campaign game structure. Once this Campaign begins, you are put right into the action on the planet Thyferra. You have Darth Vader and a complement of ground troops to engage and defeat the Rebels in this system.

An Organized Resistance

BRIEFING

You have been ordered to Thyferra to find clues as to the identity of the traitor who is giving military secrets to the Rebellion.

TASK

Eliminate the Rebel presence on Thyferra.

Assault on Thyferra

BRIEFING

1. *Slay the Rebel scum and burn their buildings to the ground.*
2. *Lord Vader must survive.*
3. *Destroy the communications array.*
4. *Destroy the Rebels' power generator.*

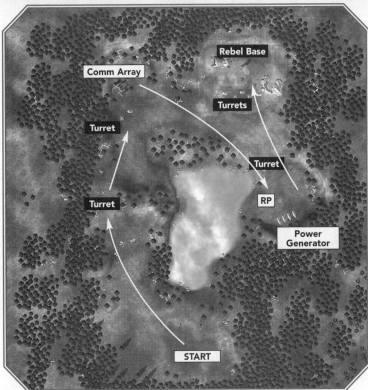

LEGEND

RP	Reinforcement Point

An Imperial army arrives on Thyferra with Darth Vader in command. During this mission, you become accustomed to Imperial ground tactics. If you have played the Rebellion Campaign, you'll see that you have different types of units that require you to play a bit differently. At the start, you have four squads of stormtroopers and six AT-STs along with your hero character, Darth Vader. Organize your units into three groups, with each group composed of a specific type of unit. Now get moving to the north. Lead with Darth Vader.

Vader can use his Force push ability to eliminate nearby enemy infantry.

You come across a couple squads of enemy infantry. Use Darth Vader's Force push ability by clicking on the ability icon as Vader nears the two squads. A red circle expands outward from Vader, eliminating enemy infantry as it passes over them. As a Jedi with the power of the dark side of the Force, Vader is a very powerful unit on the battlefield all by himself.

Continue until you come across a Rebel T2-B tank. Once again, you use Vader's special abilities—this time Force crush. Click on the icon and then on the enemy vehicle. Vader single-handedly destroys the vehicle using only the Force. With these demonstrations of the power of the Force completed, move your entire force north toward the first turret. You run into more infantry squads along the way.

Your stormtroopers have the take cover ability, just like Rebel infantry. Use it when you engage enemy units to reduce the damage you take. The AT-STs have a barrage area ability that lets you target an area onto which the selected AT-STs power down some serious firepower. AT-STs can also walk over and kill enemy infantry. Try this out as you advance, then use the barrage area ability on the first turret you come across as you advance.

Send your force in to destroy the communications array as well as the Rebels defending it.

TIP

Darth Vader is also proficient at destroying turrets. Order him to attack one while still at a distance. He moves forward and uses the Force to destroy the turret. While this takes several seconds, he does not take damage from the turret because he shuts it down while he attacks, which also prevents it from firing on other units.

Move Darth Vader or some stormtroopers over to take control of the build pad where the turret was. Then build either a bacta healing station or a repair station depending on which units need help getting back to their initial strength. Then lead your force north toward the communications array. Defending this structure are a couple squads of Rebel soldiers, a T2-B tank, and an anti-infantry turret. Order your AT-STs to attack the turret while Vader uses Force crush on the tank. Then move in your stormtroopers to deal with the enemy soldiers before you destroy the communications array to complete one of your objectives. At the build pad, construct the other station you did not build at the previous build pad and get all of your units fixed up or healed. If Vader has taken any damage, heal him at the bacta healing station along with the stormtroopers.

A shield covers the Rebel base, making it difficult to attack the units and structures inside.

With your force ready for more action, advance east. The Rebel base is protected by a shield generator. You can't fire lasers through the shield, and moving through it is slow. Therefore, continue east and then south to the power generator. Once it is destroyed, the shields will be deactivated. The power generator is defended by a turret, some tanks, and soldiers. Approach with Vader until you can see the enemy, then call in a bombing run with your TIE bombers. Click on the bombing run icon, then move the targeting reticle over the area near the turret and tank and click. It takes a few seconds for the bombers to arrive, but they seriously damage the Rebel defenders. Now move in your troops and take them out. Finally, attack the power generator to lower the shields.

A second reinforcement point is near the power generator. Move Darth Vader near it to take control. You are rewarded with some reinforcements—a platoon of TIE maulers. While they lack the shields of the Rebel T2-B tanks, TIE maulers are great for taking out infantry with their laser cannons. However, because they are fast, they are even better at running over and killing enemy infantry. Just be sure to keep them away from turrets and enemy tanks. Their special ability is to self destruct. Click on this icon and the selected TIE mauler blows up a few seconds later, damaging any nearby units. If you have a damaged mauler, move it next to a turret or a group of enemies and self-destruct. Remember that it takes some time for the explosion to occur and if the enemy destroys the mauler first, the explosion is prevented. After the maulers land, you are attacked by Rebel tanks from the north. Take them out with your AT-STs and Vader.

NOTE

Notice that the AT-ST and TIE mauler do not have shields as the Rebel tanks do. Therefore, they can't take as much damage as a comparable Rebel unit. However, they do have a bit more firepower to make up for it.

Now it's time to attack the Rebel base. Lead your force north and hold off as Vader moves ahead to locate the two turrets. Call in a bombing run, targeting right between the two turrets. If they are not destroyed outright, move your AT-STs in to finish them off. Order your TIE maulers to move in and run over the enemy soldiers moving about the base as your AT-STs use barrages to attack enemy units and structures. After a building is destroyed, Rebel soldiers usually run out. Bring in your stormtroopers and Darth Vader to help mop up. The mission is complete once all Rebel units and structures have been destroyed.

TIE maulers are speedy, making them great for running over enemy infantry before it can move out of the way. Just watch out for Rebel Plex missile soldiers. They can cause a lot of damage to the lightly protected maulers.

Crush, Kill, Destroy

BRIEFING

The Rebels have captured Fondor. Send your forces there and crush their pitiful uprising. Teach those Rebels a lesson they won't soon forget.

TASK

Build a ground assault force and recapture Fondor.

After conquering Thyferra, you are taken to the galactic view. There you can see that the Empire controls four systems—Thyferra, Abregado-Rae, Anaxes, and Coruscant. Take some time to build up your infrastructure before you invade Fondor. Build space stations at all four planets and upgrade them to level 2. On the surfaces of the planets, start building structures. You need a light vehicle factory and barracks on Thyferra and Anaxes, the same on Coruscant plus an officer academy, and a cantina on Abregado Rae. Fill in empty slots with mines because you can always sell them later to open up slots for other structures. By doing this, you can increase your daily galactic income from around 500 credits to more than 3,000! More than three-quarters of that income is a result of your mines.

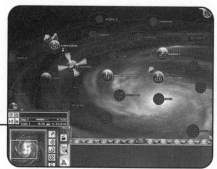

You have four systems under your control at the start. However, you soon increase your control over the galaxy one system at a time.

You also need some combat units if you are going to take over the galaxy and eliminate the Rebel Alliance. Build a couple Acclamator cruisers and a couple Tartan patrol cruisers at each planet for your space fleet. You need to create a ground invasion force as well. From the planets with barracks and light vehicle factories, you need to recruit and send enough units to Darth Vader on Thyferra so that he has at least four platoons each of stormtroopers, AT-STs, and TIE maulers, and two platoons of scout troopers. A field commander from the officer academy at Coruscant also comes in handy. Be sure to include at least one Acclamator cruiser with Vader's fleet so he has access to TIE bombers for bombing runs during ground battles. Once you have done all this, move Vader's fleet to Fondor for the attack. There is no enemy fleet in orbit, so once your fleet arrives, drag it down to the surface slot.

The Invasion of Fondor

OBJECTIVE

1. The local humans are allied with our enemies. Destroying them and their structures will go a long way to helping our cause.
2. Destroy all Rebellion land forces and structures to win.
3. Find and destroy the Rebel training facility to weaken the Rebellion's units.

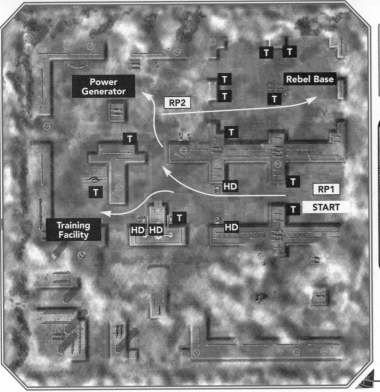

LEGEND

RP	Reinforcement Point
HD	Human Dwelling
T	Turret

The civilians on Fondor have turned against the Empire. They must be taught a lesson.

Your scout troopers land first near reinforcement point 1 in the southeast corner of a city. Quickly click on the reinforcements button and bring down a platoon of AT-STs, a platoon of TIE maulers, and two platoons of stormtroopers. Send the troopers to take control of the build pads west of the landing area. Build a repair station at one and an anti-infantry turret at the other. Also leave two squads of stormtroopers between these two pads, ordered to take cover and protect the reinforcement point. The Rebels and their allied civilians will try to take control of it so you can't bring down reinforcements to replace losses.

Destroying the training facility makes your job a lot easier and lets you focus more on the attack and less on defending against infantry squads rushing your reinforcement point.

Start off by sending a scout trooper out ahead to the west. Locate a turret, and if you keep going to the area's western side, you find the training facility along with another turret. Use the scout troopers' thermal detonator to damage either the facility or the turret before returning to your base to repair. Call in a bombing run on the enemy turret closest to your base on the way back. Now order your AT-STs, maulers, and a couple of stormtrooper squads to move west to attack the first turret and take out the four civilian structures. That decreases the number of enemies that attack you. Use your TIE maulers to run over the masses of enemy soldiers and then send them back to the repair station as they take damage. After taking out the Rebel turret, build an anti-infantry turret of your own on the build pad. Then push forward to the training facility. Once you take it out, you decrease the waves of enemies coming at you. If you take losses, bring in reinforcements and use your bombing run as often as it's available.

Once you have destroyed the training facility and the nearby turret, build an anti-infantry turret there, then pull back to the central section in the south. Repair any damaged vehicles and then assemble them in the central area, ready to push north to the second reinforcement point. However, before you can do that, you need to eliminate the turret near the entrance to the northern central section. Bombing runs soften it up for you to destroy. Then move in your stormtroopers, along with the vehicles, to take control of the reinforcement point. That doubles your troop capacity and allows you to bring down Darth Vader, a field commander if available, and two more units.

Use the TIE bombers to make runs against enemy turrets and concentrations of enemy infantry.

The shield generator is west of the northern reinforcement point. Take it out with some AT-STs while the rest of your force watches for enemies approaching from the east. Now all that remains is the Rebel base in the northeast. Send Vader forward to locate a couple turrets near the entrance and then call in a bombing run on them, followed by an AT-ST barrage area attack. All that remains is to move your force into the base to wipe out any remaining vehicles and structures. Their total destruction results in an Imperial victory and the completion of the mission.

Rooting Out the Pirates

BRIEFING

The transmission logs from Thyferra and Fondor have led the Empire to a potential pirate nest on Ilum. To retain the element of surprise, Lord Vader has ordered a probe droid dispatched to Ilum.

TASK

Build a probe droid at a system with the space station and send it to Ilum.

Now that Fondor is under your control, put it to work. You need a level-2 space station there, plus several mines on the surface. Spend some time building up Vader's invasion fleet and replacing your losses with units recruited at other planets. After you have accomplished this, and recruited garrisons for each of your planets in case the Rebels try to raid or invade them, build a probe droid at one of your systems. When it is complete, drag it into the spy slot near Ilum. Upon arrival, the probe droid informs you that Ilum has pirates both in orbit and on the surface.

Send a probe droid to Ilum to see what is in the system. You will find pirate forces in orbit as well as on the surface.

The Pirate Menace

BRIEFING

Boba Fett has been hired for a hefty price to aid the Empire. He will scout the pirate defenses and neutralize their warning systems before the main fleet enters the area.

TASK

Build a fleet and escort Boba Fett from Coruscant to Ilum.

Send Darth Vader's invasion fleet to Coruscant and add Boba Fett to it. Then send the combined fleet to Ilum. There you have to fight against pirates who may have been supporting the Rebels.

Ilum Space Battle against the Pirates

OBJECTIVES

1. Boba Fett must survive.
2. Destroy all the pirate sensor pods.

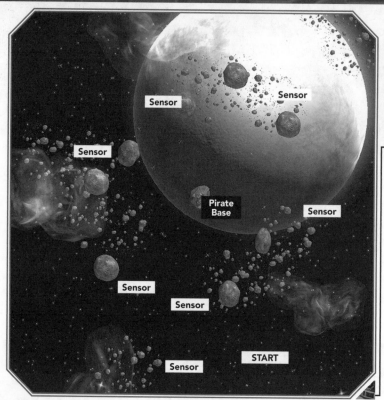

The Slave I is a very capable ship. It can single-handedly take out six sensor pods and 12 squadrons of pirate fighters.

Boba Fett jumps into the Ilum system in his own ship, the *Slave I*. This ship has a seismic charge ability. Clicking on this icon drops an explosive that detonates after a few seconds. It creates a blast wave that destroys all nearby pirate fighters. This is a lot faster than having

Boba Fett chase them and shoot them down with his lasers. Because you begin in the southeast, move west to attack the first sensor pod. As the pirate fighters approach, release a seismic charge. By the time it detonates, they should be nearly on top of it and will be destroyed. The sensors also will be eliminated after only a short attack. Wait for your seismic charge to reload before heading to the next two sensors to the north a bit. If you drop your charge between the sensors, you can often catch the four squadrons of pirate fighters guarding them in a single seismic charge. Then finish off the sensor pods.

The seismic charges wipe out entire squadrons of pirate fighters.

TIP

It is vital that Boba Fett stay far away from the pirate base in the map's center. If you are detected, the pirate leader tries to flee and you will have a hard time bringing in the Imperial fleet in time to stop him.

Continue west, and then north through a nebula to get to the next sensor pod. Use the same tactics to destroy it and the other remaining pods, careful to stay as far away from the pirate space station in the center as possible.

Once all sensor pods have been destroyed, it is safe to bring in the rest of your invasion fleet. The best place for your ships to enter is between the asteroid fields to the east of the pirate base. Open the reinforcement window and bring in four Acclamator cruisers and four Tartan patrol cruisers. The Acclamators each launch a squadron of TIE fighters and TIE bombers. Order all of your units to move forward and attack the pirate base. Target the shields first and use your cruisers' ability to boost weapon power. Once the shields are down, pound the base until it is destroyed. You may want to move Boba Fett to a safe corner to prevent him from being destroyed and thus ending the mission in failure.

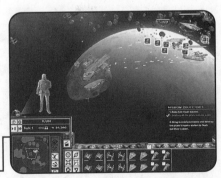

Concentrate all of your fleet's fire on the pirate base until it is destroyed.

After the pirate base is in ruins, its leader tries to escape. Order all of your units to fire on the pirate vessel to destroy it before it can escape. Because of the asteroids around the pirate base, the enemy must get his ship to the northwestern corner to jump to hyperspace and get away. Use everything to disable the pirate and capture him for interrogation to complete the mission.

Keep your fleet attacking the pirate vessel to prevent it from escaping the system.

Subjugating Geonosis

BRIEFING

Grand Moff Tarkin has assigned Darth Vader to acquire the resources of the planet Geonosis. To take full control of the planet, both space and land must be secured.

TASK

Build a fleet and escort Darth Vader to Geonosis. You will need a significant number of vessels to successfully invade.

Send your invasion force down to Ilum to take control of this planet from the pirates.

TIP

As you conquer the revealed planets of the galaxy, it's a good idea to create two different fleets. One should have a fleet commander and only space vessels. This fleet is used for clearing out the space areas around systems. The second fleet is for ground invasions. Darth Vader should be in this fleet along with a field commander, your ground units, and at least one Acclamator cruiser and a few Tartan patrol cruisers. That ensures that you have some protection if you run into an enemy fleet, and the Acclamator provides TIE bombers for bombing runs during ground missions.

The successful raid on the pirate base has revealed much useful information on Rebel activities. However, the Rebels have worked very hard to conceal the conspirator, who still eludes the Imperial intelligence agents. So, Darth Vader must continue his hunt.

Before you send your fleet to Geonosis, take the time to invade all of the planets that have been revealed. Many of these have pirate forces in orbit as well as on the surface, so you have to fight. However, not only does this add to your income and the number of units you can support, it also provides security against the Rebellion.

Start off by taking control of Ilum by landing a ground force. You have to fight against pirates, but it's not too tough. Next go for Byss. You can take this system without a fight. Corulag, Sullust, Bestine IV, and Taris all have pirates that you must defeat to take control of the planets. Endor is fairly easy, though you may have to take out a space station. Bespin has some Rebel forces, but it is only a space battle because the planet is a gas giant with no surface. Follow it up by taking control of Dagobah, Naboo, and the Vergesso Asteroids.

Replace your losses and then send your fleet to Eriadu. This has Rebels in both space and on the surface. Be sure to build space stations at all of the planets you just captured and garrison them with some troops for defense against Rebel raid fleets. Build mines on empty slots and the credits begin to pour in. In fact, you should have at least 10,000 credits coming to you each day.

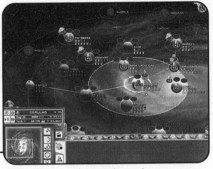

Before you move on to Geonosis, build your fleet back up. Because Darth Vader must move with the fleet to Geonosis, combine your two fleets for the invasion. You should have at least six Acclamator cruisers and eight Tartan patrol cruisers. While this may be overkill, it is always better to go in with more than you need. Now, lightspeed to Geonosis!

Several new planets have been revealed. Take control of all of them before you move on to Geonosis.

Space Battle over Geonosis

OBJECTIVE

1. *Lord Vader must survive.*
2. *Quash the Rebel space station.*

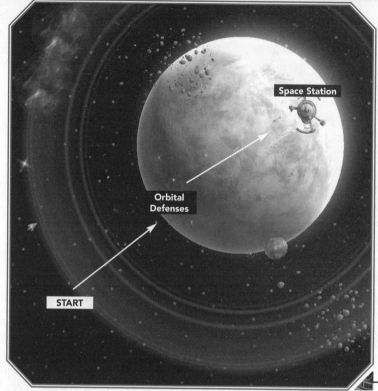

Space Station

Orbital
Defenses

START

Keep your fleet at a distance until you destroy the Rebel fleet.

The space battle over Geonosis is the largest one you have faced so far in this Campaign. Your fleet begins in the southwest with the Rebel space station in the northeast. Two large asteroid fields are in the opposite corners with orbital defense satellites across the middle. While the space station will launch its own garrison of fighters and frigates, the Rebels also have some additional space units. The key to winning this space battle is to be patient. If some transports come in with your fleet, send them to a far corner where they will be safe. Organize your fleet into homogeneous groups so you can quickly order all of a specific type of unit to attack or move.

TIP

Darth Vader fights during this space battle. He flies a specially modified TIE fighter and leads a squadron of TIE fighters. His ability is to call for wingmen. While he has his squadron around him, he does not take damage. However, after they have all been destroyed, Vader becomes vulnerable. Click on this ability icon to bring a new squadron to follow and protect him. He is best used against enemy fighters. However, keep an eye on him and pull him back if the fighting gets too intense. You might even want to leave him with the transports to protect them from Rebel fighters.

Use your Tartan patrol cruisers to target the satellites and enemy fighters. Your Acclamator cruisers are best for enemy frigates and corvettes. Send your TIE fighters after the Rebel fighters and your bombers against the frigates. The goal is to take out the Rebel fleet while staying out of range of the space station. When it seems the enemy is weakened, move your forces toward the space station. Target the shield generator first, followed by the hangar to prevent more garrison units from being launched. Then work over the space station, starting with proton torpedo and concussion missile launchers because they can penetrate your ships' shields. Keep up the pressure until the space station is destroyed and the battle is an Imperial victory. Now order your fleet to land units on the surface of Geonosis.

When the Rebel fleet has been destroyed, move all of your combat units in to take out the space station. Remember to use the boost weapon power ability on your cruisers to increase damage to the enemy.

Ground Battle for Control of Geonosis

OBJECTIVE

1. The Geonosians are revolting against their Imperial masters. Dispatch any Geonosian structures that you come across for a bonus.
2. Destroy all Rebellion land forces and structures to win.

RP3

GD

Rebel Base

GD   GD

GD

GD

RP2

RP1   GD

START

LEGEND

RP	**Reinforcement Point**
GD	**Geonosian Dwelling**

Your first unit lands on Geonosis at reinforcement point 1. Quickly bring down one platoon each of stormtroopers and TIE maulers, as well as two platoons of AT-STs. There is a Geonosian dwelling near your landing area, so destroy it. Then move your force toward reinforcement point 2. Halfway there, you have to take out some enemy turrets. Call in bombing runs and use your scout walker's barrages to eliminate them as well as the two nearby dwellings. Send your stormtroopers to take control of the build pads and build your own anti-infantry turrets there.

The Geonosians can be trouble, especially in large groups. Destroy the dwellings where they spawn to reduce their threat to your invasion.

Next send your stormtroopers and a platoon of AT-STs to take control of the second reinforcement point. You have to take out a turret, but it shouldn't be too difficult. Taking this control point adds two to your maximum capacity for units, so bring down Darth Vader. Near reinforcement point 2, there is an abandoned mine. Take control of it for some bonus credits. Near this area, build a repair station so you can start fixing your damaged vehicles. Leave a stormtrooper squad at each of your reinforcement points to guard them and then get ready to advance.

It is hard to stop several platoons of AT-STs—and watch out for their combined area bombardment. Nothing can survive that for long.

In the center of the battlefield are a couple more Geonosian dwellings with lots of natives about. Rush your TIE maulers through them or call in a bombing run to take them out and then destroy the dwellings. Because only one more dwelling remains, the Geonosians that come to attack will be severely limited. Now move your forces along the western canyon to reinforcement point 3. There are a couple pairs of turrets along your path. However, bombing runs and Darth Vader make short work of them. Take control of the reinforcement point and destroy the nearby turrets. You can also call in more units. Bring down a field commander and other units as you need them. Destroy the last dwelling to prevent any more Geonosians from showing up to fight.

The Rebels are now confined to the northeast quadrant. Build anti-infantry turrets along your borders with this area to deal with Rebel soldiers moving to take over your reinforcement points. The Rebels have a base in the northeast corner as well as on a plateau a little farther south. Start by taking out the turrets and buildings on the plateau. Then continue by finishing off the rest of the Rebel

Use Darth Vader for taking out enemy turrets, then claiming the build pads. Leave your stormtroopers back at the reinforcement points to defend them.

structures to the north. Once all Rebel structures and units have been eliminated, the mission ends and Grand Moff Tarkin has more labor for building the Death Star.

With the fall of Geonosis, all revealed systems should be under Imperial control.

Attack on Mon Calamari

BRIEFING

The Emperor believes that the fiercely independent people of Mon Calamari will inevitably aid the Rebellion if they are allowed the choice. The planet must be subjugated to prevent their interference.

TASK

Take control of Mon Calamari space. A fleet of significant size is required. Ensure that your controlled planets have adequate defenses while doing this.

Before you head off for Mon Calamari, notice that several planets have been revealed. Some are Rebel-controlled while others are havens for pirates. Because there is no rush to move your fleet to Mon Calamari, secure these planets for the Empire. You already have an army and fleet at Geonosis, so build some production facilities on this planet (it has seven slots for structures). This can be your main production facility in the Outer Rim. You can also now upgrade your space stations to level 3, which allows them to produce Victory and Broadside cruisers. Start building these two types of ships to add to your space fleet. The Victory can carry more TIE fighters and bombers and is a more powerful capital ship. The Broadside is a missile cruiser that has a powerful bombard area ability. Build several of both and add them to your invasion fleet to increase its firepower as well as to let you practice using them before you invade Mon Calamari.

It is time to expand the control of the Empire throughout the galaxy. Work your way toward Mon Calamari, planet by planet.

Test out your new ships against the pirate fleets.

Ryloth is your first target. Send your space fleet to clear the orbit of enemies, then send your invasion fleet to land on the surface and secure it. Watch out for the rancor that roams around on this planet. The Rebel base is in the northwest. Because it has a shield generator, take out the power generator in the northeast. Next move on to Nal Hutta where you face a fairly large pirate fleet in orbit, but a weak army on the surface. Secure and garrison both of these planets before moving your fleets to Corellia. Then take control of Kuat, Kessel, and Korriban. Build and upgrade space stations on all of these worlds because they are on your borders. Finally, build up a strong space fleet with at least seven Victory cruisers, six Broadside missile cruisers, and additional ships for escorts. Once your fleet is ready, send it to Mon Calamari.

The indigenous Hutts may be large, but they are no match for Imperial firepower.

Ambush at Mon Calamari

OBJECTIVES

1. *Crush the Rebel scum and their space station.*
2. *Eliminate all Mon Calamari capital ships.*

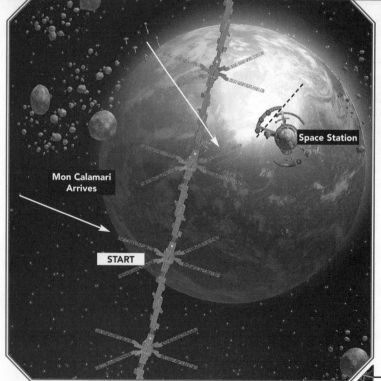

Space Station

Mon Calamari
Arrives

START

Don't be lured in to attack the space station with your entire fleet. Just send in your smaller ships to work over the defenses.

Your fleet exits from hyperspace in the southwestern quadrant. The enemy space station is in the northeast. However, do not rush right at it. Instead, send some Tartan cruisers and Acclamators toward the space station to engage the enemy corvettes and satellite defenses. However, try to stay out of range of the space station. Go ahead and send your TIE fighters and TIE bombers to attack as well. However, keep your Broadside and Victory cruisers out of range of the space station's defenses. The reasoning for this tactic becomes apparent after a while. Several Mon Calamari cruisers appear on the scene—some near the space station and others in the southwest behind your starting point.

TIE fighters can swarm all over enemy ships. Though they don't cause a lot of damage, they divert the enemy fire from your capital ships.

TIP

Mon Calamari cruisers have no shield generator hard-point. Therefore, you can never take down their shields completely—they always start to recharge. Use missile cruisers to hit them hard because the missiles go right through the shields and cause structural damage.

The Mon Calamari have tried to lure you toward the space station and then surround you with their cruisers. Once this occurs, pull all of your fleet away from the space station and concentrate on the Mon Calamari cruisers in the southwest first. As you have capacity created by units being destroyed, bring in more Victory and Broadside cruisers. Group the Broadsides together and have them all fire area barrages of missiles at the enemy cruisers.

Once you have cleared the southwest, cautiously advance toward the cruisers near the space station, moving just far enough to engage the enemy at long range while trying to stay out of range of the space station. By this time, you should have lots of TIE fighters. Order them to attack any remaining small ships and then the space station itself. This forces the space station to fire at your fighters while your capital ships come in for the attack. Take out the shield generator and then the hangar to prevent more enemy ships from spawning as a garrison force. Then open fire with your entire fleet on the space station. Remember to order your Victory cruisers to boost weapon power.

With the Mon Calamari cruisers destroyed, move your fleet in to finish off the space station and take control of Mon Calamari.

Once the space station and all enemy capital ships have been destroyed, the battle ends. With the destruction of their fleet, the Mon Calamari surrender, giving you control of their planet without even having to land troops on the surface.

Trouble on Kashyyyk

BRIEFING

A passionate rogue named Solo who had defected from the Empire some time ago has freed the Wookiees from their prisons. In his irrational defiance, he is attempting to get them off-planet. We cannot afford to lose the labor force we have established on Kashyyyk.

TASK

Stop the Wookiee outbreak on Kashyyyk.

One more planet is added to the Empire.

After taking control of Mon Calamari, build a space station, upgrade it, and build some structures to help defend it. By defeating the Mon Calamari, you have denied the Rebellion access to their powerful cruisers. Your next mission is a short distance away. Kashyyyk is next to Mon Calamari. There are no planets revealed, so you should control all of the galaxy that you can at this point. Because the Empire still controls the orbit over Kashyyyk, you only need ground units. However, be sure to take along an Acclamator so you have access to bombing runs. You need at least four companies of AT-STs, a couple companies of 2-M repulsor tanks, some TIE maulers, and artillery, as well as several companies of stormtroopers. It is a good idea to have a field commander as well. Once you are ready, send your invasion fleet to the Wookiee homeworld and begin your ground assault.

Prison Defense

OBJECTIVE

1. Protect the Imperial prisons.
2. Stop Han Solo from freeing the Wookiees.

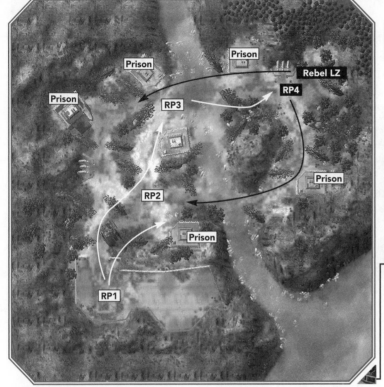

Quickly send a company up to reinforcement point 3 to secure it against a Rebel attack.

For this mission, you have to move fast. There are five prisons and you must prevent at least two from being destroyed. As soon as the mission begins, send whatever unit you begin with—usually the 2-M tanks—to reinforcement point 3. Then start landing two companies of stormtroopers, four companies of AT-STs, another company of 2-M tanks, a company of artillery, and a field commander.

Move a company of two squads to reinforcement point 2 and the other company to reinforcement point 3 so you can take control of these locations as well as the build pads near them. Build anti-vehicle turrets at each location. Follow up by sending two companies of AT-STs to each reinforcement point. Move your artillery to a position between the two points and leave your field commander back at your landing zone.

The Rebels land troops at reinforcement point 4. You have to deal with infantry and T2-B repulsor tanks as well as the freed Wookiees. Organize your units at each location to cover the area where the Rebels must cross the stream to get to the prisons on the western

Position your units to prevent the Rebels from crossing the stream and getting to the prisons in the west.

half of the battlefield. You cannot hold the prisons on the eastern side, so let them go. As soon as you see rebels, order all of your AT-STs to barrage the area where the enemy is crossing the stream. This makes a death zone through which they must travel to get to the stream's western bank.

Order your stormtroopers to take up position along with the AT-STs and to take cover. Then place your 2-M tanks behind your forward units to deal with anyone who breaks through. Hold off on your bombing run for a time when the Rebels break through with a large group. Don't use it too early and then be waiting for your next bombing run while you are being overrun. During the attacks, order your artillery to attack where the Rebels are hitting you the hardest.

When the Rebel units bunch up against your forces, call in a bombing run to wipe out the massed enemies.

TIP

If you see Han Solo during the fighting, order your units to attack him. He has some abilities that can be disabling to your force. The sooner you eliminate the smuggling scum, the better.

After repelling some large attacks, push on to reinforcement point 4. Hold at the southern crossing while massing your northern group to cross the stream and take control of the Rebel landing zone. Bring your artillery along and set it up in the stream to support your attack. The Rebels keep trying to land units until you can control the reinforcement point. Once this is accomplished, the Wookiee prison revolt will be crushed and Kashyyyk will once again be secure.

The Rebels keep coming until you capture their landing zone at reinforcement point 4.

With the revolt over, the Wookiees are herded back into prison.

A New Weapon of War
BRIEFING

With progress on the Death Star proceeding on schedule, the Emperor has turned his attention to other weapons. Colonel Maximillian Veers is set to demonstrate a new ground assault weapon—the All Terrain Armored Transport. The demonstration is to be held on Carida, home to an important Imperial training facility.

TASK

Escort Colonel Veers from Coruscant to Carida and aid him in performing his demonstration of the AT-AT prototype.

After all that you have been though conquering the galaxy, you now have to go watch a colonel show off his latest weapon. This should be easy. However, before you leave Kashyyyk, garrison it and make sure it has some defenses.

Send both your space fleet and your invasion fleet to Carida—just in case you might need them in that part of the galaxy. Then select Colonel Veers, who is at Coruscant, and drag him to Carida. Send him to the surface of the planet to get this demonstration over with.

Carida is in the upper part of the galaxy.

AT-AT Demonstration Exercise

OBJECTIVE

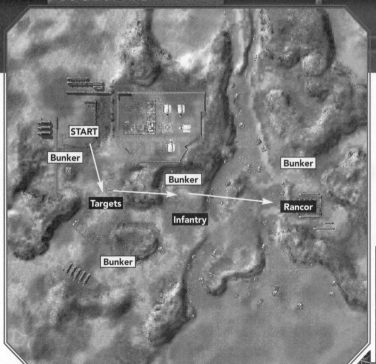

1. Select Colonel Veer's AT-AT and move it through the demonstration field.
2. Colonel Veers must survive.

Use this opportunity to see how useful an AT-AT can be to your army.

For this mission, you take command of an AT-AT. While this walker does not move very quickly, it has a lot of firepower. Start off by selecting the AT-AT and ordering it to fire at the T2-B tank to the south with other targets. Notice that it takes only a few blasts of the AT-AT's twin laser cannons to destroy this tank. Move the walker south, breaking through the low wall to destroy the rest of the targets, including more T2-B tanks as well as T4-B tanks and pod walkers.

Once all of the targets are destroyed, follow the arrow markers in the roadway to the area marked infantry on the mission map. Here you learn to use the deploy stormtroopers ability. Click on the ability icon and a squad of stormtroopers rappels from the AT-AT to the ground below. Use them along with the AT-AT to destroy some enemy infantry. They won't last long.

Stormtroopers rappel down from the AT-AT. You can then give them orders like any other unit.

TIP

You can deploy two stormtrooper squads during this mission. After the first is on the ground, and the ability is recharged, deploy a second squad. Now send one squad to each of the two western bunkers. Once they arrive, order them to take cover and be ready to defend the bunkers if necessary. Also build anti-vehicle turrets at the build pads near all the bunkers.

The next part of the demonstration is planned to show the firepower of the AT-AT against large indigenous beasts you might encounter during a ground battle. A rancor is being held in a cage to the east. Advance to the cage and fire at the rancor to kill it. Don't worry, it can't get out of the cage and attack you.

OBJECTIVE

3. Protect the four observation bunkers by defeating all Rebel invaders.

After the rancor is dead, Rebel troops start landing on Carida and try to take over the observation bunkers. The stormtroopers that you sent to the western bunkers should be able to hold out for a bit. Therefore, use the AT-AT to attack the Rebels, starting with the bunker north of the rancor. Use the maximum firepower ability when firing at an enemy vehicle. Next move west to eliminate any enemies there. Finally proceed to the western two bunkers where your stormtroopers are waiting to finish off the remainder of the Rebel units. Once all Rebels are eliminated, the mission is complete.

Rebel troops are landing on Carida. You face infantry and T2-B repulsor tanks.

The Rebel Fortress

BRIEFING

The amount of firepower used in the Rebel assault on Carida leads Veers to believe that the Rebels must have a base somewhere close. The only likely point of origin is the planet Jabiim. If any Rebel presence is found there, the planet must be made an example of.

TASK

Take control of Jabiim.

While your objective is Jabiim, five additional planets have been revealed. Take your space and invasion fleets to Fresia, Aeten II, Manaan, Dantooine, and Wayland each in turn and add them to the control of the Empire. All of these planets, with the exception of Wayland, are controlled by the Rebels. Therefore you face similar battles in each case. Wayland is somewhat easier because you face only pirates.

For the space battles, be sure you have replaced losses to your space fleet and have lots of the new Imperial Star Destroyers. Leave any Interdictors behind; you do not need them for these battles and they only take up a slot you can better use for a ship with more fire-power. When your space fleet arrives in orbit, expect a high-level space station with a fleet of frigates, cruisers, and fighters. The Rebels may also have ion cannons on the planet's surface, which they will use to disable your capital ships. Hold your fleet back at the start and let the Rebel space units come at you. Then as it thins out, move in for the attack. As you approach the space station, order your TIE bombers and capital ships to target the shield generators followed by the hangar. Keep bringing in reinforcements to replace your losses. Just be sure to bring them in at a distance because they are vulnerable immediately after entering the battle from hyperspace.

Six more systems have been revealed. Take control of the other five before heading to Jabiim.

TIP

Use the tractor beams on your Imperial Star Destroyers to grab hold of enemy frigates and corvettes so they are easier to hit with lasers and missiles.

On the surface, you can expect the Rebels to have a lot of units. However, their artillery is your biggest threat. The Rebels tend to produce quite a few artillery units. Therefore, prepare to take losses and be ready to bring down reinforcements. The only units that can withstand artillery are your AT-ATs—so land lots of them. Send them toward reinforcement points and then deploy stormtroopers from your walkers to capture the location once it is secure. Also use bombing runs for taking out concentrations of artillery and other units.

The space battles can be tough because the Rebels seem to have an endless supply of space vessels to throw at your fleet.

While reinforcement points are important so you can increase the number of units you can have on the surface, it is also important to attack the enemy base as early as possible. The sooner you can take out those vehicle factories, the less opposition you face. You might even consider sending some fast units to rush into the base—such as scout troopers on speeder bikes—just so you can have a spotter to call in a bombing run on the structures. This is a suicide mission in many cases, but it can save you a lot of trouble later. It may take a couple bombing runs to take out a structure, but the broad path of destruction means you will probably take out a lot of their units and hit other structures as well.

Locate the factories that produce the artillery units and then call in a bombing run to halt the destructive artillery bombardments by the Rebels.

Once the planets are secure, build a space station and leave behind a company of stormtroopers. It is unlikely that the Rebels will be in a position to go on the offensive at this point in the game. Build up strong space and invasion fleets and then head for Jabiim, with the space fleet going in first to clear the orbit.

Space Battle at Jabiim

OBJECTIVE

1. Destroy all Rebellion space forces to win.

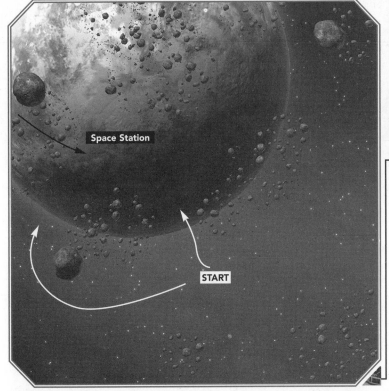

Space Station

START

Asteroids form a barrier to the space station and limit your access to it.

This space battle is very similar to the ones you just encountered while taking those five other planets. Jabiim's orbital area has a lot of asteroids that form a line from northeast to southwest with a few breaks in it. The Rebel space station is in the northwest while your fleet enters in the southeast. This limits your access to the space station. As before, hold back and engage the fleet before you move into range of the space station. However, you also want to start dividing your fleet into two groups. Have one move to take up position at the western gap while the other group stays near the central break.

Ships jumping into a system from hyperspace are vulnerable to attack for a few seconds after they arrive. This is because it takes time for them to bring their shields online. The Rebel fleet enters to the west of the space station. Therefore, your western group is tasked with attacking Rebel ships as soon as they enter. The central group will advance toward the space station and attack it directly. This tactic essentially allows you to concentrate on the space station without much threat from the Rebel fleet. This battle is won after you destroy the space station and all Rebel units.

A gutsy tactic is to wait until you have lost several units, then bring in reinforcements to the northwest of the space station. Order them to enter as close to the edge as possible and then you will have the station surrounded. Your TIE bombers have a straight, short run at the space station's hangar.

After you control the orbit around Jabiim, bring in your invasion fleet to deploy on the surface.

Ground Assault on Jabiim

OBJECTIVE

1. The local humans are allied with our enemies. Destroying them and their structures will go a long way to helping our cause.
2. Destroy all Rebellion land forces and structures to win.

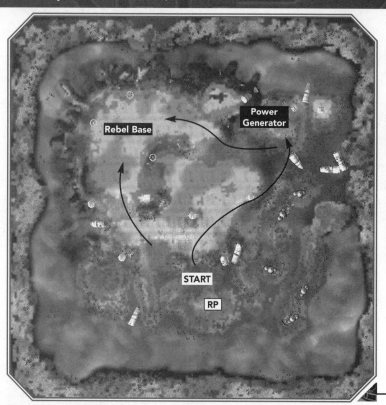

LEGEND

RP   Reinforcement Point

Land a large force all at once at the start of the battle.

This is really a typical land battle much like the ones you have previously fought. Jabiim has only one reinforcement point, so you can bring down a large force all at once. Be sure to include a field commander and at least four AT-ATs. Because of the electrical storms on this planet, you can't use 2-M repulsor tanks or scout troopers.

The Rebel base is in the northwest and protected by a shield generator. However, you can take it out by sending a force to destroy the power generator in the northeast. You face a lot of artillery as before, so quickly take out the power so you can move in and start destroying the factories at the base.

Take out the indigenous structures near your reinforcement point because they continuously spawn civilians that try to take the only reinforcement point away from you. Stay on the attack and eliminate all Rebels to win this battle.

AT-ATs are important for defeating the Rebel forces on Jabiim.

The Traitorous Moff

BRIEFING

Sifting through data recovered in the wreckage of the Rebel base on Jabiim, Lord Vader finally finds intelligence he's been searching for—an Imperial moff by the name of Kalast is the one giving classified information to the Rebels! This traitorous moff has an estate at Atzerri; he must be found at once and interrogated before his execution for treason.

TASK

Defeat the traitorous Moff Kalast.

You will now be fighting another space battle. Get your space fleet back up to full strength and then send it to Atzerri. Because you control all of the planets along the way, you don't have to fight any space battles until you arrive to attack the traitor.

Arrest over Atzerri

OBJECTIVE

1. *Destroy all Rebellion space forces to win.*
2. *Defeat the traitorous Moff Kalast.*
3. *Slaughter Moff Kalast's entourage.*

Your fleet emerges from hyperspace right near the moff's Imperial Star Destroyer. Order all units to attack, concentrating on the engines. However, before you can cause much damage, the moff jumps into hyperspace to escape. There is nothing you can do to stop him. However, he left behind a Rebel space station and fleet.

The moff is right where you can hit him hard—before he jumps to hyperspace.

Though you can't catch the moff this time, you must now wipe out the Rebels and take the Atzerri system. This is the same type of space battle as you have fought before, so you should have no trouble. After the orbit is clear, bring in your invasion fleet and take control of the planet to deny its benefit to the Rebel Alliance.

To prevent Moff Kalast from escaping again, the Emperor is providing you with a new Interdictor cruiser. This ship carries a gravity well generator that prevents ships from jumping into hyperspace during a battle while this device is activated. The Interdictor will be in orbit over Coruscant. Send your space fleet to pick it up and replace any losses. Then you must wait until Imperial intelligence finds Moff Kalast's location. As soon as you get it, send your space fleet to get him. If you wait too long, he will jump to another system.

Keep your Interdictor safe along the map's edge. You may also want to keep some of your units nearby to protect it if it comes under attack. If the Rebels knock out its gravity well generator, the moff will escape once again.

When you arrive, start off by ordering your one and only Interdictor to move to a map edge away from the battle. Once it's there, activate the gravity well generator ability as well as its missile jammer. Once these are activated, the Interdictor can't move. Now send the rest of your fleet after the moff's Star Destroyer. Take out the shields and engines first and order your Marauder missile cruisers to barrage the area around the Star Destroyer. When it is destroyed, take out the remaining Rebel units to complete this mission. This is usually an easier space battle than those you have most recently fought.

Attack the moff's Star Destroyer until it is disabled, then deal with the rest of the Rebels.

An Engagement with the Emperor

BRIEFING

Emperor Palpatine believes that the Bothan spynet is ultimately responsible for leaking Imperial information to the traitorous Moff Kalast and thus helping the Rebellion. As such, he has decided to deal with the situation himself.

TASK

Escort the Emperor to Bothawui and show the Bothans of the error of their ways.

For this mission, you need the Emperor and the Emperor alone. Make sure he is in orbit over Coruscant by himself. If you try to take other units with him to Bothawui, he scolds you for your lack of faith in his powers. Drag his fleet to Bothawui and get ready to watch a Sith Master at work.

Traitors Will Be Punished

OBJECTIVE

1. *His Excellency Emperor Palpatine must survive.*
2. *Exterminate all of the Bothan rabble and their structures.*

The Emperor shows his displeasure.

The Emperor arrives on Bothawui with two of his Imperial guards. The Bothans sent to greet him soon learn the cost of treachery. For this mission, you begin with only the Emperor and his guards.

However, that is more than enough. The Emperor can fight with his lightsaber as well as his two special abilities. Force lightning kills groups of infantry with a single strike. Force corrupt, on the other hand, turns all nearby enemies to your side. You gain control of them; however, the corrupting influence of the dark side of the Force causes these units to slowly lose health until they are destroyed.

The Emperor alone can destroy the buildings. Order your other units to attack the Bothans while he is using the dark side of the Force.

Because you begin in the center of the city, start off by moving east to toward the first Bothan building to destroy it. When you come across a large group of Bothans, use Force lightning and then order the Emperor to attack the buildings while his guards deal with the Bothans. The Emperor uses the dark side of the Force to destroy the building. When your Force lightning recharges, use it on the Bothans and then continue destroying the building.

NOTE

The Emperor only regenerates health when he is near enemy infantry, as he drains the enemy's life to replenish his own.

TIP

Hold off on using Force corrupt the first time until you get to the Rebel LZ. It takes much longer than Force lightning to recharge.

Once the first building is destroyed, head north to repeat the process using the same tactics as before. You receive word that the Rebels are landing on the planet. When they do, move next to where the Rebel transport lands. While waiting for it to unload its cargo of T2-B tanks, use Force lightning on the nearby Bothans. Then, when the tanks are on the ground, use Force corrupt to add them to your force. These are the only vehicles in the mission, so once they are under your control, you do not have to worry about other vehicles.

Proceed around the city destroying buildings and killing Bothans. Every time your Force corrupt recharges, move into a large group of Bothans and use it to take control of more units to use to fight against the remaining enemies. Once all structures and Bothans are destroyed, including those under your control (which die off on their own due to Force corrupt), the mission has been won and you have seen the power the Emperor wields on his own.

Capturing a Princess

BRIEFING

Hoping to save his homeworld from suffering a similar fate to Bothawui, a scared Rebel deserter has revealed that an Alliance agent was going after the Death Star plans. By process of elimination the Empire believes the princess is the only one who could have received this transmission. A small fleet has been dispatched to Tatooine to intercept her, but undiscovered pirate forces have suddenly attacked. Darth Vader must remove the pirates before the princess enters the system, or she will escape.

TASK

Build a fleet and escort Darth Vader to intercept and capture Princess Leia at Tatooine. You need to use the tractor beam from an Imperial Star Destroyer to catch her.

For this mission, you need a powerful fleet with several Imperial Star Destroyers. Though you eventually need an Interdictor, don't worry about including one in your fleet. Some will be provided for you at Tatooine. Remember that Darth Vader must be included in this fleet. When it is ready, move the fleet to Tatooine.

NOTE

You receive a technology upgrade that allows you to build AT-AA walkers as well as Interdictor cruisers.

Seize the *Tantive IV*

OBJECTIVE

1. *Save at least one Interdictor.*
2. *Eradicate all pirate vermin and their space station.*
3. *Lord Vader must survive.*

TIP

Use the stop command on your ships to make sure they stay put in the nebulae in which they are hiding.

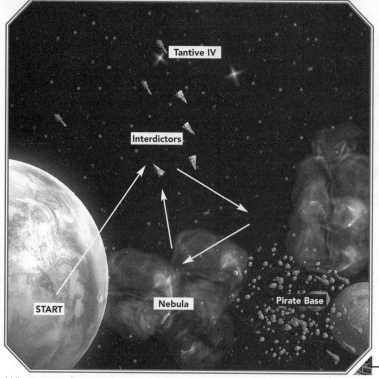

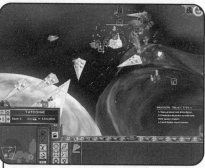

Quickly move the Interdictors to safety as the rest of your fleet fights the pirates.

When your fleet arrives over Tatooine, several Imperial Interdictors are under attack by pirates. Quickly move your fleet to attack the pirates while you order the Interdictors to move southwest away from the pirates. After destroying the pirates near the map's center, move your fleet to attack and destroy the pirates' asteroid base. It is surrounded by small asteroids, so your capital ships have to attack from a distance.

After the pirates have been eliminated, you receive word that Rebel scouts are approaching Tatooine. Quickly get all of your units into the nebula in the south and then wait.

OBJECTIVE

4. Hide your fleet in the nebula.
5. Wait until the princess receives the data transmission.
6. Activate and protect your Interdictors.
7. Capture the princess with a tractor beam from one of your Star Destroyers.

A couple squadrons of X-wings appear and check out the area.

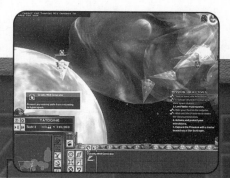

Hide your fleet in the nebula.

Because your fleet is hidden in the nebula, you will not be detected by the Rebels. The *Tantive IV* carrying Princess Leia will arrive. Wait until after the data has been received, then quickly move your Interdictors south from the nebula. Once they are clear, activate their gravity well generators and missile jammers. As long as the Interdictors are operational, the *Tantive IV* can't escape into hyperspace. Send your fleet, including a Star Destroyer, after the corvette, until you can get it locked down with the tractor beam. Once you have the *Tantive IV* caught, the mission ends and Darth Vader can begin the interrogation.

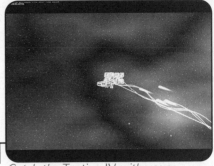

Catch the Tantive IV *with your tractor beam.*

The Destruction of Alderaan

BRIEFING

A suitable demonstration of the Death Star's power is necessary. Princess Leia has unwillingly picked the target—her homeworld of Alderaan.

TASK

Build a fleet and escort the Death Star to Alderaan.

After capturing the princess, go ahead and invade Tatooine. There are only pirate forces on the surface, so you should have no trouble. Then assemble your space fleet at Coruscant and add it to the same fleet spot as the Death Star. Order this combined fleet to move to Alderaan. The Death Star moves much slower than normal fleets. But it will still get there.

Demonstration of the Death Star

OBJECTIVE

1. Obliterate Alderaan. Fire the Death Star once it is in range.

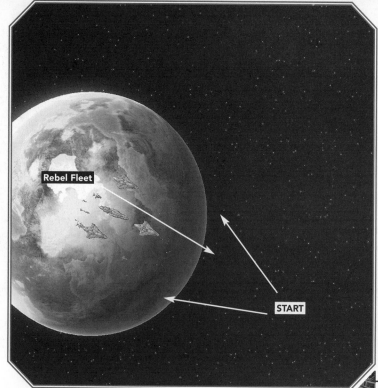

Rebel Fleet

START

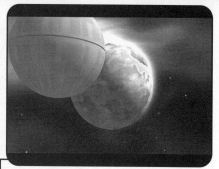

The Death Star approaches Alderaan.

When your fleet arrives in orbit over Alderaan, the Death Star is still moving into position. You have to keep your fleet alive for more than a minute before you can use the Death Star's super laser on the planet. The Rebel fleet includes several Mon Calamari cruisers. While the Rebels will come at you directly, split up your fleet and send the two groups around the Rebel fleet to surround them and hit them from several sides at the same time. Order your fleet to concentrate fire on one Mon Calamari cruiser at a time and then move on to the next target once the first is destroyed. As soon as the Death Star is in range, click the firing icon to unleash the power on Alderaan. With the planet destroyed, the mission is complete.

Attack the enemy fleet.

Alderaan is destroyed!

End of the Rebellion

BRIEFING

With the Death Star fully operational and tested on the planet Alderaan, the Rebel forces are attempting a desperate plan to engage the Empire before more systems suffer the same fate as Alderaan. Imperial intelligence has identified five potential positions for their base. With these planets eliminated, the Rebellion will be no more.

TASK

Take full control of Alzoc III, Polus, Shola, Hoth, and Yavin 4. Use the Death Star to eliminate difficult ground conflicts.

Your final mission is to destroy the five remaining Rebel bases. Replace any losses to your fleet that escorts the Death Star and then send it to Yavin 4, the closest target. Again, you have to fight the Rebel fleet while the Death Star moves into position. The Rebels have ion cannons at each of these planets that they will fire to disable your capital ships. Therefore, destroy the planet as soon as you can to eliminate this threat. Unlike at Alderaan, you then have to fight the rest of the Rebel fleet and destroy their space station to win the battle.

Because there is no planet left on which to land, after each space battle, the system is then under Imperial control. Replace losses to your fleet and then move to the next Rebel base until all are destroyed and the campaign is complete.

You have to fight five more large space battles. However, by now you have the skills that you need to win. Remember to destroy the planet as soon as the Death Star comes into range. There is no advantage to waiting. Plus, if you destroy the fleet first, then you don't get to fire the Death Star and destroy the planet.

Say good-bye to Yavin 4.

NOTE

You do not have to use the Death Star on each planet. Instead, you could send a space fleet to secure the orbit and then an invasion fleet to take control of the planet. It all depends on whether you want to fight some more land battles before the campaign is concluded.

The Galactic Civil War is over and the Empire is victorious.

GALACTIC CONQUEST

Playing a Galactic Conquest Game

Galactic Conquest is a free-form type of game that starts off with a number of planets, an amount of credits, and a certain technology level—all of which vary according to the game you choose to play. This can also be considered a sandbox-style game where you can play however you want to complete the primary objective necessary to win the game. You choose which planets you conquer and how to go about doing it.

It is a good idea to play through at least one of the Campaigns before embarking on a Galactic Conquest game, because the Campaigns in essence teach you how to play a Galactic Conquest game through a series of set missions. Galactic Conquest games, on the other hand, do not have set missions that must be completed to win. Instead, secondary objectives are offered during the course of the game. If you choose to complete the objective, then you receive a reward of some type. However, there is no penalty for skipping a mission.

Because no two Galactic Campaign games are the same, it is impossible to provide a step-by-step walkthrough for each game. Instead, this chapter includes general strategies to help you win these games as well as specific strategies for each side that will help you maximize your advantages and minimize the effects of your disadvantages. Finally, information on each of the original Galactic Conquest games helps you get off to a good start.

Galactic conquest games are very open and allow you to choose your own strategy for taking over the galaxy.

General Strategies for Victory

You can choose from eight different Galactic Conquest maps. Because you can play each as either the Empire or the Rebels, that makes a total of 16 different games. While each has its own unique situations, you need to remain focused on four main factors throughout any of these games. Consider these the golden rules of the galaxy. Neglecting any of these will allow your enemy an advantage you may not be able to afford and could cost you a victory.

It's the Economy

One of the most important factors in winning a game is the economic aspect. To win, you must conquer systems, and for that you need space and land units as well as the structures to recruit or produce those units. All of these things cost credits—the galaxy's monetary system. Therefore, in order to win, you must maintain and even increase your income.

Mines are a great source of income. Build lots of mines on planets that do not border enemy systems.

You can earn credits in a number of ways. Each system you control provides a number of credits to your account at the end of every galactic day. Some systems are worth more credits than others. In addition, if a system you control is connected to one or more of your other systems by a trade route, each connected system route produces a bonus number of credits daily. A third source of daily income is a special structure you can build on your planets—mines. Mines produce even more credits. The final way to earn credits is through expansion. Every time you take control of a planet, you gain a reward that can range from a few hundred credits to more than two thousand credits. These awards are realized only when you take control of the planet, and they are not received daily. However, with the planet under your control, you then add its daily production to your income. See the table below for a listing of planets that provide more credits each day and also receive a boost in credit production for each mine.

PLANETS WITH INCOME BONUSES

- Aeten 2
- Alzoc III
- Bespin*
- Bonadan
- Coruscant
- Kessel
- Polus

* Because Bespin is a gas giant, you can't build mines there. However, the income from controlling the system alone is considerable.

Given a set number of systems under your control, the only way to increase your income is by building mines on your planets. The amount of income you receive from a mine varies from planet to planet. Mines on some planets produce a lot more credits than others. Therefore, build as many mines on these more-profitable planets as possible, and use the less-profitable planets for producing units. While you have to spend credits to build mines, this is a one-time cost and it's usually recouped in the form of increased income within a matter of days. Therefore, the sooner you build your mines, the sooner you start bringing in more income. If you maximize the number of mines in your systems, they can provide 75 percent of your income or even more!

TIP

After building the structures you must have on a planet to defend it or for unit production, fill in the rest of the slots with mines. Don't worry about not having slots for other structures later. You can always right-click on your mines and sell them to open a slot for another structure. As a general rule, if you have an open slot, build a mine there.

Another way to increase your economy is to make your credits go farther. Each faction has a hero that decreases the cost of units and structures by 25 percent at the system where they are located— Mon Mothma for the Rebels and the Emperor for the Imperials. If possible, move these heroes between the systems you control and make sure they are at a system before placing an order for units and structures. The heroes need only be at the system when the order is placed—they do not need to stay around during the production. At the beginning of a game, when your income is limited, this discount can really increase your purchasing power. Just be careful with these heroes because in some games, if they are killed during a battle, you lose the game.

Some systems also give you a 20 percent price reduction for certain types of units. These price reductions are good at all of your systems as long as you control the system providing the reduction. Combine that with the discount you get with Mon Mothma or the Emperor, and these units cost only 60 percent of their original price! Therefore, if you have to choose from two or more planets to invade, see which offers you the best benefits. The "System Unit Discounts" table lists these systems and the units they discount.

Planets such as Mon Calamari provide discounts for specific types of units. This discount is good galaxy-wide for your faction.

System Unit Discounts

System	Unit Discounted	Faction
Abregado Rae	AT-STs	Empire
Anaxes	Victory Star Destroyers	Empire
Bestine IV	Acclamator cruisers	Empire
Carida	Infantry	Both
Corellia	Corellian corvettes	Rebel
Corulag	Infantry	Both
Eriadu	T4-B tanks	Rebel
Fondor	Assault frigates	Rebel
Fresia	A-wing fighters	Rebel
Geonosis	MPTL-2a artillery	Rebel
Ilum	SPMA-T artillery	Empire
Korriban	2-M repulsor tanks	Empire
Kuat	Imperial Star Destroyers	Empire
Mon Calamari	Mon Calamari cruisers	Rebel
Sullust	Tartan patrol cruisers	Empire
Taris	T2-B repulsor tanks	Rebel

Controlled Expansion

As mentioned in the previous section, to increase your income, you need to take control of systems and add their daily credits to your total. However, expanding too fast or randomly can be dangerous and end up costing you rather than providing profit. Therefore, it's important to keep your expansion under control.

As you increase your control over the galaxy, you need to defend your possessions. Don't start taking over a string of systems and allow your enemy to surround you on all sides. This forces you to defend at each of your systems. Instead, try to take control of a section of the galaxy. This way, you can place defenses on only those systems that border your territory. Use systems that have no connections to the enemy's territory to produce units or make them mining centers to increase your profits. By doing this, you can keep your fleets at the borders and keep them stronger because you have fewer systems to defend. Build defensive structures such as ion cannons, shield generators, and turbolaser towers on your border planets—you do not want to lose them.

Expand cautiously. Try to maintain a solid border with the enemy so that no one planet is more vulnerable than the others.

As you expand, scout out neighboring systems along your borders. The Imperial probe droids are great for this job. The Rebels can use R2-D2 and C-3PO, Han Solo and Chewbacca, or even smugglers for this job because they all travel in stealthy ships that can move about the galaxy without being detected. Some planets may be heavily defended by your enemy or pirates. On the other hand, you may find planets with no one controlling them. You can quickly move a fleet there, land a few units, and gain the system for few or no casualties. Go for these "freebie" systems at the start of a game because you immediately get the reward for taking control of them. You can then spend that reward on structures there—even if they are only mines. If all bordering systems are enemy-controlled, see which has the fewest defenses and attack there. Don't waste your units by attacking where the enemy is strongest. Instead, hit them where they are weak or least expect it.

Pirates can be good neighbors. While they are often not too hard to defeat to take over their systems, they also do not attack your systems. Therefore, you can use pirate-controlled systems as buffers between you and your enemy because the enemy must conquer these systems to get to your neighboring systems. Early in a game, leave the pirates in place unless you really need their system. Concentrate on capturing "freebies" and building up your fleets and defenses. Wait until your enemy moves in and attacks the pirates, then quickly move in your fleets to take the planet before your enemy can replace losses and build up defenses. If you rush a fleet in right away, the enemy will not have had time to build a space station or planetary defensive structures. Therefore, keep a fleet along your border with the pirates to take advantage of this strategy.

Momentum

Another important aspect to Galactic Conquest games is maintaining a constant momentum. You have to play offensively to win. Therefore, instead of spending all your time and credits building defenses on all of your planets, build powerful fleets. You can use these to defend against enemy fleets attacking your systems, and also to advance on and capture other systems. By staying put and going on the defensive, you limit your income to its current level. If you allow the enemy to expand, their income will increase and they can build larger fleets and armies and attack at will.

You have to invade and take control of enemy systems at a regular pace to keep your income increasing as well as to continuously pressure the enemy.

As soon as you capture a system, start scouting out neighboring systems and planning your next move. If the enemy takes over one of your systems, quickly move in a fleet to take it back before they can build defenses and reinforce their occupying units. Remember that for every system you take away from the enemy, you gain the income and bonuses that system provides while your enemy loses those same things.

Along the same lines of momentum in expansion, you should also be increasing your technology. The quicker you can gain access to more advanced and powerful units, the sooner you can turn them against your enemy. If you can keep your technology higher than your opponents, you have the advantage when it comes to battle.

Objectives

The Campaign games were driven by missions and objectives. They helped guide you and at the same time limited what you could do during the game. Galactic Conquest games also periodically offer missions. Often they require you to capture a specific system. Once you accomplish the objective, you receive a reward in addition to the credits you earn automatically for capturing the system. The mission reward could be credits, units, or something else. However, it's important to remember that you are not required to complete any of the objectives given during a Galactic Conquest game, except the initial objectives required to win. Therefore, when a mission is given, see if it is feasible. Is the reward worth the risk? If it is a weak neighboring planet that you need anyway, go for it. However, don't advance clear across the galaxy through enemy territory for the sake of a free capital ship added to your fleet. Also, be sure to check out a system before sending in your fleet. Even if the mission states that a planet is undefended or lightly defended, it still pays to scout it out first. Intelligence is not always accurate. Use discretion and you will be fine.

Objectives in the middle of a game can offer rewards or advice. However, you do not need to heed all of them.

Playing as the Empire

Each faction has different types of units that require different styles of play. Therefore, what works for the Empire may not work as effectively for the Rebels and vice versa. The Empire starts out with stronger units that offer abilities for increasing firepower at the cost of defenses. Their spaceships and ground units can dish out a lot more than they can take. Therefore, when playing as the Empire, stay offensive and on the attack. Use your increased firepower right at the start to cause as much damage as possible before the Rebels can hurt you back.

Use the Empire's advantage in firepower and space units to wipe out Rebel fleets before they can invade your systems.

The Empire has access to the Death Star. With this, you can destroy enemy planets, reducing the credits they provide your enemies as well as the production capabilities of those systems. Therefore, when playing as the Empire, your main goal should be to build the Death Star as quickly as possible. To do this, first build a research facility and then research technology upgrades until you can build the Death Star. While this is going on, you still need to build up a strong fleet and be conquering systems to increase your economy and income so you can afford the research and the cost to construct the Death Star. Once you get the Death Star, escort it with a strong fleet and begin attacking enemy planets. Remember that you do not have to destroy every planet. Send a probe droid in first to see what kind of defenses they have on the ground. If defenses are light, wipe out the space defenses and send in an invasion force to take control and add to your economic income. However, if the enemy has a lot of units and defensive structures, just blow up the planet and move on to the next system.

The Death Star is the ultimate weapon. The Empire should make every effort to get this weapon and use it to wipe out the Rebel Alliance.

Playing as the Rebel Alliance

The Rebels have a tougher time in direct combat with the Empire. Most of their units are made for hit-and-run raids or are specialized for certain tasks. The Rebel space units either offer boosts to speed or to shields rather than firepower. Therefore, the Rebels must take on the tactic of hitting hard and then fleeing to fight another day, or at least until your shields are restored.

As technology increases, the Rebels acquire some heavier firepower. Therefore, it's important to keep R2-D2 and C-3PO busy at all times.

Raid fleets are a great tactic for the Rebels to use.

Use them to scout out systems before you attack and especially for stealing technology. Even if the list of technology to steal does not have anything you currently want or need, keep stealing because once you have all of the items at one level of technology, you can then begin stealing at the next highest level. If the Empire is going for the Death Star, you need to get to the highest technology level so you gain Red Squadron, which is the only unit that can destroy the Imperial's massive and powerful space station.

The Rebels must also expand as quickly as possible to increase their economy and income. The more you take away from the Empire, the less they have to spend on their own weapons and research. You also want to create a defensible border. As soon as you can, build ion cannons on your border planets. This can give you a great edge if the Imperials come to invade because you can disable their most powerful space units—preventing them from using the firepower of these units, yet also taking up capacity so the Empire can't bring in more units.

Because the Rebels have trouble going toe-to-toe with Imperial fleets, especially in the beginning, the Rebels should use raid fleets. These are fleets consisting of only a few ground units. Heroes do not count against the total number of units, so send along Obi-Wan Kenobi, Kyle Katarn, or Han Solo and Chewbacca because they count as free units for the sake of raid fleet numbers and have some powerful abilities that allow your raid fleets a chance at success. Raid fleets, because they are small, can move through enemy-controlled systems without starting a space battle with enemy units or space station. While you don't have a lot of units in a raid fleet, they are intended to hit the Empire at their weak planets and go for easy victories. Try to choose planets with inhabitants who are friendly to the Rebels—such as Sullust, Geonosis, Naboo, and Kashyyyk—because you get automatic infantry at these planets that you can use for taking control of locations such as reinforcement points, build pads, and abandoned or mercenary structures. In some Galactic Conquest games, you can win by killing the Emperor. Because this unit is often safe on a planet away from the borders, once you identify his location, send raid fleets with the sole purpose of assassinating this Imperial leader. This is often effective at the start of a game because the Empire will often be building up space units and structures rather than expecting a raid against their leader.

Bring heroes along during invasions so you can use their special abilities as well as their longevity on the battlefield.

TIP

There are a couple great ways to use raid fleets. One is to simultaneously send out raid fleets to several different systems, forcing the Empire to try to put out scattered fires at once. Another is to put several raid fleets in orbits around your planets and then send them to the same target one after another. Before each raid fleet is destroyed, they should try to cause as much damage as possible to structures and enemy units. Then another raid fleet arrives shortly after the battle and before the enemy can produce more units or replace destroyed structures, continue attacking, taking up where the last raid fleet left off before it was destroyed.

The Galactic Conquest Missions
The Lines Are Drawn

Conditions

Planets	8
Tech Level	3
Initial Credits	20,000

The eight planets on this map are evenly divided between the Rebels and the Empire. Due to the positioning, each side has two safe planets with the other two bordering the enemy. To win, one side must remove the other side from the galaxy.

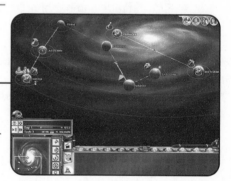

Because there are no empty or pirate-controlled planets, this game requires combat with the enemy to expand. The strategy for both factions is basically the same. First, build space stations at your border planets to provide some defenses against an early attack by an enemy fleet. This usually helps you thwart enemy invasion attempts. The overall strategy is to capture a couple of the enemy's planets to limit your exposure to enemies, then with the majority and the credits it brings in, build a force to finish them off.

Rebel Tips

After ordering space stations for all planets except Hoth, organize your ground units into two groups—one at Atzerri and the other at Tatooine. Then create raid fleets to invade Taris and Bothawui simultaneously. The citizens of Bothawui will help you fight against the Empire, and the quicker you can get your troops on the ground, the less time the enemy has to recruit or produce new units and defensive structures. As your raid fleets are moving to their destinations, produce ground units at all of your planets that you can, then use them for additional raid fleets as needed.

Imperial Tips

Because the Empire has the slight advantage in space units, group them and quickly send them to either Atzerri or Tatooine before the Rebels can upgrade a space station. Then quickly bring in ground forces and land them on the planet to take control of it. This gives you some quick credits and an advantage against the Rebels.

Alderaan's Demise

Conditions

Planets	10
Tech Level	5
Initial Credits	30,000

For this mission, the Rebels control the northeastern part of the galaxy while the Imperials are in the southwest. Alderaan and Eriadu represent the forward planets for each side. The pirate-controlled systems of Ryloth and Nal Hutta also separate the two factions. As with the previous map, there is not a lot of room for expansion without having to fight. Both sides start out with all of the technology and heroes, so you do not need to spend credits on either researching technology or stealing it. Instead, it is a race to build up fleets and units and then attack.

Rebel Tips

The Rebels' best strategy is to upgrade the space station at Alderaan for defense and keep Red Squadron there, because that is where the Empire will most likely send the Death Star first. The Rebels also need to build up their fleet and create a number of raid fleets to begin attacking all of the Imperial planets. Target the enemy planets with the highest level space stations, because those are the ones capable of building the Death Star. While you can take over the pirate systems, they are better left as a buffer between you and the Empire so you can concentrate your defenses at Alderaan. To win, either capture all of the Imperial-controlled planets or destroy the Death Star.

Imperial Tips

As the Empire, you need to work on the Death Star as quickly as possible. Because it costs 20,000 credits to begin construction, move the Emperor to where it is being built so you can reduce the cost to only 15,000 credits. A good place to construct it is at the Vergesso Asteroids; the Rebels can't send a raid fleet there because there is no surface. Heavily defend Eriadu because that is your border with the Rebels. Taking control of the pirate systems is a possibility because you can create a powerful fleet. However, that means diverting units from the defense of Eriadu. Building mines on your secure planets is a better way to earn credits than through invasion.

For a great opening attack, assemble all of your space units at the start at Eriadu and then send them to Alderaan. Your Interdictor can prevent the Rebel fleet at Alderaan from escaping, and then you can destroy Red Squadron as well as Ackbar's *Home One* in one swift swoop. Then build up a ground attack force and send it in to secure Alderaan for the Empire. This one conquest makes it much tougher for the Rebellion to fight effectively against you for the remainder of the game. Remember to make sure Red Squadron is eliminated before firing the Death Star's super laser. If the Death Star is destroyed, you lose. To win, you must take control of all the Rebel planets.

Closing on Coruscant
Conditions

Planets	10
Tech Level	1
Initial Credits	5,000

On this map, each side gets three planets and there are four pirate-controlled planets. In addition to wiping out the enemy or destroying the Death Star, you can also win by taking out the enemy leader—either Mon Mothma or the Emperor. The pirate planets can be tempting. However, with all planets along a border with the enemy, except for Rebel-controlled Sullust, defense is key and sending units off for invasions can weaken your defenses.

Rebel Tips

Because Sullust is behind the border with the Empire, build lots of mines there to bring in credits. Build up space stations at Corellia and Corulag for defense against Imperial fleets and get ion cannons for those planets as soon as you can steal technology for them, which R2-D2 and C-3PO should be doing at every possible moment. Raid fleets are a great way to force the Empire to waste resources garrisoning the surfaces of their planets instead of spending money on research or building fleets. Also consider sending small space fleets to harass the Imperial fleets in orbit over their planets, because they start out rather small.

Imperial Tips

The Empire must not only build up fleets and space stations for defense, but also make sure that each planet has enough units to defend itself from Rebel raid fleets. Build up your space fleet and then send it to take control of the orbits of each of the three Rebel planets. This prevents the Rebels from building up space fleets and allows you to then invade each planet at your pleasure. Because it takes so much research and credits in this game to build the Death Star, you are better off spending your credits on conventional units.

The Shipyards of Kuat

Conditions

Planets	15
Tech Level	3
Initial Rebel Credits	10,000
Initial Empire Credits	15,000

This is a fast-paced game. The Rebels must capture Fondor, Fresia, and Kuat within 20 galactic days to win the game. The Empire, on the other hand, must eliminate the Rebels completely within 20 days.

Rebel Tips

The Rebels need to move quickly. Right at the start, send a single ground unit to Aeten II to take control of this unoccupied planet and score some free credits. Then assemble your fleet and some ground units and take Fondor from the pirates. Build up your fleet to take on the enemy at Fresia and then Kuat. Use Han Solo and Chewbacca to scout out planets while R2-D2 and C-3PO steal technology.

Imperial Tips

You start out with a fairly strong fleet of space units. To get to the Rebels, you have to take control of pirate systems. You have lots of heroes, so use them. With a strong space fleet, you can quickly move in and take out the Rebel fleets and space stations, then land troops to capture their planets. Be sure to build AT-ATs for your invasion forces.

The Conflict Begins

Conditions

Planets	21
Tech Level	1
Initial Credits	8,000

On this map, each side controls only a small part of the galaxy and must expand to find the enemy or even just to reveal most of the planets. It is a bit slower than some of the other maps because you do not need to be worried about being attacked right away. Lots of pirate systems act as buffers between the two factions.

Rebel Tips

The Rebels begin with Hoth and Yavin 4 at opposite sides of the galaxy. The only unoccupied planet you can grab at the start is Bespin. However, it provides a lot of credits initially as well as each day. Build up your forces on each of your initial planets and begin taking over the galaxy one planet at a time. Remember, you can't steal technology until you find an Imperial-controlled planet.

Imperial Tips

The Empire begins with Thyferra and Coruscant. You can quickly take control of Anaxes, which is unoccupied. From there, begin attacking pirate systems either toward Hoth or Yavin 4. Your strategy is to wipe out one half of the Rebel force, then turn your full | attention on the other half. If you push hard, you can let the pirate systems cover your flanks while you concentrate on advancing in one direction.

Empire Surrounded

Conditions

Planets	25
Tech Level	3
Initial Rebel Credits	15,000
Initial Empire Credits	9,000

This is an interesting map where the Empire controls the Core Worlds while the Rebels have the Outer Rim. Pirates control many of the worlds in the middle. Kuat and Corellia are the only two planets where the factions border one another and thus both become the front line and should be defended. Winning means total control of the planets in this mission.

Rebel Tips

The Rebels should begin by building up defenses at Kuat to ensure that this planet does not fall to the Empire. Then begin by taking Jabiim from the pirates. This helps connect your two groups of systems and also gives you a back door into the Imperial-controlled Core Worlds. Leave the remainder of the pirate systems alone to act as buffers.

Imperial Tips

Assemble all of your space units at Corellia at the start, and upgrade the space station as much as possible. The Rebels will stage an attack against Corellia. Repel it and then go on the counterattack to take Kuat. From there, work your way around the Outer Rim capturing all of the Rebel systems. Be researching and then building the Death Star while you are advancing so you can use it later to continue your path of destruction in the Outer Rim.

Empire at War
Conditions

Planets	35
Tech Level	1
Initial Credits	6,000

This map places the Rebels along the eastern and western sides with the Empire in the middle. Several unoccupied planets can be quickly taken at the beginning to give your side an economic boost. There are also several border planets where the Rebels and Empire come in contact with one another.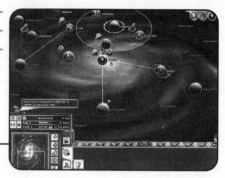

Rebel Tips

The Rebels need to act quickly to grab Bespin, Polus, Ryloth, Shola, and Wayland while they are unoccupied. These moves add lots of credits to your account without any risk. This is a good game to try to win by assassinating the Emperor. He begins on Byss and is usually around there somewhere. Send several raid fleets in quick succession so they arrive one after the other, giving the Imperials no time to reinforce the planet. The first fleets should concentrate on knocking out defensive structures such as turbolaser towers and shield generators to make it easier for follow-up raid fleets.

Imperial Tips

The Imperials can grab Kuat, Anaxes, Carida, Bestine IV, Eriadu, and Tatooine at the beginning with no opposition. Quickly secure these planets against attack from the Rebels and then begin going after one Rebel system at a time. If you can find the planet where Mon Mothma is located, surround it and try to end the game quickly by eliminating the Rebel leader. Otherwise, research and build the Death Star and then destroy Rebel bases one by one.

Galactic Conflict
Conditions

Planets	43
Tech Level	3
Initial Credits	10,000

This is the big Galactic Conquest map with all 43 systems. In addition, all systems are controlled by either the Rebels or the Empire. There are no pirate systems. Therefore, many of the systems border the enemy, making it hard to secure. The Empire begins primarily in the middle with the Rebels on the outer systems.

Rebel Tips

The Rebels should begin by focusing their attacks on Imperial systems such as Bonadan, which are off by themselves and surrounded by Rebel systems. This creates safe planets in the Outer Rim that the Imperials can't get direct access to. Use these as your mining planets to make credits for your cause. Next focus on taking control of half the galaxy and concentrating your fleets along this front, continuously pushing the Empire back at all times.

Imperial Tips

The Empire should also concentrate on securing a section of the galaxy at the time. Begin by invading the northern systems until the Empire controls the northern half. Then push along the southern front. The Death Star make this job a lot easier, and because you begin at technology level 3, you already have a head start. Don't worry much about losing the planets you begin with in the south. Just put up a fight and make the Rebels pay for everything they gain.

STAR WARS
EMPIRE AT WAR

In addition to the Campaign and Galactic Conquest games, you can also play individual tactical battles or play against other humans in multiplayer games. This chapter gives you the information you need to start playing these different types of games, as well as tips for how to beat your opponents. Finally, Skirmish maps can be found at the end of the chapter. These show important locations and features to help you plan your victories even before you begin a battle.

Skirmish Games

Skirmish games are quite a bit different from the Campaign and Galactic Conquest games. The main difference is that Skirmish games do not have a galactic mode. The entire game takes place on one land or space map. Without the galactic mode, all production takes place during the tactical battle. You earn credits during the course of the game, which you can then spend on units and upgrades for your force.

Skirmishes allow you to concentrate on a single tactical battle and are a great way to practice with different types of units.

TIP

Before playing a Skirmish game, it's a good idea to go through Tutorials 6 and 7. These are non-interactive, but they provide a good introduction to the differences in the Skirmish games as compared to the Campaigns and Galactic Conquest games covered in the previous five tutorials.

To purchase new units, you must first select a structure. For space battles, all units are purchased at your space station. However, during land battles, you must purchase your units at the appropriate structure. For example, you can get infantry at the barracks, T2-B repulsor tanks at the light vehicle factory, and artillery at the heavy vehicle factory. After ordering a unit, it still takes time for it to be produced. However, it does not roll out of the factory upon completion.

Instead, it goes into your reinforcement pool. You can then deploy your units as you would in the other games—at either a reinforcement point on land or in open space near your units or space station for space battles.

Purchase units, upgrades, and even heroes at your structures.

You can also purchase upgrades during a Skirmish game. As with unit production, upgrades are purchased at structures. Upgrades provide bonuses for your units, such as increased firepower, speed, and armor. You can increase your technology level in the same way by paying for a technology upgrade. This gives you access to new, more powerful units and heroes. All of your current upgrades are displayed along the screen's right side. During team play, only one player needs to pay for the upgrade and it is shared by all players of that same faction. However, if a structure that produces upgrades is destroyed, all upgrades from that structure are lost.

You need credits to purchase units and upgrades. Therefore it's important to have a source of income. Take control of abandoned mining facilities and resource pads on land, and asteroid mining facilities in space, by moving infantry or space units adjacent to them with no enemies around. Then you can pay to construct or rebuild these facilities. Each one you have provides a steady stream of credits to your account. Mining facilities can also be upgraded to increase their production. The more sources of income and the higher the rate of production, the faster you receive credits. For team games, all players share the income and receive the same rate—though each has his or her own account and spends credits individually.

You need mining facilities and resource pads to earn credits during Skirmish games. Because it costs credits to rebuild or construct these structures, don't use up all of your money at the start on units and upgrades.

Reinforcement points are important in land Skirmish games as well. During a game, your unit capacity is always set at 10. Capturing reinforcement points does not increase your unit capacity at all. Instead, they offer locations where you can deploy your reinforcements.

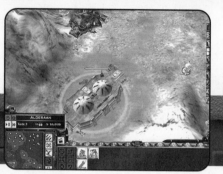

NOTE

Each faction has one reinforcement point that can't be captured. However, all other reinforcement points are fair game.

 Victory conditions for Skirmish games can vary depending on the type you are playing and the options selected. To win in the standard land Skirmish, you must destroy all enemy structures, destroy all enemies, or both. For land control Skirmish games, you must take control of all reinforcement points on the map, with the exception of your enemy's permanent reinforcement point, and hold them all for 30 seconds. Space Skirmish games require you to destroy the enemy space station, destroy all enemy units, or both. Be sure to know what the victory conditions are for your game before you begin. You don't want to waste a lot of time and units destroying a space station when all you needed to do was take out the enemy's space units.

Cantinas on Skirmish maps allow you to purchase pirate vehicles as soon as you take control of this structure.

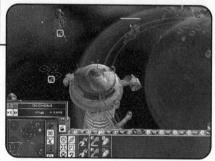

Reinforcement points are vital to victory during land control games.

Multiplayer

***Star Wars:* Empire at War** offers several different types of multiplayer games. Most of the Skirmish maps and types of games can also be played in multiplayer, with up to eight players divided into two teams—the Empire versus the Rebels. You can also play a Galactic Conquest game versus another human player with one side taking the role of the Rebel Alliance while the other commands the Galactic Empire. Several of the galactic maps are different than those for the single-player Galactic Conquest. The same tactics for Galactic Conquest games and single-player Skirmish games apply to the multiplayer games. The only difference is the unpredictability of a human opponent.

Space stations are the only structure you need to destroy during space Skirmishes. They have their own defenses, such as Hangars, that deploy fighters, so attack with caution. You have to purchase your units at the space station.

Tips for Land Skirmishes

NOTE

Many of these tips for the Skirmishes, which apply to both single and multiplayer games, were provided by the testing staff at LucasArts. Thank you very much for all your help.

Watch out for indigenous creatures, such as the rancor and the Sarlaac. They will kill your units if you get too close. You can kill the rancor with a lot of firepower, but the Sarlaac is there for the duration.

- Grab as many reinforcement points as you can as quickly as possible. This gives you more deployment options and makes it more difficult for your opponent to know where you are.

- Also capture as many build pads as you can. Turrets slow the enemy down and let you know where they are.

- Always save enough money to build mining facilities and resource pads early on. Don't spend all of your money on units or upgrades. Still, build a healthy mix of technology level 1 vehicles and infantry early on. Build infantry to take over build pads and reinforcement points, and build vehicles for added firepower.

- Resist the urge to upgrade your technology as soon as the game starts. This costs a lot of money and time at the crucial beginning stages of the game.

- Use heroes to your advantage. An army with a hero or two in it always has an advantage over an army without one.

- When playing as the Empire, use Mara Jade and the Emperor to steal the enemy's army with their Force corrupt ability.

- When playing as the Rebels, use Kyle Katarn and infiltrators to attack enemy structures using their thermal detonators. A few infiltrators can cause a big mess in the enemy's base. On the Empire side, Mara Jade also carries thermal detonators and can be used the same way.

- Use friendly indigenous units to occupy landing points. Because they keep respawning, you can continue throwing them in no matter how often they die.

- Rebel airspeeders are great for attacking turrets and structures. Therefore the Imperials should build some AA turrets near their base.

- During land control Skirmish games, you need more infantry units because they are the only units that can take control of reinforcement points. Race to grab as many as you can with the infantry you begin with. Then send more infantry and vehicles as reinforcements to hold those positions.

- Because reinforcement points are so critical during land control games, build turrets at nearby build pads to help defend, and take advantage of good ground when available.

Tips for Space Skirmishes

- When targeting hard-points on enemy capital ships or space stations for your bombers, always target the shield generators first so that your other units can target hard-points sooner.

- If going for a more conservative approach, strike an equal balance between producing defensive units and capturing as many mineral asteroids as possible. Tech up when your funds are replenished.

- If going for a tech rush, select the tech upgrade as soon as the game starts. Send your squads out and capture as many asteroid mining facilities as possible. Try to distract your opponent with your aggressiveness. When you lose your forces, hopefully your opponent will focus on building up his or her economy and units, and not attempt to counterattack right away.

- If there are any merchant space docks on the map, seek them out as soon as possible. You can get units that are the equivalent of technology level 3 units when you are still at technology level 1.

- Always harass enemy asteroid mining facilities. This is best done with disposable garrison units, most notably the fast X-wings and corvettes for the Rebellion or the disposable TIE fighters and bombers that deploy out of the Empire's capital ships and space station.

- If you need a large fleet at a specific location in a hurry, always send a fast-moving unit in first, then warp in your fleet around it. As a general rule, always warp in ships as close to your specified destination as possible. This works great for bomber rushes because they fly rather slowly and can take a while to get to your target on large maps.

Imperial TIE bombers with an escort of TIE fighters perform an attack against an enemy space station. Target the shields first, then the laser and turbolaser hard-points. Even if you have to destroy enemy units as well, once their space station is destroyed, the enemy can't produce any new units and all the upgrades they paid for are eliminated.

- Missile cruisers are good for offensives but they're even better for defense. If an opponent is approaching your space station with a large fleet, warp in some missile cruisers behind your base out of the opponent's sight range. After they have all warped in, order them to barrage various areas around the enemy fleet. This ability can completely decimate an entire invading force.

- In space, after destroying the weapon hard-points on a ship, don't destroy the ship. Let the useless ship eat up your opponent's population cap.

- Take out all corvette-sized units defending a base before moving on to the base itself. Frigate units have a good blend of speed, maneuverability, and firepower and can overwhelm attacking forces if used in numbers.

- If present on a map, build both laser and missile defense satellites near your space station and asteroid mining facilities. This adds to your available firepower and gives the enemy something else to concentrate on while you coordinate your attacks against the invading force.

STAR WARS
EMPIRE AT WAR

Land Maps

Alderaan at War

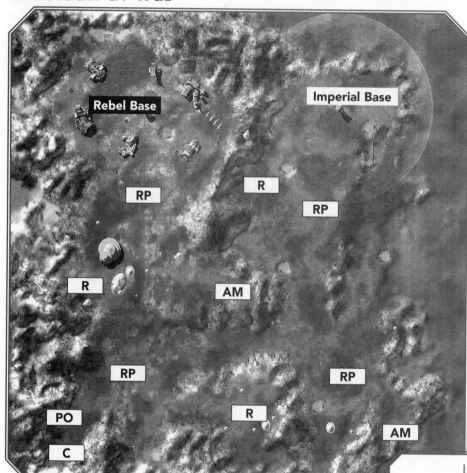

Rebel Base

Imperial Base

RP

R

RP

R

AM

RP

RP

PO

R

C

AM

LEGEND

AHV	Abandoned Heavy Vehicle Factory
AM	Abandoned Mining Facility
AS	Abandoned Sensor Array
AT	Abandoned Turborlaser Tower
C	Cantina
PO	Pirate Outpost
R	Resource Pad
RP	Reinforcement Point
S	Abandoned Shield Generator

Bothan Bonanza

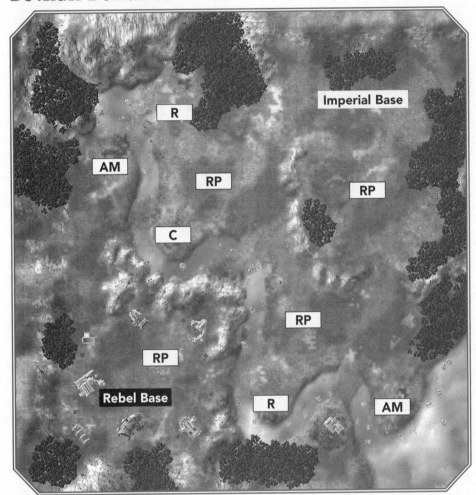

AHV	Abandoned Heavy Vehicle Factory
AM	Abandoned Mining Facility
AS	Abandoned Sensor Array
AT	Abandoned Turborlaser Tower
C	Cantina
PO	Pirate Outpost
R	Resource Pad
RP	Reinforcement Point
S	Abandoned Shield Generator

LEGEND

Clash on Tatooine

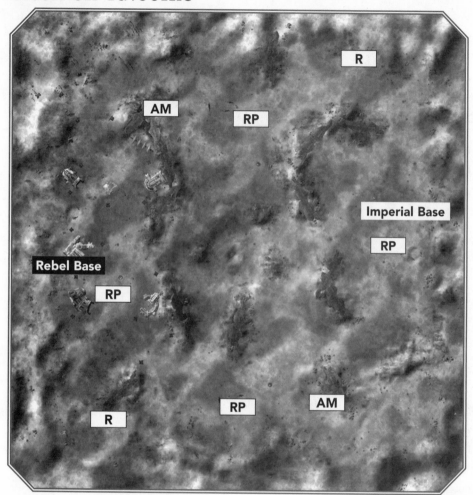

Map labels:
- R
- AM
- RP
- Imperial Base
- RP
- Rebel Base
- RP
- R
- RP
- AM

LEGEND

AHV	Abandoned Heavy Vehicle Factory
AM	Abandoned Mining Facility
AS	Abandoned Sensor Array
AT	Abandoned Turborlaser Tower
C	Cantina
PO	Pirate Outpost
R	Resource Pad
RP	Reinforcement Point
S	Abandoned Shield Generator

Dagobah Rush

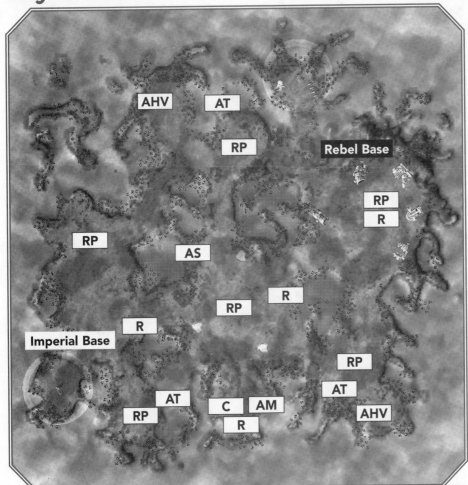

AHV

AT

RP

Rebel Base

RP

R

RP

AS

R

RP

R

Imperial Base

RP

AT

RP

AT

C AM

AHV

R

LEGEND

AHV	Abandoned Heavy Vehicle Factory
AM	Abandoned Mining Facility
AS	Abandoned Sensor Array
AT	Abandoned Turborlaser Tower
C	Cantina
PO	Pirate Outpost
R	Resource Pad
RP	Reinforcement Point
S	Abandoned Shield Generator

Yavin Training Grounds

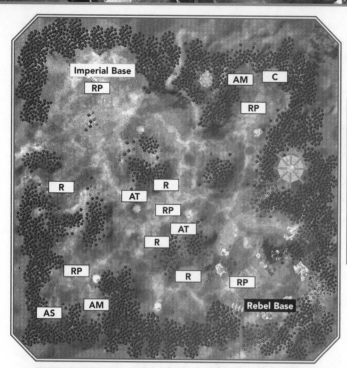

LEGEND

AHV	Abandoned Heavy Vehicle Factory
AM	Abandoned Mining Facility
AS	Abandoned Sensor Array
AT	Abandoned Turborlaser Tower
C	Cantina
PO	Pirate Outpost
R	Resource Pad
RP	Reinforcement Point
S	Abandoned Shield Generator

Assault on Hoth

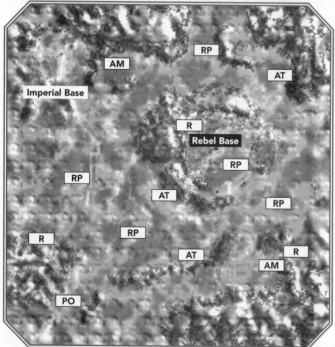

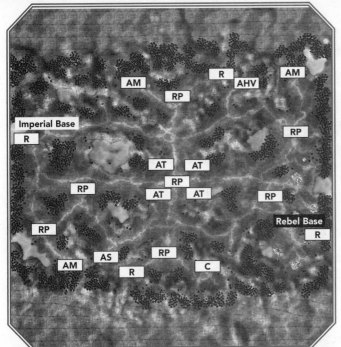

Endor Xpress

LEGEND	
AHV	Abandoned Heavy Vehicle Factory
AM	Abandoned Mining Facility
AS	Abandoned Sensor Array
AT	Abandoned Turborlaser Tower
C	Cantina
PO	Pirate Outpost
R	Resource Pad
RP	Reinforcement Point
S	Abandoned Shield Generator

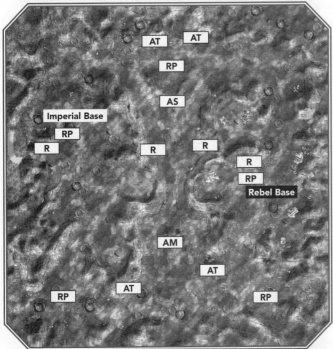

Kessel Run I

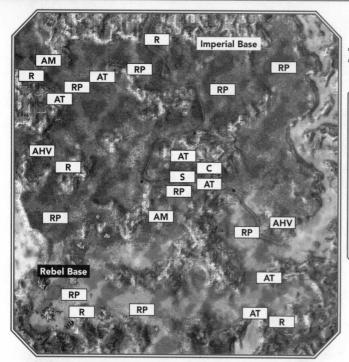

Dantooine Uprising

LEGEND

AHV	Abandoned Heavy Vehicle Factory
AM	Abandoned Mining Facility
AS	Abandoned Sensor Array
AT	Abandoned Turborlaser Tower
C	Cantina
PO	Pirate Outpost
R	Resource Pad
RP	Reinforcement Point
S	Abandoned Shield Generator

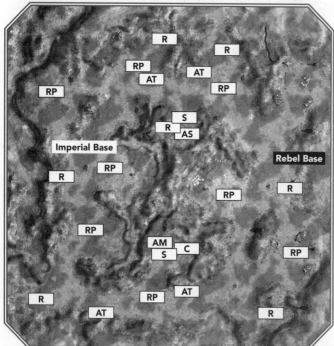

Marooned on Geonosis

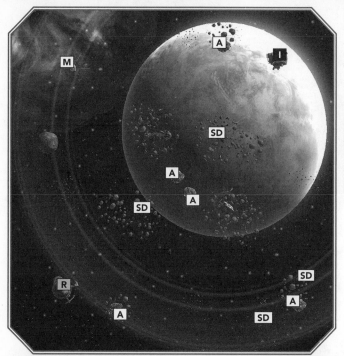

Space Maps

Battle Over Geonosis

LEGEND	
I	Imperial Space Station
R	Rebel Space Station
A	Asteroid Mining Facility
M	Merchant Space Dock
SD	Satellite Defense System

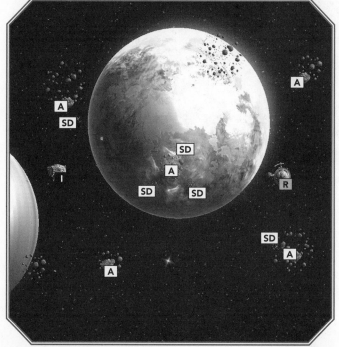

Endor Ablaze

Bothan Frenzy

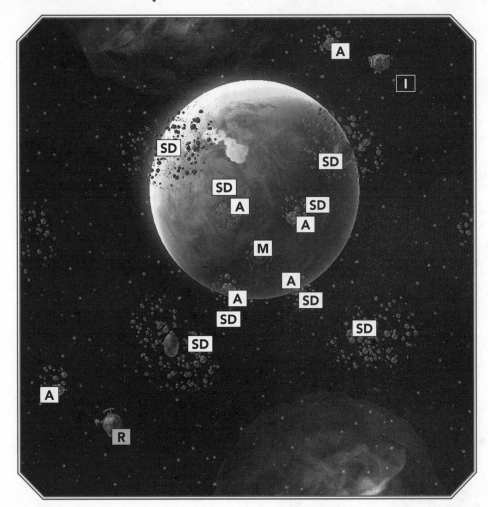

LEGEND

I	Imperial Space Station
R	Rebel Space Station
A	Asteroid Mining Facility
M	Merchant Space Dock
SD	Satellite Defense System

Dagobah Under Fire

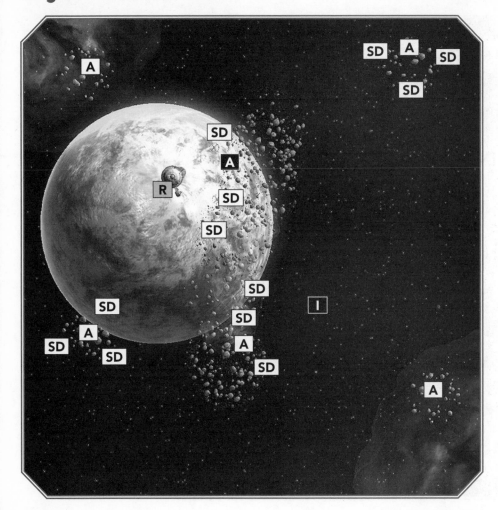

LEGEND

I	Imperial Space Station
R	Rebel Space Station
A	Asteroid Mining Facility
M	Merchant Space Dock
SD	Satellite Defense System

Alderaan Defense

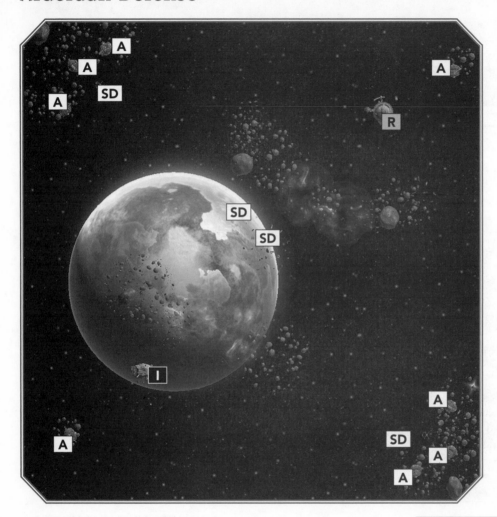

LEGEND

I	Imperial Space Station
R	Rebel Space Station
A	Asteroid Mining Facility
M	Merchant Space Dock
SD	Satellite Defense System

Coruscant Siege

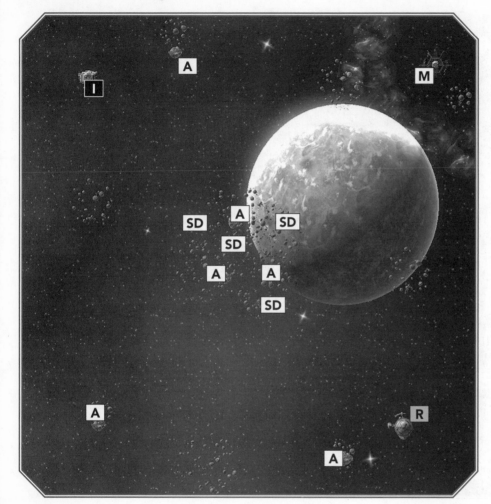

LEGEND

I	Imperial Space Station
R	Rebel Space Station
A	Asteroid Mining Facility
M	Merchant Space Dock
SD	Satellite Defense System

Resistance Over Shola

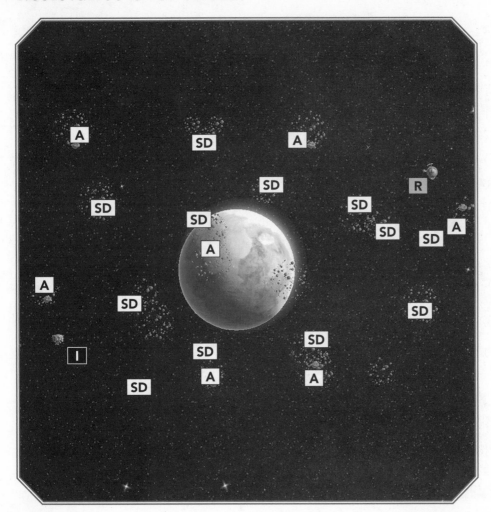

LEGEND

I	Imperial Space Station
R	Rebel Space Station
A	Asteroid Mining Facility
M	Merchant Space Dock
SD	Satellite Defense System

Hoth Conflict

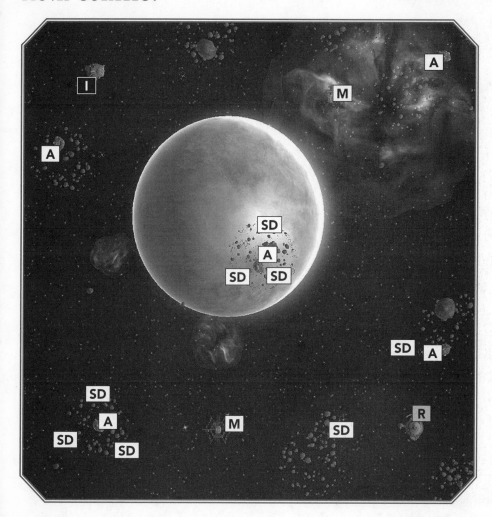

	L E G E N D	
I	Imperial Space Station	
R	Rebel Space Station	
A	Asteroid Mining Facility	
M	Merchant Space Dock	
SD	Satellite Defense System	

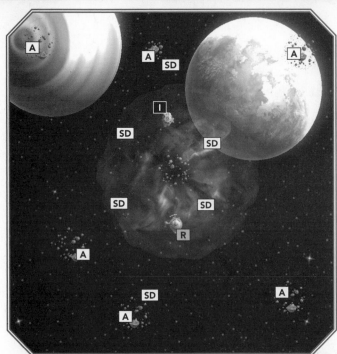

Yavin Lost

LEGEND

I	Imperial Space Station
R	Rebel Space Station
A	Asteroid Mining Facility
M	Merchant Space Dock
SD	Satellite Defense System